MY RECORD OF MUSIC

Compton Mackenzie in 1923 when he founded *The Gramophone*

MY RECORD OF MUSIC

COMPTON MACKENZIE

WITH 4 ILLUSTRATIONS

LONDON

HUTCHINSON

Hutchinson & Co. (Publishers) Ltd.

178–202 Great Portland Street, London, W.1

London   Melbourne   Sydney   Auckland
Bombay   Johannesburg   New York   Toronto

First published 1955

144220

*Printed in Great Britain
by The Anchor Press, Ltd.,
Tiptree, Essex*

To
CECIL POLLARD
and his son
ANTHONY
whose devoted steering of
the paper boat I launched
thirty-two years ago has
helped it to become the
full-rigged ship of today

The Gramophone
April 1923–1955

31 Drummond Place
Edinburgh

Chapter 1

I BEGIN with an apology. I have no right to call this book *My Record of Music* because it seems to imply that I have played an active part in music, which I have not done; it also seems to imply that my life now in its seventy-third year has always been musical, which it has not been. However, thanks to the gramophone and radio thousands of people who once upon a time were never able to develop their musical appreciation from the few concerts they used to attend, often under protest, have discovered in themselves a capacity for enjoying music which they would never have suspected fifty years ago. When sometimes I am inclined to curse the infernal ingenuity of man which has produced the atom bomb I remember the boon of music available for all at any time, and I bless that ingenuity.

Some thirty years ago I wrote an account of my earliest musical memories that began with a recollection of the Pan-pipes played by a Punch and Judy showman at Lowestoft, which instrument was followed immediately by the appearance of Punch and my being led away from the performance in an appropriate condition of panic. My mother remembered the panic at Lowestoft but told me that there had been a previous panic over Punch and Judy at Cork a year before when I was about a year and eight months old. She went on to recall that this panic had been soothed by the performance of a street hurdy-gurdy player, and that I had told her in a rapture about the 'moogit'; which was as near as I could get at that date to 'music'.

That hurdy-gurdy player in Cork over seventy years ago was the last response I was to make with my whole being to music for a long, long time. Indeed, within a short while music was to be a hostile intrusion upon the pleasures of existence. It began with the kindergarten I began to attend in 1887. Here I sat in a stuffy little room, the kind of room that dentists used to choose for their work once upon a time, in which, after a year of five-finger exercises and the scale in C major, I was taught to play the treble in a series of duets known as Diabelli's Exercises. I remember the mistress, a lean red-faced young woman with blue hands, getting much annoyed whenever, in the course of our joint effort, my left hand collided with her

7

right, and I remember thinking how unreasonable her annoyance was and how much more unpleasant it was for me to touch her clammy hand than for her to touch mine.

As I look back on those earliest exercises it seems in memory that all the treble part was written for minims to which one had to count two and entirely devoted to the space notes F, A, C and E. The minim presented itself to me as a face, a curious, fat, humpty-dumpty kind of face which was always going to be attacked by the black goblins of crotchets and quavers I could see over my left shoulder in the bass being played by the red-faced music mistress. The treble compared with the bass seemed to me a safe part of the world and I could not understand why it should have a complicated shell to indicate it when the menacing and unimaginably difficult bass was shown by a C, which being my favourite letter of the alphabet struck me as unsuitable for the evil bass. As well as of being faces I used to think of the minims (oh yes, and the semibreves to which one counted four) as pieces of silver money, and I remember hearing a person speak of somebody's silvery treble and wondering how this person had pierced one of my secrets.

Then came the fatal day when Miss Hunt informed me that I must begin the bass clef. Simultaneously with being introduced to the bass clef I was introduced to the crotchet, and the full burden of learning to play the piano was felt. I left behind the friendly E G B D F, so like a boy's name, and the friendly F A C E to wrestle with the demon G B D F E and that queer poisonous nut A C E G. The crotchets were now all nuts; the association must have been between nutmeg and aceg.

I was naturally left-handed, and perhaps if I had been tactfully and solicitously introduced to that cursed bass clef I might have enjoyed music long before I did; but for nine years it was to be my bane, and to this day, when I can still read at sight an easy passage in the treble, I have to spell out the bass with as much difficulty as I used to spell it out in the distant past. That dreary little room at the kindergarten was to be the preliminary to the drudgery of getting up early in the morning to practise for an hour before school. This purgatory endured from the year 1891 to the year 1897, and all that remains to me for those endless hours of boredom is the ability to play atrociously ten bars of an infamous composition called the *Retreat March*.

I cannot remember the name of the first composition I learnt to play; but I remember clearly that the second was *Le Carnaval de Venise* and the third *Rosalie the Prairie Flower* which came out of an old volume with marbled boards that belonged to my American grandmother. Walker Street, New York, was the address on the fly leaf, and from it my mother had learned to play the piano as a little girl in Brooklyn.

Five-finger exercises and scales were the staple occupation of practising. I had to begin at half past six in the summer and at seven o'clock in the winter; an abominable business, that practising by candlelight, when I look back on it. Fortunately I discovered a way to make the time pass more quickly by putting a book on the music holder which I read as my fingers went up and down the keyboard playing scales. I did not falter over two or three sharps even when reading *Huckleberry Finn*, but of course C major was the ideal accompaniment without a single sharp to miss at exciting moments. However, too long with C major used to bring our governess out on the landing of the floor below to clap her hands for my attention to her question how many more times I was going to play the scale of C.

The nursery piano was a Brinsmead, the front being of fretted walnut and pleated crimson silk. The drawing-room piano was a Metzler of yellow satinwood, which had a curiously muffled touch as if the soft pedal was always down. That question of pedals was a great injustice of early practising; the loud pedal was permitted only very rarely, and the soft pedal never. In fact, it was not until I learnt the *Retreat March* that I was allowed to use the soft pedal, by which time I was fourteen and very soon to be released for ever from the purgatory of practising.

The Brinsmead had an experience which perhaps few pianos enjoy. It was moved down from the top floor when the old nursery became the bedroom of my brother and myself to the schoolroom in the basement where the meals of the juveniles were eaten. My brother and I used it as a place of concealment for the fat we had managed to slip from our plates into our napkins. It was believed presently that a rat must have died under the floor, and then when discovery seemed imminent it was decided to move the Brinsmead piano down to Hampshire so that my eldest sister could practise in her holidays. I do not remember who or what was blamed when the decayed mess was discovered, but the gods aiding us, my brother and I somehow escaped detection. Sam Weller once reflected on the fact that nobody had ever seen a dead donkey or the grave of a dead postillion. What has happened to the pianos of the Victorian age? We can still see charming pianos of the early part of the nineteenth century and spinets of the eighteenth century, but what happens to instruments like that maltreated Brinsmead or to that muffled

Metzler which took the Brinsmead's place for a year or two in the schoolroom after being supplanted in the drawing-room by an Erard grand? A grand or an upright piano cannot be such an easy affair to dispose of; yet all those old pianos must have been disposed of somehow.

Practising on a piano was bad enough, but then my mother took it into her head that it would be jolly for us to learn to sing glees. The first attempt to beguile us into what we thought was an abominable abuse of liberty was to have us learn a German composition called *Johnny Smoker* in the course of which a variety of instruments had to be imitated. We felt that we were being made fools of by having to sing 'Ich kann spielen, ich kann spielen' and then proceed to a shamemaking imitation of flute and fiddle and trumpet in onomatopoeic German. If Johnny Smoker himself had appeared we should have slain him and hidden his corpse in that old Brinsmead piano. We did not want to sing ourselves and we did not want to hear other people singing. Those were the days when people were asked after dinner if they had brought their music with them and when there was a dinner-party we used to look at the guests' rolls of music in the hall and pity the misguided grown-ups who would have to listen after dinner to the singers. Occasionally we were involved in having to listen ourselves if we failed to dodge my mother's At Home Day. The At Home Day! That is an occasion to which the happy youth of to-day is not exposed. To come back from school and be made to change in order to go into the drawing-room because This, That or the Other was there who wanted to see us, ugh! And then perhaps to have to listen to somebody singing:

> I had a message to send to her,
> To her whom my heart loved best,

or

> Just when the red June roses blow
> She gave me one a month ago,
> A rose whose tender breath revealed
> The secret that her heart concealed.

We were nauseated.

There was, however, one visitor who, if we could persuade her to perform, enchanted us. This was Mrs. Barker, the mother of Harley Granville-Barker, who used to give exquisite imitations of birdsong. She was the daughter of an Italian physician and was a woman of singular charm. Granville-Barker must have owed much to his mother.

We put up with the singing at school concerts for the pleasure of boisterously applauding from the gallery. I do not recall any great singer who started his career at St. Paul's School, but I see across the gulf of sixty years a pink-faced rather plump cherub in Eton jacket and white silk tie and hear him singing in a beautiful treble *Cherry Ripe*. That was Sir Otto Niemeyer of to-day who after a brilliant career at the Treasury was entrusted with the job of putting their finances right for several countries and rose to Everestian heights of financial eminence.

In 1896 when I was thirteen we went for the summer holidays to Scarborough where Meyer Lutz was conducting the Spa Orchestra. He composed the famous Pas de Quatre for a Gaiety burlesque danced by Fred Leslie and three other comedians who were dressed as ballet-girls and made up to look like Irving, Toole, Edward Terry and Wilson Barrett. Irving was offended and in deference to his protest the make-ups were altered. I was much impressed to meet this genial old gentleman who had composed a tune to which we had all danced the Barn Dance at dancing-classes. Indeed, so popular was it that for some years the Barn Dance was always called the Pas de Quatre.

The dancing-class was not quite such a trial for youth as practising the piano or singing glees, but it was a trial, at any rate for boys. My earliest memory is of the one held at the kindergarten and dames' school. To this, being about five or six, I was sent in a black velvet suit with a vandyke collar. This horrid costume for small boys was the result of the success of Mrs. Hodgson Burnett's play *Little Lord Fauntleroy*; I remember being laughed at by magnates of seven and eight in white sailors' tops. 'Oh, to wear a white top,' I sighed to myself on the way home in the dusk of a winter's afternoon. Next week when I left at five-and-twenty minutes past two for the dancing-class I decided that, however much it hurt, I must do something to achieve a white top. So I flung myself down in the gutter and successfully ruined the black velvet suit at the cost of cutting and grazing my knees on the kerbstone. It was not considered economical to buy me another velvet suit and the following week I was in a white top like the rest.

Later I attended a dancing-class at my preparatory school which was presided over by an elderly gentleman called Lawson, who wore evening dress with a crimson silk handkerchief stuck in the opening of his waistcoat. He was rather a fierce old

gentleman with a face that sometimes turned as red as his handkerchief, but he was a very good master, who taught one to dance the
Ladies' Chain by banging on the head with his fiddle-bow any boy
who hesitated which hand to offer. He had an unpleasant habit, if one
was dancing fairly well, of fetching one out into the middle of the floor
to show the other boys how it should be done, during which ordeal
he used to play a rapid *pas seul* on his violin. He had an equally
unpleasant habit of fetching one out into the middle of the floor if
one was dancing badly, so that one never escaped those solos. Then
there was the detestable ordeal of walking across the room to ask
one of the little girls sitting demurely on the other side to dance.
One had to walk as we thought mincingly up to the lady of one's
choice, bow deeply, and ask in clear accents, 'May I have the pleasure
of the next dance?' Unless this ritual was perfectly fulfilled one was
banged violently with the fiddle-bow.

We learned to dance the Quadrille, the Lancers, the Waltz, the
Polka, the Mazurka, the Pas de Quatre, the Highland Schottische
and the Circassian Circle, but the only tune to which we danced
that I can remember is that Pas de Quatre of Meyer Lutz.

The happy day when I was told I could give up the piano was
for me a complete emancipation from any kind of music. From that
time on for many years I was bored by music. To be in a room and
hear somebody invited to play something filled me with dejection;
I do not recall a single performance that gave me the faintest pleasure. I was taken to the famous musical comedies of the 'nineties
like *The Geisha* and *The Circus Girl* and light operas like *Les Cloches
de Corneville* and *La Poupée*, but the serious music in them was something to be put up with as a boring interruption of the comedians.
I went to performances of *The Bohemian Girl* and *Maritana* by the
Carl Rosa Opera Company and decided that even the ineffable
tedium of school was more endurable.

Then sometime in my seventeenth year I went to see a performance of *Tannhäuser* given by the Carl Rosa Opera Company during
a short season at the Lyceum Theatre, and I remember the amazement with which it dawned on me that people really might enjoy an
opera. I fancy that my pleasure in *Tannhäuser* was entirely in the
drama, and had nothing to do with any development of musical
taste because I made no effort to hear other operas or even to attend
concerts. Yet that performance of *Tannhäuser* did bequeath to me the
right to claim, with the half comic, half pathetic self-importance of
adolescence, that without caring much for music I did enjoy Wagner,
and in 1899 to enjoy Wagner was to move out of insularity into

the wider air of advanced European opinion comparable with appreciating Ibsen and Mallarmé, Maeterlinck and Paul Verlaine.

It was a month or two after *Tannhäuser* that I made friends with a younger brother of Maurice Hewlett, whose lovely romance *The Forest Lovers* had been published in the previous year. William Hewlett had musical genius but he had lacked the diligence and concentration to make the most of his great gift. He had a marvellous facility for playing the piano by ear, and could give a performance of a Wagnerian opera merely with his fingers. Hewlett did his best to get into my head that music did not begin and end with Wagner, and he was at last successful in winning from me an admission that Beethoven's Waldstein Sonata and Chopin's Ballade in A flat did give me pleasure.

I do not think it was merely emotional pleasure; even to this day, with rare exceptions, I do not enjoy music emotionally. I think that I enjoy it for the way it occupies and cultivates the waste ground of the mind. In saying that I am anticipating a theory I propose to discuss more fully later. At the time of which I am writing I was finding in poetry all I required from art emotionally and from painting all that I required to satisfy the aesthetic side of myself. If somebody had suggested to me that I could get from Chopin what I was getting from Swinburne, Rossetti or Keats I should have laughed at such an absurd notion.

It was about this period that my first musical friends grew much excited over Tchaikovsky, and I well remember trying to discover the magic that was distilled for them from the Sixth Symphony. It seems incredible now when I look back at myself in those days that there really was once a period in which with absolute sincerity I could declare that I perceived no melody anywhere in the Sixth Symphony of Tchaikovsky; I seem to be confessing that about this time I was unable to perceive that sugar was sweet. I recall a dripping grey morning in February, a genuine Tchaikovsky morning, when I called on an Irish friend who was studying to be a professional pianist and was determined to get the melodies of the Pathetic Symphony into my head. Over and over again he played the first movement upon the piano.

"Do you mean to say you can't hear the melody?" he demanded. I shook my head.

"It's an affectation," he cried, using every moment a richer brogue, "to pretend you like the Waldstein Sonata and then have the damned impudence to tell me you can't recognize the melody in that movement."

And off he went again, playing the phrase over and over again in the treble with one hand. Hewlett had come in by now and he took over from Wolseley Charles, but it was no use. I could not perceive any melody.

A ludicrous incident occurred on one occasion while Hewlett and Charles were trying to convert me to Tchaikovsky. The landlady suddenly opened the door and gasped, her face pallid, that there was an enormous monkey in the bathroom.

"Don't be so ridiculous, Mrs. Burton," Hewlett told her. "You thought it was a monkey!"

"For God's sake, Mr. Hewlett, the animal's sitting there half as big as the bath and if I hadn't slammed the door it would have got hold of me."

"I'll go up and see what Mrs. Burton thinks she saw," Hewlett said.

"Whistle that opening of the Pathetic Symphony to it," I urged, "and see if this mythical creature is impressed."

Presently Hewlett came downstairs again. "Mrs. Burton wasn't dreaming," he announced. "There is a whacking great baboon sitting at the end of the bath. It looks pretty fierce, too. I slammed the door as quickly as Mrs. Burton."

And in fact it was a big baboon which had escaped from the Earl's Court Exhibition and climbed up a drainpipe to enter Mrs. Burton's bathroom on the first floor and occupy it. The operation of getting it out again and back into its cage at the Exhibition was long and difficult but it was accomplished at last by the baboon's keeper under the presidency of a London policeman.

Chapter 2

WHEN I went up to Oxford I had the advantage of being in a musical set, but out of perversity, or simply because I was still unable to enjoy music, I gained nothing from my association. I would not join the Oxford University Musical Club where I should have heard chamber music played by visiting artists of the first rank; I would not even attend the Sunday evening concerts at Balliol. Music remained a bore. Once a musical friend of mine asked another of my musical friends to play him Elgar's *Pomp and Circumstance*, whereat my musical friend protested at being made the exponent of such a cheap theme, and I remember wondering to myself how on earth he had arrived at finding something in which I could not perceive any tune at all so obvious as to seem cheap, but my heart was hardened and I was content to go on disliking music and making no effort to like it.

Now I look back to those days at Oxford fifty years ago and ponder the wasted time and lost opportunities so far as music was concerned, for the damage done by such perversity and silly complacent ignorance can never be repaired now. It was the same with singing, which I could tolerate even less patiently than instrumental music. Well, the moment was not ripe and it is idle to lament not having taken advantage of something that did not exist; it is only when I look back to the time before my musical life began that I realize in what a desert I existed.

In May 1904 I met Donald Tovey[1] at a lunch during Eights Week and left as soon as possible afterwards because he was playing Beethoven sonatas to an enraptured audience. Tovey was in his thirtieth year by now but he looked no older than the average undergraduate. He had eyes like those of a startled deer and spoke in a high echoing voice, rolling those startled eyes at infinity. He was in fact his natural self but he seemed to the less respectful of us to be affecting the airs of genius. Later on that afternoon with Raymond Wavell, a first cousin and exact contemporary at Winchester of the late Field-Marshal, I went to tea somewhere else that afternoon, and found to my dismay that Donald Tovey had also arrived. Presently, when thinking with relief of the sonatas I should be escaping, I said

[1] The late Sir Donald Tovey.

15

that Wavell and I must go down to the barges to see the First Division row at six o'clock; I was taken aback to be told by my host that Donald Tovey would be going with us. Wavell and I looked at one another in consternation. We both attached importance to preserving certain conventions, particularly Raymond Wavell, who about this date once bought me a cigar because I was proposing to walk with him down Bond Street with a pipe in my mouth.

The prospect of escorting this wild-eyed genius down to the barges under the critical eyes of our fashionable young contemporaries was not a welcome one. The reality proved far worse than our gloomiest forebodings. All the way down the High Donald Tovey conducted an imaginary orchestra, occasionally stopping to deliver some phrase of music in a kind of transcendental hoot. Wavell and I gazed at one another in despair as disapproving undergraduates with their relatives and friends turned round to stare at this strange figure in the sunlight of a late golden afternoon in May.

The embarrassment of Mr. Smauker in Bath when he was escorting Sam Weller to the 'swarry' and Sam started to whistle was no greater than ours. Like Mr. Smauker I felt inclined to beg Donald Tovey to take my arm, but that might have made matters worse because he would still have gone on conducting an imaginary orchestra and tootling away to himself like a cracked French horn.

Presently a crisis was reached when the ghostly scherzo Tovey was conducting involved an unusual energy of movement and he almost conducted one of those picture hats young women were then wearing right off her head. This was too much for Wavell and myself. We simultaneously discovered that we had forgotten to leave word about something in the opposite direction from which Donald Tovey was going and we left him to conduct his own way down to the barges.

In the following year I was lunching with Arthur Ponsonby,[1] who had just given up the diplomatic service in order to take part in the great Liberal revival that was imminent, when I met Donald Tovey again. The dining-room at Shulbrede was the refectory of the old priory, a large vaulted room. Tovey, who had been tramping over the highlands of Haslemere with F. C. Schiller,[2] arrived with the Pragmatist philosopher after we had waited a quarter of an hour for lunch and had at last, quite a dozen of us, taken our seats round the long table. Arthur Ponsonby was at the head of it with his back to the windows.

"Oh, what a wonderful room for sound!" Tovey exclaimed, as

---

[1] The late Lord Ponsonby of Shulbrede.
[2] Afterwards Professor of Philosophy at the University of Southern California.

he cupped his hands and started to make a noise between a trumpet and a dog baying the moon.

The guests at lunch gazed with astonishment at his progress round the old refectory followed by Schiller, who looked as if he wanted to take his seat anywhere as quickly as possible.

"Toota-ta-toot!" Tovey trumpeted.

Behind him, open-mouthed, was Arthur Ponsonby's small daughter Elizabeth aged about five and dressed in a sort of Kate Greenaway frock. She wanted to reach her father, but between her and him was this strange tootling creature whom she feared to pass. So Elizabeth swung right about turn and with short rapid steps hurried round the long table until she reached her father on the other side from Donald Tovey. She tugged at his arm and he bent down to see what she wanted.

"Elizabeth does not like that man," she confided, her eyes wide with dismay, her voice tremulous with distaste.

To return to Oxford. Every week in *The Isis*, the representative of undergraduate opinion in term time, used to appear the brief biography of some prominent young figure in University life under the title 'Isis Idol'. In February 1904 I appeared as the 259th Isis Idol and in the course of it my biographer wrote:

"He confesses to an indifference to music except as represented by Mr. Dolmetsch."

That enjoyment of period music was the result of going up to Cambridge during the Long Vacation to play in a dialogue of Thomas Heywood called *Worke for Cutlers* which had been discovered by A. Forbes Sieveking in the library of Trinity Hall. The parts were Rapier, Sword and Dagger. I played Rapier, and carried a genuine rapier of Elizabethan times, a difficult weapon to manage gracefully, for it was more than six feet long. The piece was performed in the garden of Trinity Hall and to lighten the wooden dialogue encrusted with conceits Arnold Dolmetsch was there with his orchestra, a family affair. Arnold Dolmetsch had a workshop in Haslemere where he made harpsichords, clavichords, lutes, viols and recorders; on these instruments for which it was written he used to give concerts of old music.

On this occasion in the Hall garden the Dolmetsch party were all dressed in Elizabethan costume and I recall the rigorous discipline he enforced. For myself I was enchanted by the 17th-century music and the antique instruments—the viola d'amore and the viola da gamba, the lute and the virginals.

From that time onwards I used to maintain that at last I had

B

discovered the music that really appealed to me. Nowadays I sometimes wonder if some of those would-be extremely musical people who affirm that they can only stand Bach may not be at the same stage of musical taste as I was in during my early twenties. I have often found that the pleasure they claim to be getting from Bach is really the pleasure of literary association, the same kind of pleasure that I still get from pre-Raphaelite painting. Let me quickly add that I am not referring to people who, having experienced the whole of music, return in the end to Bach as the master of them all; but I am always suspicious of perfect taste that has not been reached by a good many leagues of bad taste. I do believe that, unless at some time or another one has revelled in Macaulay's Lays or Longfellow's Psalm of Life, that one cannot possibly appreciate the best poetry.

Some thirty years later I would be writing about Handel's Sonata in C for viola da gamba and harpsichord:

"The tone of the viola da gamba is something between that of a violoncello and a viola, with a quality of its own that I hesitate to call unmistakable when I remember how many musical people I have heard fail to identify far more familiar instruments. This sonata is early Handel, and it is the early Handel which I like best. I am not attempting to question the greatness and the grandeur of him later on, even if on me personally it makes the impression of a Salvation Army leader in full-bottomed wig and full-skirted coat. There is no doubt that he expressed the musical ideals of the English nation in *The Messiah*, and though I wouldn't walk five yards to hear *The Messiah* (indeed, I would walk five miles not to hear it) I recognize the kind of brassy inspiration which it gave to English emotion. It is the kind of music which I feel the butcher Cumberland could enjoy. It is the music of port wine and apoplexy. It is the music I hear when I am turning over an album of Hogarth's plates, and if in the countenances of any of the characters I detect a faint expression of human nobility, I am willing to give the credit to Handel's music. If Income Tax collectors ever indulge in community singing, I have no doubt that they sing the choruses from *The Messiah*, for *The Messiah* is the first great anthem of man's enslavement by materialism. But this early sonata, written long ago at Hamburg when Anne was Queen of England, has a wistful beauty, a poignancy and a grace, which make any attempt to describe it or convey it in words as idle as an attempt to convey in words the perfume of pinks in a June garden. And that is what these old instruments possess, a curious spicy fragrance that their successors have lost. In aiming so much at fruit, instruments have lost their flowery quality."

When I left Oxford in 1904 I went to live at Burford in the Cotswolds where, in an Elizabethan house called Lady Ham, I spent a year in seclusion, reading hard and writing a good deal of verse. The only interruption was the production of *The Clouds* of Aristophanes by the Oxford University Dramatic Society in February. While I was rehearsing for this I stayed with Logan Pearsall Smith in a small and ancient house in Grove Street. He had recently invented that exquisite form of prose expression which he called *Trivia* but he was also much preoccupied with the sonnet.

The music for *The Clouds* was written by Sir Hubert Parry, and the overture contained what all my musical friends declared were some magnificent parodies of Richard Strauss, who at this date was the representative of modern music most familiar to British audiences, these parodies being in perfect accord with the spirit of Aristophanes' mockery of contemporary taste. My inability to appreciate the point of that music piqued what I suppose can be called my vanity and made me wonder if it were not time that I applied some of my diversified energy to acquiring a taste for and knowledge of music. The personalities of Sir Hubert Parry and of Dr. Hugh Allen[1] made a profound impression on me and I began to apprehend what I was missing by my ignorance.

Hugh Allen who was directing the chorus had been organist at New College for three years and was aged thirty-five at this date. He was soon to be recognized as the most inspiring choral conductor anywhere. When Hubert Parry died in 1918 Allen succeeded him as Director of the Royal College of Music and later he was to become Professor of Music at Oxford. What Hugh Allen was able to do with those choruses in *The Clouds* was almost miraculous. At that date it was a rigid rule of the University that only Shakespeare and Greek tragedy and comedy could be performed by undergraduates and even these plays only by the O.U.D.S.; another rigid rule was that no undergraduates could play female parts. At Cambridge the exact opposite was the rule; no women were allowed to perform in the productions either of the A.D.C. or on the Footlights which were the two undergraduate dramatic societies.

The Clouds who form the chorus in Aristophanes' play are female, but the Vice-Chancellor made a grand exception and the

[1] The late Sir Hugh Allen, G.C.V.O.

undergraduates taking part were allowed to wear wigs of feminine hair. The opening of one chorus, which began 'Ye heavenly clouds', has remained in my memory for fifty years and I have wished many times that I could hear it again. I have never found anybody that knew where the music of *The Clouds* composed by Parry is to be found. Dr. Vaughan Williams' overture to *The Wasps* has been recorded and it is often played, but Parry's overture to *The Clouds* has passed into silence. He also composed music for *The Frogs*, *The Birds*, and *The Acharnians* of Aristophanes, but none of it is ever heard.

The President of the O.U.D.S. when *The Clouds* was produced in 1904 was Alec Cadogan[1] but he did not play a part. I played Pheidippides, the dashing young racy man, whose wealthy father Strepsiades sends him to study the New Thought under Socrates. Strepsiades was played by C. W. Mercer who under the pseudonym of Dornford Yates was to become a very popular romantic novelist.

Sir Hubert Parry was just fifty-seven in that February. He was a burly rubicund man with a tremendous laugh and looked much more like a jovial country squire than a composer. He was the grandfather of that little Elizabeth Ponsonby who was so dismayed by Donald Tovey's tootling.

One dusky afternoon Parry stopped at Lady Ham on his way to Gloucestershire to have tea with me. Motoring was still enough of a rarity then to make his big car an event in Burford. He was wearing a fur coat and wrapped up in all the extra shawls and mufflers that wintry motoring in open cars called for.

After tea we somehow got to talking about Maeterlinck, and I read him some bits of a parody I had just written, something about the Princess Migraine and Prince Aspirin and Prince Cocaine. I remember that one of the characters had to say portentously, "I think there will be a blue moon to-night," followed by a stage direction in brackets (*A blue moon rises*). Suddenly Parry jumped up to seat himself at the piano where he began to improvise a skit on the music of Debussy's *Pelléas et Mélisande* which had been first performed some eighteen months earlier. It was so cold in the stone-flagged hall of that Elizabethan house where I was living that Parry put on his fur coat and sat roaring with laughter at some musical joke which of course I could not appreciate. He had laughed with such warm kindliness at my jokes that I was mortified not to be able to laugh with obvious spontaneity at his. It may well be that this was the actual moment when I decided that my almost complete ignorance of music was no longer to be tolerated.

[1] The Rt. Hon. Sir Alexander Cadogan, G.C.M.G., K.C.B.

What a delightful man Parry was and how surprising it was to hear somebody who looked and talked like a boisterous fox-hunting squire so eloquent about music and literature! I see him now waving to me from his big car as it goes noisily up that old High Street of Burford towards the bleak Cheltenham road westward bound, and people peering from lamplit doorways to find out what the unusual sound can be. To-day on a summer's afternoon the wide High Street of Burford seems narrow on account of the cars parked all the way along it, and the noise of them is continuous night and day.

The opportunity to cultivate the enjoyment of music came when my friend George Montagu,[1] as he was in those days, imported to the small house he had taken close to Lady Ham the instrument, now I believe almost extinct, known as an aeolian. This was to the organ what the pianola was to the piano. The music was on rolls and one pumped air into it by pedals, the hands being left free to manipulate the various stops. To listen to the aeolian being played by somebody else was torture; but to play it oneself was a delight, combining as it did stiff exercise with what one believed was artistic accomplishment. The repertory of rolls was a large one, and in George Montagu's collection there were complete rolls of the Third and Fifth Symphonies of Beethoven and of the Fifth and Sixth Symphonies of Tchaikovsky. That whine in the first movement of the Pathetic Symphony with the *vox humana* stop pulled out would have moved a heart of stone, and when I reflected that only four years earlier I had been unable to perceive the existence of that yearning melody I found my former insensitiveness incredible. However, it was the Fifth Symphony of Beethoven that for me as for so many others opened the gates of music. One hesitates to claim that any experience changed one's whole outlook on art and life. Yet when at the end of August 1904 I heard for the first time the Fifth Symphony of Beethoven played by an orchestra at a Promenade Concert in Queen's Hall that experience was like the sudden turning of a key which seemed to admit me in one sublime instant to the whole company of human nature. That sudden unlocking of my heart in the presence of a great audience could never have been experienced in the isolation of my own room. I was sitting in the right-hand corner of the top tier at Queen's Hall, leaning over the orchestra and seeming positively to be floating on the music. I was not caught up to any seventh heaven of my own personal raptures, but rather I was, as it were, absorbed into the expression of humanity which was visible all around me. I recall that close to my own place there were

[1] The Earl of Sandwich.

sitting a young man and a young woman, very much in love with one another. She was dressed in an 'arty' green gown of the period, and he was the kind of farouche young man with tumbled hair, thin face, and bright hungry eyes who may be seen by the dozen in any artistic quarter, busy hoping to become famous one day. And when Fate came knocking at the door in that opening first movement I lost all consciousness of my own petty egoism, and heard Fate knocking at the door for those two young people, and presently for the mass of that audience. The whole world seemed in love that afternoon, the whole world seemed hoping to become famous one day.

I went back to Burford to play that Fifth Symphony of Beethoven over and over again on the aeolian.

Chapter 3

THE Promenade Concerts at Queen's Hall seemed to me, at the beginning of the twentieth century, to express with the significance of a mighty group of sculpture an eternal gesture of humanity. In their unchanging manifestation of a phase of men's essential unanimity, in their capacity for evoking emotion from the mere spectacle of so many hundreds of people gathered together for one purpose, they exceeded anything I had beheld, whether in a cathedral it was some solemn and simultaneous gesture of worship or at a political gathering the spontaneous expression of popular desire. They possessed that enchanted tranquillity of action crystallized by art which displays in stillness the moment of its most intense activity. They possessed the quality of those immortal petrifactions of sublime motion like the frieze of the Parthenon and the dance of the three Graces in the Primavera and the serenade of the angels in Piero della Francesca's Nativity; or that incommunicable poignancy of stilled life that Keats nearly communicated in his Grecian Urn ode and perhaps did communicate in that fragment of the Ode to Maia.

Twenty years later I should write these words:

"I am fresh from revisiting the Promenade Concerts after a long interval of years. Beyond the fact that it now costs twice as much to stand in the Promenade as in days gone by and that I could no longer perceive either an egg-headed oboe player or a violoncellist of supercilious and celestial exterior, I could detect no change. The very coffee that was served in the bar during the interval might have been brewed twenty years ago and warmed up for the evening. Sir Henry Wood looked if anything younger than twenty years ago; and when one evening Sir Edward Elgar's thrilling arrangement of Bach's great fugue in C minor for orchestra was applauded and applauded again, and when Sir Henry Wood turning to the audience announced that he should have great pleasure in giving an encore of the piece in a few days' time, I felt that if he had announced he should have great pleasure in giving an encore of the fugue five hundred years hence, he would not have been overestimating either his longevity or his youthfulness.

"On one evening I sat luxuriously in the circle close to the orchestra, so that I could watch the hands of the players in that concerto of Bach for three pianos. It was then that I confirmed the absence of the egg-headed oboe player and saw in his place Leon Goossens, a master of his difficult instrument, who played upon it all through the Seventh Symphony of Beethoven as deftly and as beautifully as a faun. This second visit was my last, for I never had time to go again and sit where I once used to sit twenty years ago, in a corner of the upper circle, omnipotent and omniscient as Zeus himself gazing down upon this poor earth from the summit of high Olympus. But now, as I think of myself sitting up there twenty years ago, I suddenly realize that there is one great change in the orchestra, which is the introduction of a number of women into the strings. I wish they would not wear low-necked dresses and leave their arms bare, for by doing so they destroy all the beautiful black and white austerity that ought to make an orchestra resemble an immense pianoforte come to life. Incidentally, I noticed with disapproval that several of the male players were dressed more suitably for golf than for music. This may seem fractious criticism; but the loss of external decorum implies a deplorable indifference to form. I should not mind the orchestra's donning tweeds, or even pyjamas, to play most contemporary music; but I do strongly object to Bach in anything but the orthodox black and white of evening dress."

That was written thirty years ago. Let me again go back fifty years to recapture, if I can, the impression made upon me in that August of 1904 by the Pathetic Symphony when for the first time I heard it played by an orchestra.

I am fully aware how dangerous it is for a writer to attempt to put into words what a particular piece of music meant to him once upon a time, for such an attempt is liable to be as wearisome a failure as an attempt to relate what struck oneself as such an amusing dream the night before. The complete unification of form and matter in music means to say that every individual will derive from it an individual impression so intensely peculiar to himself that he cannot hope to generalize that impression. At the same time, a composer like Tchaikovsky has expressed so perfectly that *fin-de-siècle* weariness at the close of the nineteenth century, a weariness in which many of us during our adolescence found it necessary to immerse ourselves, that I must make some attempt to express what this particular symphony sounded for my inner ear. I no longer believe that the tragic bassoon which groans forth during the introduction a protest against the unendurable complexity of modern life is really tragic. I believe now that it is merely neurasthenic, which is not quite the same thing. But fifty years ago, when those strains pierced the blue haze of the tobacco smoke and reached my heart, what a divine philosopher that bassoon seemed! I know now that what it really reached was my solar plexus, and I know now that the whining melody on the strings which repeats and repeats itself through the first movement was not charged with all the human grief that ever was but with a kind of epileptic irritability of mind. Yet fifty years ago, all sorrow, all hope deferred, all the tragic sense of human failure

> Where Youth grows pale and spectre-thin and dies,
> Where but to think is to be full of sorrow
> And leaden-eyed despairs,

were in the first movement of the Pathetic Symphony, and if I wanted to heap the Pelion of neurotic prose upon the Ossa of neurotic music, could I not go home when the concert was finished and read Dostoevsky until the sparrows chirped in a dripping London dawn. It is all very well to laugh at the shrouded and confused horizons of youth, but when one looks back on them from the damnably swift stream of old age that bears one along to the edge of life they appear so much more enviable and beautiful, and so much more richly fraught with magical potentialities than the clear-cut, heavy, thunderous horizons of middle-age. So why should I not go on believing that bassoon to be a tragic and philosophic bassoon, and believing that melody so many times repeated to be a wail and not a whine, and believing that my heart is still being played upon by the tears of things and that my solar plexus is not being troubled by uncomfortably low vibrations and that the first movement of the Pathetic Symphony does express with supreme mastery grief and not merely a grievance?

If the first movement led one's imagination through dripping, grey and hopeless dawns, through what sombre and subtle twilights was one led by the second movement! In those days it was the fashion for writers, whether of verse or prose, to perceive in the barrel-organ one of the great illustrators of human emotion, and by how many French symbolists and by how many English decadents was a barrel-organ playing at twilight held up as the most intimate expression of human heartbreak! I am sure that the barrel-organ which served Huysmans, Mallarmé, Laforgue, Verlaine, Arthur Symons, George

Moore, and I know not how many more besides, always played the second movement of the Pathetic Symphony. Soon after the piccolo, like a romantic errand-boy, has gone whistling past in the twilight we hear that tragic bassoon again, trying to interrupt the barrel-organ by wishing that it had never been born. Fifty years ago I thought that the pizzicato note on the violins which brings the movement to a conclusion was as dramatically inevitable as the click of the shears of Atropos, but now when I listen to it I sometimes wonder if it was not the click of Tchaikovsky's tongue in his cheek.

Even in the relatively cheerful third movement Tchaikovsky manages to convey an impression of the human soul's imprisonment in modern life, and to make its cheerfulness resemble the cheerfulness of a squirrel running round and round in its wheel. And if for a moment the audience is allowed to cherish an illusion of human joy, circumscribed though it be, the gloom of the last movement is as gloomy as anything could be. And gloomiest of all is that tragic bassoon, again making as shamelessly direct an appeal to the human emotions as a lame beggar outside a cathedral.

Earlier in 1904 I had been taking every opportunity I could find of writing to music, and I produced a series of impromptus in free verse as the result of surrendering myself to the playing of Chopin nocturnes by a friend. Those impromptus have long ago been ashes, and I have only the faintest recollection of what they were about beyond an autumnal melancholy in the mood of Verlaine. A Russian friend in one of the regiments of Guards admired them, but he was in a melancholy mood, having been ordered East at the outbreak of the Russo-Japanese war, and having a presentiment of death which was fulfilled.

These impromptus, written at extreme speed while the music was being played, were quite formless, and, though rhyme and metre were used as much as possible, they must have included a large amount of bad overstressed prose. I hope that an admiration for construction and design and a radical preference for line rather than colour would not have allowed me to continue producing these jellies much longer; but in any case, the absurdity of such a method of composition was brought home to me once and for all by the second performance I heard of Beethoven's C minor Symphony later that autumn.

I had read that the opening four notes were intended by Beethoven to represent fate knocking at the door. And fifty years ago I was more easily taken in by such phrases, but when the music began

I forgot all about phrases and interpretations, and understood that the symphony did not represent anything except itself. I do not pretend that I could appreciate its construction at this date, in spite of my own performance on the aeolian. Yet, although I was entirely ignorant of its technical triumphs, I did apprehend that it was a titanic piece of construction, and I was as much aware of its grandeur as I should have been aware of the grandeur of the Parthenon without knowing its measurements. I came away from that performance with only one idea in my head—to plan, to construct, and to complete a vast literary work. I immediately conceived a trilogy of novels (this was several years before trilogies became the stock-in-trade of every young novelist, though no doubt Merejkowski's trilogy had already made its impression), the first of which was to be called Love the Destroyer and the other two Love the Something Else, but just what I cannot for the life of me now recall. This great work, the details of which I have entirely forgotten, was no mere affair of titles, for I remember meeting a friend in Oxford and going for a long walk with him and sketching out in detail for his benefit the theme of the three volumes. This friend was working on the *New English Dictionary* and had just come back from the north coast of Siberia where, like a hero of Defoe, he had been left behind for a year by the ship in which he had sailed. He had suffered extreme privations among the wretched inhabitants with whom his lot was cast, and I remember to this day his description of the grass he had to smoke. It amuses me now to think that not even the titles of two volumes of my trilogy remain in my mind and that the theme of the whole work is utterly obliterated from my memory, whereas the adventures of my friend to whom I confided my literary project remain fresh and vivid to this day. There is an excellent moral in this little tale for any of my young readers who hope to become great writers.

To return to the Fifth Symphony of Beethoven. I took the first opportunity of going to a third performance, and this time I remember that I had a strange impression of the whole of the audience at the Queen's Hall as existing within the music like a congregation in a cathedral, or perhaps more accurately as the life of birds, beasts and insects exist in a wood. It is obvious from the way in which I am qualifying my comparisons that I am attempting to convey an impression of a condition which it is not in the power of words to give except symbolically and by faint adumbrations of the reality. Moreover, I am trying to convey in the present what was at the time a revelation of the meaning of life which was inexpressible then and which paradoxically by the comparative facility I have since acquired in the use of words is even more inexpressible now. It sounds bombastic and pretentious to say that I perceived in that audience in the Queen's Hall the pattern of human life, or even to say that I perceived the countless diversities of the individuals composing it as a whole momentarily unified. Try as I will, my attempts to describe what I experienced remain a jumble and stumble of words; but I know that I came out from that performance with the profound faith that I could, if I may so express myself, do something with humanity. The next step to this was an equally profound conviction that to suppose I could do anything with humanity in verse was a delusion. After the C minor it can easily be imagined that my autumnal and melancholy improvisations to Chopin's nocturnes were as little satisfying as my previous method of harnessing myself to an academic emotion and allowing the diction-ary to hold the reins.

I should like to be able to confess proudly that my enjoyment of the C minor was the prelude to a systematic and passionate explora-tion of the whole of Beethoven's work. Alas, it was no such thing, and I must regard my enjoyment—I scarcely dare call it appreci-ation—of that mighty symphony as a happy accident; just as I have often come across people with a detestable taste in literature who have nevertheless managed to enjoy inexplicably, but quite sincerely, some acknowledged masterpiece of poetry. It is difficult for me now when fifty years have gone past not to attribute some of my present musical feelings to that younger date; yet I think I should be wrong if I were to refuse to credit my younger self with no more than a rhythm, a tune if you will, that took its fancy. That younger self was certainly deeply impressed by the scherzo in which the double-basses play the melody. Even as I write these words I have in my mind's eye the vision of those grave and elderly players plunged into the goblin round, and I can see a kind of supercilious disapproval in the countenances and attitudes of the violoncellists waiting to join in the dance and rescue it from the eccentricities of such pantaloons.

A day or two after hearing for the first time Beethoven's Fifth Symphony played by an orchestra I heard one of the first perform-ances in England of Richard Strauss's tone-poem *Till Eulenspiegel's Merry Pranks*. I heard a Queen's Hall audience which had cheered the C minor cheer what seemed to me a pandemonium of unpleasant noise. I read the programme and was infuriated by what it claimed the music was doing. It is strange to reflect that fifty years later

Till Eulenspiegel's Merry Pranks present themselves to my ear as a string of obvious tunes.

I was inclined to be discouraged about the development of my musical taste when I found other people's enjoyment of the music of Richard Strauss incomprehensible. Moreover, in spite of having played it over and over on the aeolian, the Eroica Symphony did not make upon me anything like the impact of the C minor. I was beginning to believe that an ability to be awed by Beethoven's Fifth and to be moved by Tchaikovsky's Sixth were accidents when I heard the first performance of a work by a composer whose music many years later was to bewitch me, and that composer a contemporary of the fateful five decades through which we were to live.

At the beginning of 1905 I and my future brother-in-law, Christopher Stone, who had been sharing the Burford house with me, decided that we ought to live in London if we were going to earn any money by writing. Having given up writing verses I was resolved to write plays; Christopher Stone, who had also given up writing verses, was resolved to write novels. We took two rooms at 7 Grosvenor Road, Westminster, the sitting-room looking out over the river to Lambeth Palace, the bedroom window opening on the stables of the London General Omnibus Company where, very early in the morning, inspectors jangled bells and stamped on the steps to test those vehicles that already seem as remote as mammoths. For these two rooms we paid 9s. 6d. a week. It was now the early autumn of 1905 and I was depressed by the thought that I had reached the age of twenty-two without having achieved fame and without any immediate prospect of attaining it. One evening I had gone to a Promenade Concert at Queen's Hall and, being very hard up, could not afford more than the shilling it cost to stand in the promenade. Feeling tired, I resolved to leave in the interval, and then my eyes were caught by an announcement that in the second part of the concert a work by a Finnish composer, Sibelius, would be performed for the first time in England. I was taken by the story of the Black Swan of Tuonela in the programme and decided to stay and hear it, though without hope that the music would appeal to me, so much prejudiced had I been by my inability to enjoy the programme music of Richard Strauss. From the first note to the last *The Swan of Tuonela* cast upon me a spell, so powerful a spell indeed that now looking back to fifty years ago I am puzzled to explain why I did not make a pilgrimage to Finland that I might hear all the music the great composer had written up to that date, when he was forty years old, fortunate in being the native of a small country whose government had provided for him since he was thirty-two.

I shall have more to say about the music of Sibelius later. At this stage in my musical life I could not have put forward even the most remotely plausible reason for being attracted to it.

Chapter 4

ON November 30th of that year 1905 I married the sister of Christopher Stone, which meant that I had married into a musical family. The first lesson I had was that chamber music could be enjoyable. It was during that winter of 1905–6 that I heard Frank Stone with the violoncello, Lucy Stone with the violin and my wife at the piano play the Mendelssohn Trio in D minor. I was so much exhilarated by my ability not merely to enjoy the Mendelssohn Trio but even to be able to preserve some of the melodies in my own head that without any of that leaden weight of anticipated tedium I went without protest to concerts at Wigmore Hall of the Norah Clench Quartet in which Lucy Stone with a Stradivarius was the second violin.

All went fairly well with Beethoven and Mozart, but when the Quartet gave the Debussy Quartet in G, I was as much bewildered as I should have been in trying to follow and appreciate the music of the Far East.

Although this was 1906 and Debussy's Quartet had been published as long ago as 1893 it was still hardly known in London.

"It's interesting, don't you think?" Lucy Stone said to me when friends were gathered behind the platform afterwards to congratulate the Quartet on their concert.

No doubt, with the feeble good manners that have been such a handicap to freedom of expression all my life, except when I am armed with the pen, I agreed with her that the Quartet was interesting. Yet something of my bewilderment must have been apparent, for she added quickly, "but strange".

"Very strange indeed," I declared.

The Debussy Quartet has ceased to sound strange for many years now, but it has never roused affection in me, and indeed I can say as much about all the music Debussy wrote. I can admire without loving just as the other way round I can love Grieg without always admiring him. Nevertheless, I resent Debussy's witty description of his music as frozen fondant, for, though that description may be abominably true the music of Grieg has helped such a lot of musical lame dogs over the stile that leads to the wide green meadows of appreciation beyond.

For most of us in those days when the gramophone was regarded as an expensive luxury on which to listen to certain singers if one could afford to pay perhaps as much as a guinea for one single-sided disc, the road to the enjoyment of music was the piano, and the pianola was accepted as the mechanical aid which would open the door to a wider and deeper knowledge than could be obtained in any other way. Ernest Newman, the greatest musical critic of the time, had given the pianola his blessing and by ignoring the gramophone had implied a disbelief in its ability to serve as anything more useful than a rich man's toy.

It was in 1909 that my father bought the latest cabinet model of His Master's Voice, which no doubt was the same as the latest model of the Victrola across the Atlantic.

The repertory included about a dozen records of Caruso in his golden prime singing solo, of Caruso singing duets with Scotti and Ancona, of Caruso in the quartet from *Rigoletto*, and, most admired of all as a miracle of reproduction, of Caruso in the sextet from *Lucia di Lammermoor* on a white-label celebrity disc which cost a guinea. There were records too of Melba and Destinn. The latter's performance of *Un Bel Dì* from *Madama Butterfly* was considered and indeed *was* a triumph of soprano recording, with which at that date the gramophone was not successful, or rather with which the sound-box was not successful; the recording was all right. Besides these we had a bunch of black-label popular ballads and three much-prized examples of Harry Lauder. And the instrumental music? There were two or three hackneyed overtures and two or three violin solos by Mischa Elman, but they were so much inferior to the singing that general opinion decided the gramophone was no use for anything except the human voice. No doubt if I had taken the gramophone seriously and searched for the better sound-box and the better internal horn or perhaps if I had gone back to the old external horn I might have dreamed of a musical future for the gramophone. As it was I accepted the judgment of the majority that it would never be much more than a medium to display Caruso's voice.

In 1924 I should write:

"If you are anxious to test the measure of Caruso's vitality, consider what he has meant to the gramophone. He made it what it is. For years in the minds of nearly everybody there were records, and there were Caruso records. He impressed his personality through the medium of his recorded voice on kings and peasants. Everybody might not possess a Caruso record, but everybody wanted to possess one, and a universal appeal such as his voice made cannot be sneered away by anybody. People did not really begin to buy gramophones until the appearance of the Caruso records gave them an earnest of the gramophone's potentialities.

"We to-day with our symphonies and quartets owe our good fortune to Caruso. Fifteen years ago when violin solos sounded like bluebottles on a window-pane, overtures like badly played mouth-organs, chamber music like amorous cats, brass bands like runaway steam rollers, and the piano like an old woman clicking her false teeth, Caruso's voice proclaimed a millennium and preserved our faith. . . .

"Yes, it was—nay, it is, a great voice. It holds within its variety the orange groves of Sorrento, the sparkling ripples of Santa Lucia, the raucous street-cries of Naples, and the calm blue expanse of the lovely bay. It is sometimes rugged as the trunks of one of the great ilex trees about Castellamare and sometimes soft (as in that mar-vellous last note of *Magiche Note*) as the sea-wind in the boughs of an Aleppo pine. It is as profoundly coloured as the grottoes of Capri, as passionate as the Italian sun, as velvety as the Italian sky, and sometimes as murky as the crater of Vesuvius.

"There are three things in this life that seem to store up the warmth of dead summers—pot-pourri and wine and the records of a great singer. As I write this, somewhere somebody is playing a Caruso record and somewhere somebody is getting from it an assurance that life is worth while. His immortality is secure, for every day, somewhere, somebody will hear his voice for the first time and say, 'This was a singer.' "

For music at this date I relied on my wife's piano and gradually I came under the spell of Beethoven and even more completely under the spell of Schumann. I developed the habit of writing to the accompaniment of music which I have retained for nearly fifty years.

In the days when emotional sustenance was required I think it is true that music provided some of it, and certainly I cannot hear Schumann's *Carnaval* without being carried back to the time when I was writing my second novel *Carnival*. A writer's second novel is a much more formidable undertaking than his first if that first novel has had even the smallest recognition. *The Passionate Elopement* had been started in November 1907 and finished some time in the summer of 1908. It was then despatched in search of a publisher but did not find one until 1910. It first appeared as a printed book in January

c

1911 and was received with such extraordinary generosity by the critics that Martin Secker the publisher was able to proclaim in his advertisements that it was the best reviewed first novel for years. This may have been very gratifying but it meant a much greater sense of responsibility for the pen that was taken up to start another novel. Luckily I was able to feel completely confident that I was going to pull it off again. Nevertheless, whatever my fundamental confidence it was inevitable that there should be many evenings when the fatigue of concentrated effort left me with the sense of failure at the end of it. Any intelligent schoolboy knows how often he has handed in his papers at an examination with gloom to find later that the very paper in which he fancied he had failed most utterly was the best he had done, and how often exactly the reverse occurred. The explanation is simple enough : easy writing makes hard reading and hard writing makes easy reading. In those moods of discouragement when all the effort was seeming unrewarded by the result I was sustained by music as a channel swimmer is sustained by liquid refreshment at intervals.

Nowadays music performs a rather different function : it occupies the waste places of the mind when I am writing. Instead of my sub-conscious attention wandering off to think about letters that ought to have been answered or bills that would have to be paid or a speech I was pledged to make in the near future that sub-conscious attention is held and rooted by music. In the moments of intense concentration of which at the age of seventy-two I am happily still capable I can hardly be said to hear the music at all, and a Beethoven quartet on a record can seem to have been played through in a few seconds before I am aware that the first bars are over. Yet in what are already coming to seem the far-off days when the discs had to be turned and changed half a dozen times in the course of a quartet I was very seldom so deeply concentrated as not to notice if a disc had been put on the turntable out of order. However, the value of this accompaniment of music is when the invention flags or the right word refuses to present itself or some confounded jingle of present participles required sorting out, for at such moments that accompaniment welcomes my attention to itself but declines to allow it to wander anywhere else. So much a part of my composition has this musical accompaniment become that whereas once upon a time I found anything more than a violin sonata or string quartet distracting I can now listen sub-consciously not merely to symphonies but even to opera.

In the spring of 1910 when there was apparently no prospect of my first novel's being accepted by a publisher my father suggested that I might have made a mistake in thinking that I was a novelist, and that it might be as well if I turned my attention seriously to the stage. A second dramatized version of *The Deemster* had been made by Hall Caine, and this play under the title of *The Bishop's Son* was to be produced at the Garrick Theatre in August. Hall Caine required somebody to play a young ascetic French priest who was cast ashore from a wreck on the Isle of Man in time to give absolution to Bransby Williams, who was playing the banished son of the Bishop.

I stipulated for a salary of £10 a week, with half a hope that this sum would be refused and so give me a chance of backing out. Some years earlier while I was still at Oxford I had refused an offer from Arthur Bourchier to sign a seven-year contract to be his *jeune premier* at the Garrick Theatre, beginning at £500 a year and rising to £2000 a year. It was exasperating to think that if I had accepted Bourchier's offer I should be drawing £30 a week by now, but even more exasperating to contemplate the intolerable boredom of acting for a livelihood. However, no sooner had I been engaged for the run of *The Bishop's Son* than Martin Secker appeared with an offer to make my first novel *The Passionate Elopement* his first novel as a publisher in the new year.

Hag-ridden all the time by acute influenza I dressed myself up as a priest to give absolution to Bransby Williams for six nights running and then mercifully the run of *The Bishop's Son* came to an abrupt end.

One of the actors, Shiel Barry, had been engaged by H. G. Pélissier of the Follies to play lead in a revue that Pélissier had undertaken to write for the Alhambra Theatre. Pélissier, who had started the Follies as a pierrot show to entertain seaside holiday makers, had gone on to make his troupe such a star turn at the music-halls that he had been able to take the Apollo Theatre and fill it nightly for his enchanting entertainment. The Alhambra management had decided to put on what was one of the very first revues staged in London, and Pélissier was commissioned to write it for production in September 1910. Shiel Barry had talked in the dressing-room we shared about the possibility of my being taken on to write some lyrics for the revue, which was to be called *All Change Here*, but I have never been a bubble-blower, and I was completely surprised when he telegraphed for me to go to the Apollo one Saturday night in that September.

It happened that I had a very bad sore throat and could hardly speak, but I made the best of it, and went off for a drink at Verrey's with Pélissier, Morris Harvey and Dan Everard. After some small-talk Pélissier gazed at me with those great eyes of his like violet saucers and said abruptly, "I suppose you understand that I shall want all those lyrics by Monday night?" "Of course," I agreed as airily as my throat would allow. "Then you'd better come back with us to Finchley now." I divined that if I were to make any excuse about the pain I was in or even to hesitate one instant Pélissier would take no more interest in me and that my chance of writing lyrics for him would vanish for ever. So off we went to Finchley.

In Pélissier's dining-room an immense cold supper was waiting with places laid for at least a dozen people. This was the Finchley use, and if I call that supper Gargantuan I am not using a trite epithet, because since Gargantua himself there was never any man who was so much Gargantua as Pélissier was. Not that he ever saw himself in the pages of Rabelais. "Do *you* think Rabelais funny?" he once asked me, and I knew by the contemptuous pouting of his lips that he did not, in spite of the luxurious edition of him he would have bought. Indeed, except over some of Dickens our literary tastes seldom coincided.

After supper, at which the host himself carved with a tremendous gusto, and which I had to pretend to enjoy, though every mouthful was an agony to swallow, we adjourned to a room that seemed full of grand pianos. "Now this is the idea of the revue." The author or inventor gave a muddled account of his conception. "And this is the first song." We wrestled with rhythms until five or six o'clock of Sunday morning, when I was allowed to go to bed. At half-past eight Pélissier's face rose like a sun above the foot of my bed. He was wrapped in a brilliantly coloured dressing-gown. "Aren't you up *yet*?" he exclaimed. "Look here, come into my room, I've got a new tune." I followed him, and found another piano at the foot of his bed. All that Sunday, interrupted by gigantic meals, games, and quantities of visitors we talked about the revue.

In the evening after a colossal supper I insisted on being sent back to the seclusion of Church Row, Hampstead, to work at the lyrics. Pélissier, when he took a fancy to anybody, wanted him or her round him all the time, and having apparently taken a fancy to me he was most unwilling to let me go. "Never mind about this damned revue. Go on talking. I like to hear you talk. You interest me." But I was determined he should have those lyrics the following evening even if I should offend him by going away to work when he wanted me to talk to him; and the following evening he did have them. After that he demanded my company all the time.

The first thing Pélissier always did when he made a new friend was to present him or her with a wrist-watch. So on Tuesday, when of course I had to lunch with him, the wrist-watch was bought. One of his traits was to be prodigally generous over presents and hospitality, but not very extravagant in his payment for work done. This attitude was not due in the least to meanness but to his deeply felt conviction that everybody round him—the other Follies, the men who wrote his words, even Hermann Finck who, by putting his tunes into musical shape, was indispensable—were really contributing nothing. No man was ever more aware of his own creativeness than Pélissier. "What does Hermann do? Nothing. It's the tune that counts." Yet even Pélissier had to admit that *In the Shadows* was a good tune, though he did his best to spoil it by making me write some idiotic words to it. "I've got a good idea for a song to that tune of Hermann's. Something like this. *You can take me if you want me or leave me if you don't,*" and on this fatuous verbal theme I had to build. But in case I am seeming to disparage Pélissier's comic genius, let me hasten to add that in nine cases out of ten he was justified in believing himself to be everything and his collaborators very nearly nothing. His fear of paying too much was thoroughly justified when one compared what he was with what we did; but inasmuch as no man ever made such exhausting demands upon other people's devotion (so that to work for Pélissier meant that one was at his beck and call for work and play for literally every hour in the twenty-four) that lack of generosity was not so justifiable. "You'll lend a hundred pounds to any actor that comes to your dressing-room and flatters you," I once told him, "but you'll argue for an hour whether you ought to pay me five pounds or six for a week's work." "Ah," said Pélissier, "but I despise *them.*" And after all there is much to be said for such a point of view, though at the time I might have put up with some of the contempt for a little more of the cash.

Somehow or other *All Change Here,* as the revue was originally and (after some fifty other titles had been debated) ultimately called, was finished; but it was a hard task in those days when the theatres and the music-halls were quarrelling over what was and what was not a stage play.[1] The Alhambra management having

---

[1] The grievance of the theatrical managers was that a play to be produced in a theatre had to be submitted to the Lord Chamberlain for his licence, whereas the music-halls were exempt from censorship.

insisted that to avoid a prosecution by the Theatrical Managers' Association there was to be no spoken dialogue, every line of the revue had to be written in verse and set to music. On top of that Pélissier, whose comedy was of the most intimate kind, was overwhelmed by the size of the Alhambra and quite incapable of constructing an entertainment in which he was not going to take the chief part himself. His own shows were essentially improvisations, and all through the rehearsals of that revue we felt that Pélissier was treating them as he treated rehearsals of the Follies with the consciousness that he would be there on the first night to fill in with his own immense personality any gaps. He declined to have a producer. He would show the principals what he wanted and, "You," he said, turning to me, "can manage the rest." Now the rest consisted of the Alhambra ballet, and my feelings when I confronted over a hundred girls in practice dress for the purpose of turning them into temporary Follies touched the poignancy of despair. I had only the mistress of the ballet to help me, and whereas she wanted her best dancers I was searching for the best actresses. I smashed the Alhambra traditions of fifty years when I picked the girls I wanted for each scene. The revue was a failure, but since it led directly to my writing *Carnival* I look back at it with an affectionate emotion that no other production ever has evoked or ever will evoke, and wherever you are now, you dancing London ghosts, I salute you with a very deep and a very humble gratitude.

The failure of the revue hit Pélissier a great deal harder than anybody knew except myself. Outwardly he was setting to work as usual to prepare a new show for the Follies at the Apollo. The immense meals, the flock of visitors on Sunday afternoons, the drives to Ramsgate or Brighton after the performance on Saturday night were as they had always been; but Pélissier himself was brooding over his first failure, and forever asking me unanswerable questions about his future. He divined that he had reached his climacteric and that from now onward the struggle to maintain himself would become harder and harder. "Some great change is coming," he would assure me, his great violet eyes seeming as large as the Pierrot moon by the light of which he had always performed, "and I shall either go completely to pieces or do something. But what I haven't the slightest idea." Then he would lie back and roar with laughter. "What on earth are you laughing at?" "Myself, of course." After this he would turn serious abruptly. "I like you, because you really do understand what I feel." Then he would gaze at me, his lips turned down at the corners, like a giant baby about to weep. "You do understand, don't you?" he would plead. And then he would sit in a melancholy, trying to solve the problems of life with the mind of a child. I guessed that the malaise which now continually oppressed him was his own premonition of adolescence. But how was it possible to say this to a man of thirty-six? Yet that was in effect what was troubling him. He had outgrown the simplicity of childhood, and he was frightened by the complications of growing up. Gradually, however, he seemed to shake himself free from the depression and doubt about himself caused by the failure at the Alhambra. The success of my book, when at last it was published, gave him tremendous pleasure. On the Apollo stage he was always introducing gags about passionate elopements to the complete mystification of the audience. Their obvious bewilderment would have been a good lesson for any young writer in danger of supposing that a few good reviews had made him and his work famous. I once asked the late William Heinemann if a novel of his had not been a great success. "Oh, yes, with the little London clique," he replied, "but that is not much use to a publisher." One hears the splash made by the pebble of one's reputation in the small pond on which the literary ducks quack, but the ripples grow faint very rapidly and they soon vanish altogether.

I alluded just now to our drives after the performance to Ramsgate and Brighton. We used to travel in two Daimlers, and the privileges of the road were taken advantage of with a kind of Dickensian relish. On the way to Ramsgate we used to reach a public-house somewhere before Blackheath called the *Marquis of Granby*. It would then be about ten minutes to twelve, so that it was a pious duty to alight and take advantage of the fact that there were still ten minutes to closing time in order to fortify ourselves with Dickensian drinks for the drive ahead. This hostelry had a curious museum of oddities collected by the landlord, and we drank amid a compendium of the late Victorian era. The next stop was about one a.m. at a roadside inn where, duly advised of our arrival, the landlady had prepared her speciality—the dish called toad-in-the-hole. I wish I could remember the name and locality of this inn, for we always ate there very heartily. Pélissier knew better than anybody how to motor. To be sure, he drove much too fast for my taste, but he made up for this by enjoying an inn, and what is more by getting the best out of that inn. I motor with other people, and we are fobbed off with a miserable ordinary; but with Pélissier even in strange country we never failed to eat and drink magnificently. I can remember the flavour of the cold lamb at Exeter after driving westward from six o'clock of a blazing July morning, and the richness of the wine in Penzance that same evening. We were only once defeated and that was by the—well, by an hotel in Southampton. There we fared abominably, and though I won a large sum over a race and heard the news after lunch, even that did not destroy the memory of the badness. But the best of all our Saturday night emigrations were those to the Albion at Brighton. We never wasted a moment on that road over so much as a gin and bitters. Nothing was allowed to take the edge of Sir Harry Preston's reception, and once more I see Pélissier as Gargantua when I recall him to my mind's eye, striding into the sitting-room and inspecting the cathedral of bottles on the sideboard. "Coronation Cuvée?" he asks, eyeing the champagne, and in response to the waiter's reverent nod of assent he beams like a schoolboy at the Christmas pudding. It was at Brighton that we used to sit up all night—Pélissier, Morris Harvey and myself—working at a new show for the Follies; and it was at Brighton that after getting to bed about seven o'clock we would be woken by Pélissier an hour later and invited to be ready to drive with him as far as Shoreham by nine. One of our troubles in those days was the difficulty of finding enough successful plays that lent themselves to being potted. We used to go and sit through a matinée, hoping to strike a rich deposit of potter's clay, while Pélissier would grow more and more like a tired baby in the darkest corner of the box, and the performers, having heard that he was in front and longing to be potted, acted for him with all their might and main. The only play at that time which really took his fancy was a Charles Hawtrey production called *Inconstant George*, and this chiefly because he looked forward to having an enormous bed constructed on which the greater part of the action was to take place. I used to argue that it was really absurd to parody a farce, but he was so anxious to go bounding about on the springs of that huge bed that he insisted on potting *Inconstant George*.

I used to hear many people express regret that the Follies were becoming so elaborate, and I am sure that they were at their best in the old days before the Apollo when they did a thirty minutes' turn at one of the music-halls. No doubt if Pélissier, without expansion, could have kept that first fine careless rapture and made all the money his temperament required, it would have been better for him and better for his audience. Unfortunately no artist can crystallize himself at the moment of his nearest approach to perfection. The real reason why towards the end Pélissier began to lose some of his hold over the public was his own boredom with the development of his Follies. He became exasperated by his own creation. He was like the father of a grown-up family who resents his children's dependence on him, but who, at the same time, resents equally their daring to suppose themselves capable of the least independence. Without the breath of his life the Follies were dolls. Even the addition of Morris Harvey overweighted them; and, just because he was not a doll brought to life by Pélissier, he always seemed rather like a professional introduced from town to strengthen the resources of local talent. Lewis Sidney, who combined with Pélissier to make the greatest comic pair our time is likely to know, was curiously ineffective without him. The Folly with most natural talent was not Gwennie Mars, as the public always supposed, but Ethel Allendale. It was she who was always given the most difficult bits to do, and she alone in my experience added anything of herself without for a moment ceasing to be a perfect Folly. She was Pélissier's incarnate whim, such a perfect Folly indeed that for the public at large she remained only a shadow cast by the Pierrot moon, and they attributed many of the impersonations they had enjoyed and remembered best to Gwennie Mars.

When my sister, Fay Compton, joined the Follies the end was already in sight. They were beginning to expire of sophistication in the attempt to keep pace with the public's enjoyment of them and to develop as their creator himself was developing. The unfortunate Alhambra revue began to seem only a temporary setback to Pélissier's ambitions. The mortification of that was forgotten at last, and he was for ever contemplating different ways to expand. He became preoccupied with the notion of writing a play in which I was to collaborate with him. The theme of this play was a situation handled at the critical moment without humour; then after a tragic dénouement the same situation was to be repeated, but handled this time at the critical moment with humour. The truth was that Pélissier was becoming so much obsessed by the importance of humour that his own humour took on a kind of grim seriousness. He had often been asked to take the Follies to America and he had always refused—rightly, I feel sure—because his instinct warned him that the Americans would not understand his methods. Indeed, for many years his instinct had been very nearly always infallible; but now even his sense of an audience was beginning to desert him. He would occasionally indulge himself in a kind of savage insolence towards the public, and if he was remonstrated with he would declare his contempt for them because they had no humour.

To the very end he remained an amateur; and, though this

amateurishness was the essential charm of the Follies, so long as
their enchantment retained its original simplicity and ingenuous-
ness, as soon as they fell victims to elaboration this very amateurishness struck the public as the contemptuous indifference of a too-
successful man. Pélissier himself did often make the amateur's
mistake of supposing himself superior to his audience, and his
frequent failures to appear without notifying the public beforehand
were typical of this unfortunate attitude. I have always felt thankful
that he did not live to encounter the First World War, for if his
humour had moved much farther along the lines he was dragging it
he might have lapsed into some tragical error of taste that would
have seemed unpardonable in that period of strained emotions.

On the other hand it is easy to imagine that if he had recovered
from his illness he might have thrown off some of that unhappy
obsession with the seriousness of humour, and expressed himself as
completely as he longed. It is a common fate of humorists to feel
themselves thwarted by the medium which has made them famous.
You may find it in Swift as much as in Dan Leno, and genius burned
so hotly in Pélissier that towards the end he fancied that the atmosphere of the Follies was stifling him. His marriage with my sister,
which at the time struck so many people as a kind of Folly joke, was
to Pélissier himself the outward signal of his resolve to conquer fresh
territories of the mind. Alas, it was too late.

Chapter 5

I WORKED for Pélissier through 1911, being occupied apart
from that with the writing of my second novel, *Carnival*. As I have
said, he was not a generous employer so far as actual salary went and
if I had not betted with assiduity and some success I should have had
even less to spend that year than I had. The prospect brightened
with the publication of *Carnival* in January 1912. How much cause
have I to bless that encounter with H. G. Pélissier after the failure
of *The Bishop's Son*! Up to the present *Carnival* has sold well over
half a million in various copies; it has been translated into several
languages; it has been mauled about in three separate films; it has
been dramatized twice; it has provided a libretto for a broadcast
opera; it has been performed as a broadcast play nine times; it has
been a book at bedtime on radio.

In the early summer of 1912 Gerald du Maurier suggested that
I should dramatize the novel for him, but Frank Curzon, his
manager, opposed the notion because the woman's part must out-
shine that of her lover. Presently Miss Grace George made enquiries
about a dramatized version with a view to producing it in America,
and early in September I sailed for New York in the old S.S. *St. Paul*.
Everybody is familiar to-day with the first view of New York thanks
to the films; in 1912 for most people it came as it came for me with a
shock of wonderment, the first vision of humanity's material future.

Ninety-one years earlier in another September my great-grandfather, who called himself Joseph Cowell on the stage after he left
the Royal Navy, had sailed from Gravesend for New York, arriving
there after a voyage lasting over six weeks. I extract from his reminiscences published by Harpers in 1844 that great-grandfather's first
impressions.

"I had put in my pockets, more for show than service, some
thirteen or fourteen English shillings: New York was then a very
different place of accommodation for travellers from what it is at the
present day; no oyster-cellars that you could stumble into at every
corner; 'restaurant' staring at you in the face in every street; and
coffee-houses, and all sorts of houses, capable and ready to accommodate a stranger. The only two places of the kind in existence then,

even when you were directed where to find them, was 'Morse's', a very humbly-fitted-up cellar, where a table-cloth was never seen, and a clean knife, only by waiting till the operation was performed, under a store in Park Row, where now, I suppose, there are thirty; and there you could find a fried beef-steak, raw oysters, or soup made of the same material, which at that time I considered sauce for codfish by another name; and one of a little better class, kept by a Frenchman, under Washington Hall, then the second best hotel in the city. After wandering about I knew not whither, 'oppressed with two weak evils', fatigue and hunger, I entered what in London would be called a chandler's shop, put some money on the counter, and inquired if they would sell me for that coin some bread and butter and a tempting red herring or two I saw in a barrel at the door.

" 'Why, what coin is it?' said a fellow in a red flannel shirt and a straw hat.

" 'English shillings', I replied.

" 'No,' said the fellow, 'I know nothing about English shillings, nor English anything, nor I don't want to.'

"I thought, under all the circumstances and from the appearance of the brute, it might be imprudent to extol or explain their value, and therefore I 'cast one longing, lingering look behind' at the red herrings in the barrel, and turned the corner of the street, where I encountered two young men picking their teeth, for which I have never forgiven them.

"The feelings created by the war with England, then long since over, was still rankling in the minds of the lower order of Americans, as if it were yet raging, and their hatred of an Englishman they took a pride in showing whenever in their power. In every quarrel, domestic or national, it will always be found that the conqueror is the last to forget, and generally the last to forgive. The language necessarily used in boasting of success rekindles the fury of a fire the dews of peace should always quench. In England the war of 1812 had ceased to be spoken of, or even alluded to.

"The turning I had made from the grocery was into a badly paved, dirty street, leading up a slight ascent from the river to Broadway, and at about half the distance, to my joy, I beheld, over a dingy-looking cellar, 'Exchange Office. Foreign gold and silver bought here.' I descended three or four wooden steps, and handed my handful of silver to one of 'God's chosen people', and, after its undergoing a most severe ringing and rubbing, the (I have no doubt) honest Israelite handed me three dirty, ragged one-dollar bills which he said, 's'help me God is petter as gould'. As all I wanted then was that they should be better than silver, my politics at that time didn't cavil at the currency, and I hastily retraced my steps to the red-shirted herring dealer, and, placing one of the dirty scraps of paper on the counter, I exclaimed, with an air of confidence, 'There, sir, will that answer your purpose?' He was nearly of the Jew's opinion, for he declared that it was 'as good as gold', and I gave him a large order, and made my first meal in the United States seated on a barrel, in a grocery at the foot of Wall Street.

"The best sauce to meat is appetite, and my herrings and bread and butter put me in a much better humour with myself and everybody else. From information gleaned from my anti-English friend and his customers, I was assured that the ship would be up by the evening tide, and anchor for the night in the stream, by nine or ten o'clock, and I engaged an owld counthryman to take me on board. Thus relieved in mind and body, I sallied forth again, up Wall Street and through Broadway. The pavement was horrible, and the sidewalks partly brick and partly flagstones, of all shapes, put together as nearly as their untrimmed forms would permit. The Park . . . I found to be about the size of Portman Square, but of a shape defying any geometrical term to convey the form of it. It had been surrounded by a wooden, unpainted, rough fence, but a storm on the first of September, the power of which we had felt the full force of, twenty days after, on the Atlantic, had prostrated the larger portion, together with some fine old buttonwood-trees, which either nature or the good taste of the first settlers had planted there, and the little grass the cows and pigs allowed to remain was checkered o'er by the short cuts to the different streets in its neighbourhood. The exterior of the theatre was the most prison-like-looking I had ever seen appropriated to such a purpose. It is not much better now, but then it was merely rough stone, but now it's rough cast, and can boast of a cornice. Observing the front doors open I ventured in, and, opening one of the boxes, endeavoured to take a peep at the interior of the shrine at which I was either to be accepted or sacrificed; but, coming immediately out of the daylight, all was dark as Erebus. A large door at the back of the stage gave me a glimmer of that department, and groping my way through the lobby, I felt, at the extremity, a small opening, and proceeding, as I intended, very cautiously, tumbled down three or four steps, and was picked up at the bottom by someone in the dark, who led me on the stage.

" 'Have you hurt yourself?' said this immensely tall, raw-boned fellow, with his shirt-sleeves rolled up over an arm the same size from the wrist to the shoulder.

" 'No,' I replied, 'but I wonder I didn't.'

" 'Have you any business here?' said he.

" 'No, nothing particular,' said I.

" 'Then you can go out,' said he, and he pointed to the opening at the back.

"I took the hint and direction, and found myself in an alley deep with filth the whole width of the theatre. I continued my walk up Broadway, and as I went the houses diminished both in size and number, and in less than a mile I was in the country. On my return, the theatre doors were open, and the audience already assembling. Phillips, the singer, was the 'star', and the performance, *Lionel and Clarissa*. The opera had not commenced, but I took a seat, with about twenty others, in the second tier. The house was excessively dark; oil, of course, then was used, in common brass Liverpool lamps, ten or twelve of which were placed in a large sheet-iron hoop, painted green, hanging from the ceiling in the centre, and one, half the size, on each side of the stage. The fronts of the boxes were decorated, if it could be so called, with one continuous American ensign, a splendid subject, and very difficult to handle properly, but this was designed in the taste of an upholsterer, and executed without any taste at all; the seats were covered with green baize, and the back of the boxes with whitewash, and the iron columns which supported them covered with burnished gold! and looking as if they had no business there, but had made their escape from the Coburg.[1] The audience came evidently to see the play, and be pleased, if they possibly could, with everything; the men, generally, wore their hats; at all events they consulted only their own opinion and comfort in the matter; and the ladies, I observed, very sensibly all came in bonnets, but usually dispossessed themselves of them, and tied them, in large bunches, high up to the gold columns; and as there is nothing a woman can touch that she does not instinctively adorn, the varied colours of the ribands and materials of which they were made were in my opinion a vast improvement to the unfurnished appearance of the house.

"Fully satisfied that I had nothing to fear, judging by the way the portion of the performance I had witnessed that evening had been approved of, I set off in good spirits to my appointment at the foot of Wall Street. The night was very dark, not a lamp was to be seen, save a twinkle from a little light through the closed glass door of a

[1] A theatre in London.

solitary chemist's shop, in the whole distance; 'twas about eight o'clock, and every store was shut: nor did I meet more than thirty persons during my walk. Look at Broadway and Wall Street now! I found my Irish Charon true to his appointment, but the ship was not expected for two hours at least. I enquired of mine host if I should be an intruder by remaining in his shop, and being answered in the negative, I ordered some more bread and butter, and a herring 'to close the orifice of my stomach', and took my old seat on a barrel of pickled shad, as it proved to be; for, after a while, the head slipped in and so did the tail of my new black coat, which I had had made out of respect to the memory of poor Queen Caroline.[1] To make myself as amiable as possible in the estimation of four or five gentlemen, short of shirt and long in beard, who may frequently be found in such places, I treated 'like a man', to two or three rounds of grog and cigars. I was then no connoisseur in the latter article, having never smoked tobacco in any shape in my life; but to act up to the pure agrarian principles I professed, I undertook a 'long nine' and a couple of glasses of 'excellent brandy', as the old red shirt said. On the passage I had never tasted wine or spirits, though those luxuries were included in the thirty-five guineas apiece cabin fare. So ill prepared, the 'long nine' soon knocked me over as flat as a nine-pounder: I was sick;

> 'The dews of death
> Hung clammy on my forehead, like the damps
> Of midnight sepulchres.'

"I was perfectly in my senses, but was incapable of sound or motion or, I should more properly say, voice or action. In these days the march of improvement in such matters would have doomed me to the certainty of having my throat cut, then stripped, and thrown into the dock; and the next day a coroner's inquest would have quietly brought in a verdict of 'found drowned', and no more would be said about the matter. But at the untutored period I speak of, they were content to take only my movables, *id est*, my hat, cravat, watch, snuffbox, handkerchief, and the balance of the thirty dollars. My incapacity to make resistance saved my coat, for I was so limber they couldn't get it off whole, and after, in their endeavours, splitting it down the back, and the tail being in a precious pickle, they concluded it would be more honourable to let me keep it—

---

[1] He had got into trouble by leading the audience at the Westminster Theatre in singing "God Save the Queen" at the time of George IV's Coronation after she had been excluded from the ceremony.

carried me down to a boat, rowed me off to the ship, and delivered me to Old Bunker, as 'a gentleman very unwell'.

"This is 'a full, true and particular account' of my manner of passing one day out of upward of Eight Thousand I've seen in the United States."

After transcribing that account by my great-grandfather I recall with a smile my own first day in New York ninety-one years later.

I was met by a representative of William Brady, the husband of Miss Grace George, with the auspicious name of Spingold who told me that Mr. and Mrs. Brady were staying at French Lick, Indiana, whither I was to proceed by train to-morrow morning. Meanwhile, he had taken a room for me to-night at the Waldorf Astoria and with the advice not to get into conversation with any stranger he left me until he should call to pilot me to the train for Indianapolis.

Unlike my great-grandfather I did not venture to go to a theatre, being unwilling to make a fool of myself by asking for seats which I feared might not exist under names familiar to myself. A cinema house in Broadway seemed easier to negotiate. It is fantastic to look back now to that dreary little place hardly a third full with an ill-lighted flickering screen on which was being portrayed an early film of jungle-life. No smoking was allowed; the seats were hard; the atmosphere was heavy with the heat of a September evening in New York. Moreover, I had already suffered two shocks to my system.

The first was when, after venturing to tackle the barber-shop at the hotel, I had suddenly been precipitated backwards in the chair for the operation of being shaved. I use the word 'operation' deliberately. At that date we were ignorant in Great Britain of the chair that presented one to the barber in a horizontal position. I felt like one of the victims of Sweeney Todd, the Demon Barber of Fleet Street. We were also ignorant of the hot towel. To this day I refuse to have my head enveloped in a hot towel, so acute was the shock of experiencing it for the first time in September 1912.

The ordeal of dining at the hotel was beyond my moral courage, and I decided to brave a restaurant. I felt that it was necessary to live up to the American half of myself, and summoning ancestral spirits to my support I asked boldly for six cherrystone clams. The waiter shrugged his shoulders compassionately.

"Have you any soft-shelled crabs?" I asked tentatively.

I learnt afterwards that I was on the very edge of the season for soft-shelled crabs. The waiter, obviously relieved to unload upon me the last of them, brought me soft-shelled crabs. I was convinced, when I tasted the dish, that the crabs were past their prime, but I lacked the courage to suggest as much. I merely decided to myself that soft-shelled crabs were a much over-rated delicacy.

It was with the memory of that first hot towel and those first soft-shelled crabs that I sat in that half-empty cinema theatre, from which I emerged to behold for the first time the sky-signs on Broadway. This was over forty years ago and no doubt the sky-signs on Broadway to-day would feel superior about their predecessors. I suppose that Piccadilly to-day could almost rival the sky-signs of Broadway at that date.

It was later on in that autumn before I repeated my great-grandfather's experience by visiting my first opera on the other side of the Atlantic. It was the first performance of Puccini's *Manon* at the Metropolitan Opera House. Caruso was the Chevalier des Grieux and Lucrezia Bori was Manon. I remember the performance but vaguely. The impression that remains most vividly is of the women covered with jewels who seemed on the verge of falling out of the boxes, so much of their posterior anatomy was bulging over the sides of them. The contrast with Covent Garden was violent.

The previous time I had heard Caruso was a year or two earlier in *Madama Butterfly* at Covent Garden with Emmy Destinn. I count her the best Madame Butterfly I ever saw. I recall from that performance to which I went with the late Sir Fisher Dilke and Lady Dilke a courageous and determined rebuke administered by Lady Dilke. When Madame Butterfly had gone behind the screen to kill herself and the child was waving little American and Japanese flags the poignancy of the scene was interrupted by two large overdressed women getting up to make their way out of the stalls before the curtain fell. Ethel Dilke leaned over and prodded one of the women in the back. "Sit down," she adjured her in a fierce whisper, and down she and her companion sat at once. People behave better at the opera to-day than they did forty years ago, but that better behaviour leads to an excess of tolerance for the second-rate.

Apropos of *Madama Butterfly* I recall my mother's giving me an American magazine some time in the 'nineties and telling me to read one of the most beautiful short stories she had ever read. This story by John Luther Long was made into a play by David Belasco which was used as a basis for the libretto of the opera.

It is not so much for opera that I remember Covent Garden in those years before the First War as for the Russian Imperial Ballet

D

which it can be said without exaggeration changed the artistic outlook of London in a night. One should always hesitate in age to praise the singers and actors and dancers that captivated one in youth at the expense of the present, and the first impact of the Russian Ballet was so tremendous that the present may be forgiven for wondering if the novelty of that experience may not have influenced our judgment. I shall not discuss the comparative excellence of the ballerinas of forty-five years ago and the ballerinas of to-day, but I must insist that Nijinsky was incomparably superior to any male dancer that has been seen upon the stage since. I can still gasp at the picture in my mind's eye of Nijinsky in *Scheherazade* bounding on like a great panther at the head of the slaves who are taking advantage of the Sultan's hunting to make love to the ladies of his harem. Nothing so superlative as an expression of physical grace had been seen like it before and nothing has been seen like it since. Indeed, it may be doubted whether anything like it will ever be seen again on any stage. To this day whenever I hear Rimsky-Korsakov's music that dark figure bounding across the stage like animated rubber preoccupies my fancy.

It may have been the exquisite combination of Nijinsky and Karsavina in *Le Spectre de la Rose* danced to the melodies of Weber's *Invitation* that has made me suppose that Karsavina in her prime was a greater ballerina than Pavlova. I should never argue the point. Moreover, I saw Pavlova first at the Palace Theatre, and the setting of Covent Garden was wanting.

I have wandered away from that visit to the United States, but it is just as well, for though it profoundly influenced me in many ways it played no part in my musical life. In spite of hearing *Alexander's Ragtime Band*, *Waiting for the Robert E. Lee* and *Hitchy Koo* as novelties which would not reach Britain until some months later I was not so much excited by ragtime as by the new word "highbrow" which I brought back with me to London in the spring of 1913 and which I suppose I must have played some part in popularizing.

All through that summer I was working hard down in Cornwall at the first volume of *Sinister Street*, sending off copy to the printers with every hundred pages completed; I look back now with amazement at the nerve both of myself and Martin Secker, my publisher. The last chapter of the first volume was called 'Music' and described a concert at which Michael Fane's sister Stella made her début on a concert platform, playing a concerto of Chopin. I quote a page or two:

"Michael sat by himself at the concert. During the afternoon he had talked to Stella for a few minutes, but she had seemed more than ever immeasurably remote from conversation, and Michael had contented himself with offering stock phrases of encouragement and exhortation. He went early to King's Hall and sat high up in the topmost corner looking down on the orchestra. Gradually through the bluish mist the indefinite audience thickened, and their accumulated voices echoed less and less. The members of the orchestra had not yet entered, but their music-stands stood about with a ridiculous likeness to human beings. In the middle was Stella's piano, black and lifeless, a little ominous in its naked and insistent and faintly shining ebon solemnity. One of the orchestra threaded his way through the chairs to where the drums stood in a bizarre group. From time to time this lonely human figure struck his instruments to test their pitch, and the low boom sounded hollowly above the murmurous audience.

"A general accession of light took place, and now suddenly the empty platform was filled with nonchalant men who gossiped while they made discordant sounds upon their instruments. The conductor came in and bowed. The audience clapped. There was a momentary hush, followed by a sharp rat-tat of the baton, and the Third Leonora Overture began.

"To Michael the music was a blur. It was soundless beside his own beating heart, his heart that thudded on and on, on and on, while the faces of the audience receded farther and farther through the increasing haze. The Overture was finished. From the hall that every moment seemed to grow darker came a sound of ghostly applause. Michael looked at his programme in a fever. What was this unpronounceable German composition, this Tonic Poem that must be played before Stella's turn would arrive? It seemed to go on for ever in a most barbaric and amorphous din; with corybantic crashings, with brazen fanfares and stinging cymbals it flung itself against the audience, while the woodwind howled and the violins were harsh as cats. Michael brooded unreceptive; he had a sense of monstrous loneliness; he could think of nothing. The noise overpowered his beating heart, and he began to count absurdly, while he bit his nails or shivered in alternations of fire and snow. Then his programme fluttered down on to the head of a bald violoncellist, and the ensuing shock of self-consciousness, which was mingled with a violent desire to laugh very loudly, restored him to his normal calm. The Tonic Poem shrieked and tore itself to death. The world became very quiet.

"There was a gradual flap of rising applause, and it was Stella who, tall and white, was being handed across the platform. It was Stella who was sitting white and rigid at the black piano that suddenly seemed to have shrunk into a puny insignificance. It was Stella whose fingers were causing those rills of melody to flow. She paused, while the orchestra took up their part, and then again the rills began to flow, gently, fiercely, madly, sadly, wildly. Now she seemed to contend against the mighty odds of innumerable rival instruments; now her own frail instrument seemed to flag; now she was gaining strength; her cool clear harmonies were subduing this welter of violins, this tempest of horns and clarionets, this menace of bass-viols and drums. The audience was extinguished like a candle. The orchestra seemed inspired by the angry forces of Nature herself. The bows of the violins whitened and flickered like willows in a storm, and yet amid this almost intolerable movement Stella sat still as a figure of eternal stone. A faint smile curved more sharply her lips; the black bows in her hair trembled against her white dress; her wonderful hands went galloping away to the right and left of her straight back. Plangent as music itself, serene as sculpture, with smiling lips magically crimson, adorably human, she finished her first concerto. And while she bowed to the audience and to the orchestra and the great shaggy conductor, Michael saw ridiculous teardrops bedewing his sleeve, not because he had been moved by the music, but because he was unable to shake by the hand every single person in King's Hall who was now applauding his sister."

When I re-read *Sinister Street* for any corrections I wished to make in a new edition of the book published nearly forty years later I changed "Tonic Poem" to "tone poem" and "clarionets" to "clarinets", but was relieved to find that what I had learnt about music since 1913 did not reveal any of those howlers which novelists have perpetrated from time to time over music. I had been cautiously vague in letting Stella Fane announce that she intended to play a Chopin concerto for her début. If I had written *Sinister Street* ten years later I should probably have given her the Schumann Piano Concerto to play, or perhaps one of Mozart's. However, considering how very little I knew about music when I wrote that chapter I got off lightly.

Chapter 6

THERE is little enough to say about music, so far as I was concerned, during the First World War. However, in Athens during part of 1916 I was able to go occasionally to the opera performed by a mixed company in Greek, French and Italian. It may have been ludicrous in *Il Barbiere di Siviglia* to hear the basso singing "Buona sera, signorina" and the soprano singing in Greek "Kalespera, kyrie". Yet I would sooner hear an Italian opera sung in Greek, French and Italian than an Italian libretto translated into and sung in English. Perhaps it is because I remember the impossibility of finding the best English words to fit the music of H. G. Pélissier and the continued wounding of my sense of language that I am more aware that so many other people seem to be of the failure of any translation I have ever heard or read to match the music. Moreover, English singers singing an English translation are rendered self-conscious by the clumsy phraseology in which they are supposed to convey emotion across the footlights. Never mind about the accent. They always sing opera better in the tongue in which the libretto was written. I am equally sure that singing in translation tends to make them enunciate badly, so much depressed are they by the words. I am referring to male voices. Operatic sopranos of any nation and in any language almost always sacrifice the words to the quality of their notes.

When opera in English is enunciated in such a way that every word can be distinguished I feel like saying what W. B. Yeats once said to me when we met in the lobby of the Theatre Royal, Dublin, during a concert given by John McCormack in 1924.

"It's been a wonderful concert, hasn't it?" I commented to the Senator in his top hat and frock coat.

"Yes, yes," the Poet replied, seeming to discard the Senator's attire and assume a bardic robe. "But oh, the clarity of the words," he moaned. "The damnable clarity of the words."

There is no doubt Yeats was suffering acutely, being, like so many poets, tone-deaf and therefore conscious only of words that he was considering an outrage upon language.

Among the operas I heard in Athens were *Norma* and *La*

53

Traviata. I record as melancholy evidence of my uncultivated taste for opera that I was bored by *Norma* and quite unaware in listening to *Casta Diva* that I was listening to the most exquisite soprano aria ever written.

I wish I could remember the name of the soprano who sang Violetta in *La Traviata*. Nobody I have seen since or whose performance I have heard broadcast or recorded greeted the return of her lover with such heartrending joy and therefore gave to the duet *Parigi, o cara* such a perfection of poignancy, although the tenor sang it in Italian and the soprano in French. I had been reading for the third and last time *La Dame aux Camélias* and, though I have never read that book by Dumas Fils since because I do not want to spoil the memory, it remains with me like my first reading of *Manon Lescaut* and *Trilby* and *Vie de Bohême* as an indestructible part of my youth.

Just before I left England in October 1914 in the hope of getting into the war Henry James said to me of my own book *Carnival* that it was in the tradition of young love in Bohemia, all roses and sweet champagne. Those words of his came back to me when I was watching the second act of *La Traviata* in Athens, and I wondered if my book would last as long as *La Dame aux Camélias*. Sixteen years later a recording of *La Traviata* for the gramophone was to produce some reflections upon it of which I should have been incapable in 1916.

"I have been thinking of *La Traviata* in relation to the music of Stravinsky and of what I have been saying about the effect of removing all taboos on art. The removal of such taboos is largely due to the greater social freedom achieved by the advance of modern thought. We should be careful, however, to distinguish between the genuine tolerance which comes from extended knowledge and the cultivation of the gentler side of humanity and, what so much of our modern tolerance is, mere laziness or indifference. Take the theme of *La Traviata*, which is the self-sacrifice of a courtesan in order to promote the happiness of her lover's family life. This theme with variations is the same as *Trilby*, as *The Second Mrs. Tanqueray* and perhaps a hundred other novels and dramas of the nineteenth century. The difficulty of reconciling the claims of love with the various other claims than can be made upon man or woman is obviously a fertile field for art. Equally, the more deeply respected the marriage bond, the greater the opportunity for the artist to invent new tunes for the eternal triangle. When society begins to criticize the conventions it has established at an earlier stage of its development, and when from such criticism it proceeds to adopt the point of view that other people's love-affairs are their own business, the bottom is so completely knocked out of the story-teller's world that he must search for a new formula. In the world of to-day a story like *La Dame aux Camélias* appears ridiculous and consequently the music which perfectly suited its emotion equally appears ridiculous.

"Violetta by her manner of life has cut herself off from the society of respectable women, or let us say of outwardly respectable women. She has left the *monde* and entered the *demi-monde*. Nowadays the *demi-monde* no longer exists, and the life of a woman like Violetta is indistinguishable from the life led by many young women who never run the slightest risk of being cast out of society on account of the late hours they keep in the company of men or of their habit of drinking champagne in night-clubs. To begin with, there is hardly any society left from which they could be cut off, and if there were any society left, it would feel, provided the young woman were not tiresome, that her morals were her own affair. The levelling down of all social distinctions which we admire as democratic progress is accompanied by an equally definite levelling down of all moral distinctions. There is still a faint prejudice against walking the streets for a livelihood, but it is the same kind of prejudice which exists against the profession of the pavement artist or the street-musician. It is not a moral prejudice so much as a feeling of contempt sweetened by pity, not for those who have failed to be good, but for those who have failed to make good.

"On top of Violetta's conflict with society comes Alfredo's conflict with family life. That sounds equally absurd nowadays. We regard as a piece of fantastic snobbery old Germont's demand that his son should give up the company of a beautiful and attractive woman because his débutante sister's engagement is likely to be smirched by her elder brother's behaviour. There is now no penalty attached to breaking the moral law so long as one steers clear of other people's cheque books and safes.

"But, somebody may argue, the theme of the *Antigone* is equally ridiculous nowadays. There the whole fuss is whether a sister shall scatter a few handfuls of dust upon the body of her brother and thus perform the ceremonial rites of burial essential to the future happiness of a corpse's soul. Her uncle, King Creon, is so determined that his nephew (Polynices) shall pass an unpleasant eternity that he makes his burial a capital offence, and the emotion of that sublime tragedy is achieved by the self-sacrifice of Antigone, who prefers death by being entombed alive to the neglect of a sister's piety.

"Sophocles was an immeasurably greater artist than Dumas Fils, but we must remember that many centuries have rolled by since the *Antigone* could enthrall a really representative audience. The *Antigone* is loved and appreciated by a comparatively minute number of human beings. Even long ago Sophocles must have already been appearing old-fashioned to the majority of his countrymen for Euripides to have produced his own tragedies with success. Take the *Alcestis*, where the theme is again the suggested sacrifice of a woman, this time a wife for a husband. The great moment in the *Alcestis* is when Admetus asks his father, then already near to dying of old age, to sacrifice himself a few years earlier to Death. He reminds him how often he has expressed a wish not to live too long, to which the old gentleman replies that one's point of view about living changes as one gets older. Euripides was already making the weakness of human nature itself a theme for drama, and a conservative poet like Aristophanes objected to his cheapening of all artistic values by such themes. Aristophanes, indeed, objected to Euripides for much the same reasons that an American highbrow critic will object to Sinclair Lewis. Yet, although Euripides might appear to artistic conservatives as revolutionary as an Athenian James Joyce, he still had plenty of conventional social conflicts against which to stage the inner conflicts of human nature.

"It is only within the last fifty years, indeed only within the last thirty years, that a variety of causes, of which speed is but one, has taken away from the artist nearly all of what may be called his familiar properties. Even since I myself have been writing, the themes which I could use when I began are now denied to me. I could not write another *Carnival*, and I am inclined to think that the failure to make it a vital film reflects this change in the popular attitude. As a book it may still be as much alive as it ever was, but I should be chary of expecting it to outlive all those readers who from their own experience could recapture the vanished world in which it was written. It is equally improbable that a century hence anybody will be moved by *Traviata* or by *Bohème*, and we who have witnessed the destructiveness of the first quarter of the twentieth century may feel doubtful whether, by the time the other three-quarters are accomplished, any works of art hitherto produced by humanity will have the least power to move those who are still unborn. We may feel equally doubtful whether Stravinsky's *Rite of*

Spring and Joyce's *Ulysses* will not appear a century hence as ridiculous as to the internal combustion of a Bloomsbury mind now appears *Lucia di Lammermoor*.

"The believers in James Joyce claim that he has stepped beyond music into poetry. The believers in various contemporary painters claim that they have stepped beyond painting into music.

"With all this merging of the arts that is now going on, it is obvious that within a comparatively short space of time the only standard will be a personal reaction to the artist's attempt to translate his intention. Such a standard will mean the final end of art because it will relegate art to the position at present occupied by dreams and nightmares. If I persuade myself to-morrow that I am a poached egg, and if I go round the world looking for a piece of toast on which to repose, I will pledge myself to find a certain number of people who are prepared to believe themselves pieces of toast; but would that justify any sincere and normal person in believing that I really was a poached egg? Might not the sincere and normal person suspect that those who agreed to consider themselves pieces of toast had hypnotized themselves into that belief because it seemed to offer them a chance of differentiating themselves from the common herd? I have taken an extreme instance, but I have just as much right to believe myself a poached egg as Miss Gertrude Stein has to believe herself a poet, and Miss Gertrude Stein is only the precursor of thousands who in the future will claim to be poets not because anybody understands what they are writing about, but because nobody does. Human nature is not likely to be indifferent to the attractions of esotericism until it is removed from the savage state by many more centuries of development. The history of literature is full of esoteric cults which have flourished for a short space and died. Music, with a much shorter history, was comparatively free from them until the twentieth century, and it is much more difficult for the normal man to dispose of musical charlatans than to dispose of charlatans in the other arts. He is always exposed to the accusation of possessing an undeveloped ear.

"When I see hanging on the walls of an art exhibition a piece of cardboard covered with blue sugar paper on which was stuck the label of a match-box, four or five matches, and some drops of red sealing-wax, and the whole labelled *Street Symphony* I can assert with a measure of security that the young painter who thus expresses himself is an impudent rascal, and that those members of the public whom I see gaping in admiration at the picture are half-wits allowed by this tolerant age of ours to utter their opinions

without being put in the stocks. When I read a sentence like this
from James Joyce's *Work in Progress*:

" ' 'Tis endless now since eye erewone last saw Waterhouse's
clogh. They took it asunder, I hurd thum sigh. When will they
reassemble it? O, my back, my back, my back! I'd want to go to
Aches-les-Pains. Pingpong! There's the Belle for Sexaloitez! And
Concepta de Send-us-Pray! Pang! Wring out the clothes! wring in
the dew! Godavari, vert the showers! And grant thaya grace!
Aman,'

I shall assert that not a single person outside James Joyce himself
could securely attach common sense to that paragraph. This, of
course, would not affect the artistic value of *Work in Progress* if, as
some of its admirers maintain, Joyce has passed beyond literature into music. At the same time those admirers must remember
that when the temperature of a human creature rises above 105°
similar verbal music flows from the lips of the delirious. But when I
hear a string quartet by the latest composer, although I can assert
with a measure of security that the effect upon my own ears is of a
quarrel among the tools in a carpenter's chest, I am aware even in
my own musical development of how easily a few years ago I might
have thought *Till Eulenspiegel's Merry Pranks* like a quarrel among the
tools of a carpenter's chest.

"Sir Osbert Sitwell has said that Stravinsky's *Rite of Spring* makes
all other music after it sound absurd. I accept that statement, but is
it quite the testimonial that was intended? I might say that the
noises which a baby dribbles above its bib makes all other forms of
human eloquence sound absurd. I might say that those shapes of
damp sand which a child turns out of a pail on the beach, and which
in the days of my youth were known as honey-pots, make all other
architecture look absurd. This argument of Sir Osbert Sitwell's
does not really lead us any farther. At the same time we who are
incapable, not so much of appreciating certain modern music, but
of even recognizing that in any sense of what we have hitherto called
music it is music at all, must face the fact that our lack of recognition
may be a sign of our being survivals from the past; a sabre-toothed
tiger might be incapable of recognizing that tinned tongue was
food.

"But if, the modern painter or poet may ask, you allow yourself
the liberty of doubting the finality of what we have hitherto called
music, why not allow an equal liberty of doubting the finality of

other forms of artistic expression? My reply can only be that every other art except music has always been dependent on the recognition of the critic or the public. The notion that the majority of painters and poets have had to wait until they were dead for their work to be understood is a fallacious conclusion reached by a hasty and superficial examination of an insufficient number of instances. The theory, for instance, that poetry was improved by being divorced from sense did not appear until the end of the nineteenth century in France. All this fuss about words and verbal association is a sign that our culture is decadent. You find precisely the same state of affairs in fourth-century Rome. A careful study of the works of Ausonius might be disturbing to the ultra-modern men of letters. Music, however, has never been hampered by the competing claims of form and matter. In music form and matter have always been one. We can talk about writing nonsense in words; but we cannot talk about writing nonsense in music, and critics who talk about the rugged common sense of a composer like Brahms are irrelevant.

"It is true that none of us knows the exact effect of Hamlet's soliloquy on his neighbour's inward thoughts, but we may all of us feel fairly confident that we have a rough idea what that effect is. The effect of Beethoven's Fifth Symphony on anybody else except ourselves is quite unknown, and what is more disconcerting, quite incommunicable. If an instrument could be invented for recording the thoughts of listeners to a piece of music it would undoubtedly register a state of mind far removed from any suggestion that music was being listened to; whereas the state of mind of listeners to a speech of Shakespeare would certainly evince symptoms of being related to, or prompted by, the spoken words. With so much diversity of reaction to accepted works like Beethoven's Fifth Symphony how dare one venture to deny the possibility that Stravinsky's *Rite of Spring* may arouse in some a genuinely intellectual or emotional response, incomprehensible perhaps to the majority at present, but perhaps to the next generation so easily comprehensible as to be commonplace? I confess I lack the courage to deny a future for the path which modern music seems to be taking. My own belief is that modern music will continue along the path it seems to have taken, but that as fast as every musician takes it his footsteps will be obliterated by the footsteps of the one immediately behind him. In other words, the music of the future will only be intelligible to, and enjoyed by, those who live at the time when it is being written, and I will add the prophecy that all art will be equally ephemeral. That is the penalty which we shall pay for destroying form. The artist

cannot be blamed for this. The world of to-day is beyond his forma-
tive capacity. Those who envy the past its great men forget that
any hope of such great men in the future has been sacrificed to their
finickin, individual comforts. Everybody cannot have hot and cold
water in every room and expect his neighbour next door to produce
a Beethoven for him. The Muses slept not on luxurious beds but in
the brakes of Parnassus. Even a happy childhood will in most cases
destroy an artist. The believer in material progress is entitled to maintain that the loss of great art is an insignificant price to pay for not
knowing from birth to death as much discomfort as his predecessors
knew in a day.

"No, I have no quarrel with the materialists if they succeed in
accomplishing the high standard of leisure and comfort for human
beings which is their aim, but they really must give up the idea that
the leisure and comfort they propose to create will result in anything
more than what I have called elsewhere a 'rich ennui'. The ultra-
modern artists of to-day are trying to discover how to intensify the
life which is being lived to-day. Alas, in order to do this they are
using stimulants, and dependence on stimulants is always a mortal
condition.

"Self-consciousness is my ultimate charge against contemporary
composers. They do not seem able to risk making fools of themselves. Whatever might be laid to the charge of James Joyce as a
writer, nobody could accuse him of cowardice. Nobody could have
accused D. H. Lawrence of cowardice. Yet there is not a single
young composer whose work does not betray signs of timidity.
Côterie literature is bad enough, but literature has hitherto survived
a succession of côteries. Côterie music will be fatal, because enough
great music has not been written to provide the world with what it
can absorb. Like the cuckoo in Matthew Arnold's poem, musicians
have despaired too quickly. The writer of to-day starts with the discouraging reflection that any addition he may make to literature is
almost certainly superfluous. That sudden and swift break-up of a
manner of life to which he had been educated by several hundred
years of progress along much the same lines has left him utterly
dependent on an ego the unimportance of which is being brought
home to him more ruthlessly every day. The young musician has
before him a virgin prairie where the young writer has nothing
bigger than a garden city. However, the idea of ploughing that
prairie never seems to occur to him. He feels safer growing bulbs in
fibre with a lot of other people.

"It occurs to me that perhaps the reason why so much modern

music exasperates the ear is because it is being written for instruments which were invented to suit tonality. A modern string quartet which so often sounds like four hens scratching about in a back-yard might sound almost sensuous played on instruments which have not yet been invented. New wine is being put into old bottles, and the bottles burst every time, though the fermented juice is thin enough. What about some new bottles?"

There was no music in 1917, most of which I spent on the island of Syra in the middle of the Cyclades. Indeed, there was no music until 1919 when the process of turning the isle of Capri into the isle of Capree began.

Fortunately the process was slow at first and during 1919 and 1920 Capri was setting in a rich sunset.

Chapter 7

IT must have been in the summer of 1919 that three musicians of international renown spent some weeks on Capri. Ottorino Respighi was living in the small cottage at Anacapri in which six years earlier I had written most of the second volume of *Sinister Street*. Francis Brett Young lived there later for a while; I believe that to-day Grahame Greene retreats to it. Respighi was an extremely modest little man and not apparently in the best of health even then. Like so many artists in every medium at that date he seemed perplexed about the immediate future for his art. We used to hear a great deal about the disastrous effect of the First War on the artists of the younger generation, but the European artists who suffered most heavily were those born early enough to have achieved a measure of success before the First War, who, having as they supposed settled down to carry out the scheme of their artistic future, were swept off their feet by the shattering interruption of catastrophe.

Respighi did not strike me as a modernist, and I have always fancied that his orchestral works were composed in a brave attempt to keep up with the bewilderingly rapid period. He considered himself first and foremost a writer of songs, and I remember he asked me to send him a copy of my poems in the hope of finding something suitable for his music. I could not get hold of a copy of them at the time, and when a couple of years later I came across one, the indolence, which always overtakes me when I have to contemplate sending off even the smallest parcel, prevented my gathering together sufficient strength of mind to send the volume to him.

The representatives of modernity on Capri were inclined to be condescending about Respighi, but I wager that his *Pines of Rome* and *Fountains of Rome* will outlive the compositions of those who, at that date, believed themselves the precursors of a musical revolution.

Marinetti, who had been preaching Futurism as early as 1908, was himself now suspect and so he was particularly severe on Respighi whom he proclaimed to be an unregenerate passatist.

Marinetti was the best of exuberant good company but his obsession with the need to erase the past could become tedious. He once said to me that the top of the biggest Faraglioni should accommodate an open-air café to be reached by lift from a boat. What value had empty rocks, however picturesque in an old-fashioned way?

I reminded him of the blue lizards that in the whole Mediterranean were found only upon the Faraglioni.

"Blue lizards!" he scoffed. "Anything might turn blue if condemned to live on those lumps of dismal grandeur."

Marinetti is no longer with us and not even yet has the isle of Capree managed to establish a café on the summit of the Faraglioni.

The handsome countenance of Alfredo Casella would smile compassionately but most courteously at the mention of Respighi's name. He himself was immersed in pianistic obscurities. Nevertheless, he could play the music of Chopin as beautifully as I have ever heard it played. The genius of Paderewski was imprisoned on gramophone records made with an Erard grand in pre-electric days. Alas, I never heard him in the flesh.

One night Casella was playing the Nocturnes in the *salone* of our villa, the guests star-scattered on the terrace in the moon's eye, a full golden moon hanging low above the serene Salernian Gulf. As we listened, each of us wandering in some magical dream of his own woven out of the music, a young Frenchman of the *avant-garde* arrived with a companion. At the door of our *salone* he drew back with an expression of agonized astonishment.

"Chopin!" he gasped. "Chopin! C'est dur."

Maliepiero was the third Italian composer in Capri that summer. He looked as distinguished as his Venetian patrician's name but I do not recall much else about him.

In 1920 I decided to forsake Capri as a permanent residence: its transformation into Capree was now merely a question of time. My first intention had been to acquire a small sailing-ship in which to wander round the world but at that moment a 60-years' lease of the isles of Herm and Jethou in the Channel Islands was offered by the Crown and I was accepted as the tenant of both. There I fancied I should be able to avoid the fever of the decade on which we were entering and yet at the same time remain in touch with the *zeitgeist*.

In the late autumn of 1921 I came to London for a brief visit from the island of Herm on which by then I was living and when dusk was setting in fast at the close of a drenching November day I found myself walking up Bond Street in a mood of depression. The drought of that blazing summer of 1921 had made farming on Herm a very expensive business. It has always been my habit when I am worried by financial problems to buy something. A defiant piece of extravagance is a tonic for such a mood. So I decided to order a new suit from my tailor in Grafton Street. It was within a few minutes of closing time, and I chose a green tweed which by artificial light seemed a modest and decent green. When I visited London next and went in to give my tailor a fitting I found by daylight that I had chosen for my new suit what with very little exaggeration I could describe as a length of billiard cloth.

"It is very green, isn't it?" I said to the cutter in a sombre voice.

"It is rather green, sir."

"I didn't realize it was going to be quite as green as this."

"No, sir," he agreed cautiously.

However, there was nothing to be done and I hoped that once the suit was out of Grafton Street it would look less green against the cliffs of Herm, In fact it looked if anything greener when grass was its background and in the end I had to have it dyed brown.

The reader may wonder why I am dragging this suit into a record of music. A little patience, and the importance of that suit will be apparent.

Sometime in the February of 1922 I came to London again and about dusk of a drenching day I again found myself in Bond Street and again in a mood of depression. This time, however, I rejected the cure of ordering a new suit. I did not want to make another mistake. So I left Grafton Street on my left and continued on my way into New Bond Street. Suddenly I found myself by the Aeolian Hall and from all but twenty years ago the memory of that aeolian organ of George Montagu's at Burford pressed upon my fancy. I would have an aeolian on my island, and forthwith I hurried from the murk and rain of Bond Street into the Aeolian establishment when it was only about ten minutes from closing time.

The manager tried not to look so much surprised as he evidently was by my proposed purchase. I doubt if he had sold an aeolian organ for some time. In fact we had to penetrate to some remote corner before I could be shown an instrument.

I said I wished to buy it on hire purchase terms, filled up the necessary forms, and asked for a catalogue of their rolls. None could be found but I was promised that one should be posted to Herm.

Two days later when I was back on the island the catalogue of rolls arrived, but alas, the symphonies of Beethoven and Tchaikovsky I remembered were no longer listed. Indeed, there was no classical music at all and the catalogue was full of selections from musical comedies already forgotten. My dream of interpreting

Some of the records when *The Gramophone* was twenty-five years old

Beethoven while the sea wind moaned round the windows of my library and rumbled uneasily in the chimney dissolved.

I wrote to the Aeolian Company to say that I had bought the organ under a misapprehension and that I wished to cancel the transaction. A letter came from them to explain that this was difficult owing to the financial arrangement they had with the hire-purchase people. Would I object to their sending me a Hepplewhite model of an Aeolian Vocalion Gramophone instead? With memories of that gramophone we had had in Cornwall fourteen years ago my first impulse was to write and ask if they thought that a few expensive records by Caruso would compensate me for my disappointment in not being able to play worth-while music to myself. Then I turned the pages of the record catalogue that accompanied the letter and realized that chamber music was now available for the gramophone not to mention many orchestral recordings which had not been thought of fourteen years ago. To be sure, the music consisted of abbreviated versions or isolated movements from quartets, and the orchestral pieces almost entirely of overtures. Nevertheless . . .

I waited for the arrival of that Hepplewhite model and the Vocalion records with growing eagerness. Then one morning in March the gramophone arrived. I put on the first movement of the Schumann Piano Quintet and listened to it in a rapture, careless of the scratch, uncritical of the way in which it had been shortened. When I rose to put on the sombre second movement, I was at the mercy of one of those passions without which Goethe says that man withers.

I asked the engineer of my auxiliary motor-boat *Aphrodite* if he knew the name of the biggest company that made gramophone records.

"H.M.V. are the biggest," he told me.

"What on earth does H.M.V. stand for?"

Adam Robertson smiled under the impression that I was pulling his leg.

"His Master's Voice," he explained when he realized that I really did not know.

I have always found that no amount of advertising makes the faintest mark on me unless I am already interested in what is being advertised. However, the theory is that by steadily keeping the name in front of the public anything can be sold. So I must be an exception.

The H.M.V. and Columbia catalogues for 1922 would look odd to the 33-year-old gramophone enthusiasts of to-day who were born in that year. In the H.M.V. catalogue there was only one

E

complete symphony—Beethoven's Fifth—played on four double-sided discs by the Berlin Philharmonic Orchestra under Nikisch. There were only a few snippets of chamber music. The strength of the catalogue was the Celebrity list printed on carmine paper at the end. In the Columbia catalogue there was a better selection of chamber music, but not a single symphony. The Celebrity list was a very short one compared with that of their rivals.

I spent about £400 in acquiring every single record from H.M.V., Columbia and Vocalion that seemed worth acquiring and within two months I had a collection of about 1200 discs all of which are extant to-day.

In early summer I visited London and found that Robin Legge, the music editor and critic of the *Daily Telegraph*, occasionally reviewed records. He suggested that I should write an article for him, which was published on September 22nd, 1922.

This is how I opened:

"Stevenson said it was only worth while being rich in order to have a yacht and a string quartet. I have personally nothing to add to these reasons, and now having just discovered the gramophone I am ready to forgo the quartet, the extra money for which will one day be spent on that yacht. I wish Stevenson could have had a gramophone in Samoa. I wish he could have played when he was in the mood that quintet of Schumann's. I feel sure that he would have become a 'gramophile', and that he would have written anxious letters to Sir Sydney Colvin about the long delay en voyage of that Schubert trio in B flat from the Aeolian Company, or enthusiastically to Mr. Edmund Gosse[1] of the unexpected arrival via San Francisco of a complete set of those glorious records of Jascha Heifetz from His Master's Voice. Yes, the gramophone is a consolation for living in the age of Lloyd Georgian verse and of being assured that Mendelssohn did not know how to make music.

"Yet I have only recently discovered the gramophone. Until lately I supposed it to be nothing but a detestable interruption of conversation and country peace, the golf of sound. Gramophony was a noise to me rather more unpleasant than would be the combined sounds of a child running a hoopstick along a railing, a dentist's drill, a cat trying to get out of a basket in a railway carriage and a nursemaid humming upon a comb wrapped in tissue paper.

"To be sure, I knew that there were such alleviations as the records of Caruso; but inasmuch as friends who produced one of

[1] The late Sir Edmund Gosse, C.B.

these records nearly always produced Tosti's 'Ideale' or Tosti's 'Addio', I came to think that the choice was a small one. I had heard old records of Mischa Elman; but violin records ten years ago were very different from what they are now. In those days the squeak of a bat would have been almost as audible. As for the bands and orchestras of those days—but let us forget them, although I regret to add that His Master's Voice still allows currency to some ancient outrages upon music. There is a ghastly record of Brahms's Hungarian Dance in D minor played by Joachim which is only fit for a museum, and even there should never be played. However, it is ungrateful to speak of such when nowadays the same company has given us that First Hungarian Dance divinely played by Kreisler and as perfectly recorded.

"My own instrument is what is called the Hepplewhite model of the Aeolian Vocalion, and I confidently affirm that neither that nor the Adam model of the same make is surpassed by any other instrument cost it three times as much. With equal confidence I affirm that it is folly to spend, let us say, £35 upon an instrument when for another £15 the perfect instrument can be obtained; and anyone who can afford £50 for an instrument can afford to pay the extra amount for good records, even if they have fewer of them."

The rest of this naïve article was devoted to discussing various recordings and offering a tyro's advice about needles and other accessories of the gramophone.

I was astonished by the correspondence my words evoked; no previous contribution of mine to the Press had brought me a tenth as much.

One letter from Percy A. Scholes which began "At last!" ought to have given me particular pleasure but the extent of my ignorance was such that I had not heard of Percy A. Scholes at this date, and was then completely unaware of the fight he had been putting up for some time to obtain some recognition of the potentiality of the gramophone from intelligent musicians.

When I came to London that autumn I was in a state of crusading exaltation, an echo of which can be heard at the beginning of another article I wrote for the *Daily Telegraph*:

"Having reached that encouraging stage in the progress of art, wisdom, and sport when a man grasps how little he really knows, I resolved to correct my ignorance by devoting a fortnight to an extensive experience of gramophones in London and to follow this up with a winter of extensive experiment in Herm. It would take much more than a column to relate my adventures with various instruments during this fortnight. Moreover, I should be chary of committing myself to a final opinion on the strength of hearing a few records played by nearly every make of instrument in existence. Therefore, whatever criticism I express in this article will be tentative, and by the time I find it expedient to set down my observations in print once again I shall probably wish to retract as much of this article as I should like to retract of the article I wrote three months ago. I have one advantage over most of the gramophiles I know, which is my omnivorousness. I like orchestras, bands, string quartets, flute solos, coloratura sopranos, and the ukulele. The last-mentioned noise puts me in mind of a squirrel complaining to his love. Why? Am I a case for psycho-analysis?"

I had found another enthusiast of my own craft in Archibald Marshall who was preparing to write about the gramophone for the *Morning Post*. Marshall was then a burly man on the edge of sixty and had enjoyed a great vogue in the United States as an authoritative exponent in fiction of country house life in England. He had been given an honorary D.Litt. by Yale and for about ten years had enjoyed a considerable financial success. Then suddenly the vogue for his books had begun to drop and he had become worried by having taken on responsibilities in the way of an establishment that with the rise in the cost of everything after the war was becoming a burden. In his worries he had found solace in music, and our combined enthusiasm produced a book of gramophone programmes for every day of the month which was published by Heinemann in November 1923.

In the course of his introduction Marshall wrote:

"This little book was devised and partly accomplished during a visit that I paid to Compton Mackenzie on his island of Herm. On that enchanted isle there is no winter, no telephone, no tax-collector, but I can think of nothing that is lacking to a life of perfect contentment. Music might be the one thing lacking to the enjoyment of an otherwise contented islander, but it had been the recent surprising discovery of us both that music of a wide range can now be supplied by the instrument which, of all others, had seemed to do most violence to music. There is no lack of it on the Isle of Herm, and there need be no lack in any other retired or lonely spot. . . .

"The scene of our easy labours was a book-lined room, in which there were two gramophones, and upon these we rang the changes for various kinds of records. The records were kept in albums, duly indexed, which is the only way to keep them when they run into hundreds. Mackenzie's library now exceeds the fifteen hundred mark, and the albums containing all this stored-up music handsomely fill a section of his book-shelves. My own collection does not reach those inspiring figures, but runs into some hundreds and contains ample material to draw from."

In the course of my own introduction I wrote:

"At the present moment we are, all of us who earn our living by entertaining the public, wondering what is going to be the effect of the broadcasting boom on our sales, and the great recording companies must be wondering more anxiously than any of us. I do not think that, if they will follow a strict policy of building up for the public a great library of good music, they need be afraid of wireless competition; but if they issue nothing except rubbishy so-called ballads, schoolgirls' violin pieces, and hackneyed orchestral compositions, they will not be able to compete for long with the rubbish that is being buzzed into the ears of the public every day by the broadcasting companies; poor material soon wears out, and the public are not going to pay for records of rubbish when they can get a change of rubbish daily. But the masterpieces are not played daily, and as long as recording companies have enough faith in the public to issue entire symphonies and concertos of Beethoven, they have nothing to fear from the future. There is no reason why, in another fifty years, it should not be possible to find libraries of music that will compare with the great libraries of literature to-day. Let the recording companies take warning from the history of publishing; let them note that no great publishing business has ever been built up by publishing rubbish, even if a brief prosperity has deluded some firms into supposing that a pander's life is longer than the wares he sells."

Those remarks of mine drew a letter from Mr. John Reith,[1] the Managing Director of the British Broadcasting Company. It was not yet Corporation. He asked me if I would call on him sometime that he might correct certain misapprehensions about the policy of the B.B.C. which I seemed to have formed. I lost no time in going round to the new headquarters that the B.B.C. had acquired on

[1] Lord Reith, G.C.V.O.

Savoy Hill and I retain a vivid memory of one of the most impressive interviews of a lifetime.

From behind a desk table that seemed as large as a mountain tarn rose the tall figure of the young autocrat, his lean face scarred from a wound he had received in action as a Sapper Major. His dark eyes looked at me with a concentration of will power that Mussolini might have envied; his stance was as rigid as that of a vigilant giraffe.

When we were seated, with the tarn between us, this remarkable Scottish engineer and son of the manse spoke about the future of broadcasting with the fervid eloquence of a fanatic offering to his listeners the contemplation of eternal life. He wound up by denouncing the folly of a Press that thought it could stem the power of this new and tremendous mundane influence. Raising his arm he brought down his fist upon the table with a bang.

"Those who think they can impede what we are setting out to do will be smashed."

John Knox, looking more like Savonarola than he might have liked, had spoken.

I assured Mr. Reith that he had completely changed my point of view about broadcasting by what he had told me; whereupon he said:

"I've just started a little paper as an experiment. Our first number was published on September 28th and I have great hopes for its future. I've called it *The Radio Times*. If you feel inclined later on to let us have an article you will find yourself in good company. Bernard Shaw, H. G. Wells and Arnold Bennett have all promised to write articles for me."

I have not yet read an adequate tribute to Lord Reith for the way in which he moulded the B.B.C. at the beginning. To few men in this twentieth century does our country owe a greater debt.

Chapter 8

ONE conviction I brought away from that interview with Mr. John Reith at Savoy Hill was that if he succeeded, as I had no doubt he would, in achieving what he aimed to achieve for broadcasting the future of the gramophone was secure, and this was then a most important assurance to have because six months before I had succeeded in bringing out the first number of a monthly review called *The Gramophone*. I knew that if my dream of making good music a profitable affair for the recording companies was to come true how vital it was to get the general public accustomed to hearing good music. If Mr. John Reith had told me that the B.B.C. could not afford to give the public anything but what it wanted I should have abandoned hope for the future of the gramophone.

As I remember the project to start a review was produced by the optimism engendered by champagne. The late W. L. Yeomans, who was then in charge of the Educational Department of His Master's Voice, was staying with us on Herm for Christmas, and to him in that mood of optimism I announced my intention. He told me that there were already four trade-papers in existence: *The Sound Wave*, *The Talking Machine News* and two others, the names of which I have forgotten. This shook me for a moment but he went on to say that he thought His Master's Voice might favour the idea of something that aspired to take the gramophone seriously.

The Managing Director of His Master's Voice was the late Alfred Clark, an American who had been a moving spirit in the great development of the company from the time it had opened its first office in Maiden Lane with a typewriter as a subsidiary product. Clark was friendly and helpful when I lunched with him at Hayes. I think he thought the whole plan was a bubble blown by a mad amateur, but he promised us three pages a month of advertisements for a year—two pages from His Master's Voice and a page from their popular-price Zonophone records—at seven guineas each.

"And we shan't object to your calling your paper *The Gramophone*," Clark added.

"Why should you?" I asked in astonishment.

"Well, it *is* a proprietary title, you know," he replied with a smile.

71

"Gramophone" was invented when Edison successfully opposed the right of exploiters of Emil Berliner's new method of recording to use "phonograph", which he had registered for the instrument that played his old cylinders, patented in 1877. I have never understood how Edison managed to establish a proprietary right to a word he did not invent.

In 1835 "phonograph" was used for hieroglyphics which represented sounds in contrast with "ideograph" which represented ideas. Then in 1863 a machine called the "electro-magnetic phonograph" was invented. This was "capable of being attached to pianofortes, organs and other keyed musical instruments, by means of which they are rendered melographic, that is capable of writing down any music played upon them".

Emil Berliner's original word was "grammophone", but the less accurate "gramophone" has won. It is curious how many people still write "gramaphone". Indeed, in that book of programmes written by Archibald Marshall and me the title on the cover was "Gramaphone Nights". I doubt if by 1923 the Gramophone Company could have sustained their proprietary right to the word "gramophone", for by that time it was in the Oxford English Dictionary. A relic of these verbal battles of long ago is the use by the Columbia Company of "graphophone" to avoid any legal difficulties with the Victor Company.

In the course of that article of mine in the *Daily Telegraph* I light-heartedly coined the word "gramophiles" for enthusiasts of recorded sound. It was a barbarism which I put into inverted commas and never expected to see in print again, but it has been in continuous use ever since (except by myself) and unless Edward Sackville-West's much better word "discophile" succeeds in ousting it, as I hope it will, "gramophile" may be found in the next supplement of the N.E.D.

I met at Hayes that afternoon the late Francis Barraud, who painted the picture of "His Master's Voice" which was to become perhaps the most famous trade-mark in the world. Obsolete may be that external horn and old-fashioned may seem that fox-terrier who sits with cocked ears listening to the voice of his master coming out of it, but I hope it will never be displaced.

After the Gramophone Company at Hayes, the next fence to tackle was Columbia. I had written to announce the publication of *The Gramophone* and invited them to send us records for review, but had received from the late Herbert Ridout, their publicity manager, a letter to say that before sending records to be reviewed Columbia wished to know how such records would be treated. I replied that such records would be treated on their merits and that if Columbia did not care to send review pressings on such terms we should buy them for ourselves and say just what we thought of them.

That brought a letter inviting me to call and talk the matter over in Clerkenwell. I found Ridout in a paper-scattered room high up in the Columbia building with a very large window looking across the roofs opposite to a wide London sky. We hit it off at once and he was to remain a devoted supporter and friend of our paper for over twenty years.

Meanwhile, I had written to my brother-in-law Christopher Stone to ask if he would like to take up the other half of £2000 to launch a new paper called *The Gramophone*. He wrote back that he thought it was rather a venturesome undertaking in view of the development of wireless which would soon make the gramophone obsolete. I do not fancy that I convinced him by my argument that wireless could not harm and would in all probability help the gramophone, but he agreed more out of good nature than conviction to become a partner. John Hope-Johnstone who was staying with me on Herm that winter was associated with the project and undertook to review the latest records.

It was a good thing that the two great recording companies were less discouraging than most of my friends and acquaintances about the new venture, or *The Gramophone* would never have become an accomplished fact.

I had been tempted to invite Sir Edward Elgar and Sir Charles Stanford to contribute to the first number, but the reception of my announcement by less exalted musical members of the Savile Club discouraged me from approaching either.

"Start a paper about the gramophone? What extraordinary ideas you do have!"

"The gramophone, did you say? But who's going to read a paper about the gramophone? Yes, I believe our maids have one, but I doubt if they'll want to read a paper about it."

"The gramophone? Surely nobody takes that horrible affair seriously?"

Stanford was by now in his 72nd year and in poor health. Indeed, he was to live only one more year. He was apt nowadays to be fierce with junior members and I did not feel inclined to risk annihilation. I shall have a tale to tell of Elgar presently.

In the end it was the ever good-natured Mark Hambourg who

gave me an article on piano-recording for the first number of the new paper.

I look at that first number, wondering how there was ever a second. April, 1923, Vol. I, No. 1. Editorial Office: Isle of Herm, Channel Islands. Publishing Office: 48 Hatfield Street, S.E.1. The latter was the private address of Cyril Storey, a friend of Yeomans who had volunteered to handle the distribution.

There were twenty-one pages of reading matter, eleven of which were written by myself under various signatures, one page by my wife, and a page and a half of reviews of some of the latest records by Hope-Johnstone under the pseudonym James Caskett.

In a brief Prologue, which reads to me now uncommonly like the preliminary announcement of a school magazine that is being published as a rival to *the* school magazine, I note that

"our policy will be to encourage the recording companies to build up for generations to come a great library of good music. I do not want to waste time in announcing what we are going to do in future numbers, because I do not know yet if there is any real need for this review at all."

Then came half a page about a Royal record, which we made our excuse for bringing out the paper when April was almost over in order that our readers might have authentic information about a record that King George and Queen Mary had made in Buckingham Palace of their Empire Day Messages to the children of the British Empire.

The 10-inch disc with *God Save the King* and *Home, Sweet Home* on the other side was to cost 5*s.* 6*d.* and all profits were to be handed to His Majesty for distribution among children's hospitals, etc.

"No other means are in existence" (the announcement continued) "by which the children of London, Inverness, Calcutta, Ottawa and Fremantle can at, say, twelve noon on Empire Day, 1923, hear speeches by their King Emperor and Queen Empress delivered in their own voices. . . . Very few, indeed, of the many millions of British subjects have heard the King speak, and fewer have heard the Queen."

This pride in the achievement of His Master's Voice expressed by Walter Yeomans may seem naïve to-day after the achievements of radio in the way of Royal speeches, but the gramophone deserves to be given a pioneer's credit.

From the very moment of hearing the opening bars of that Piano Quintet by Schumann I realized that chamber music was a gift above any other with which the gramophone could enrich my mind. I have no doubt that the difference between my musical outlook in 1903 and 1923 was the amount of Beethoven, Schubert, and Schumann I had absorbed through my wife's playing without realizing what a change had been effected. The secret is repetition and without doubt the reason why the people of this country enjoy music so much more than they did has been the opportunity the gramophone has provided to love music that once upon a time bored them because they have been able to hear it over and over again. The trained ear might enjoy a quartet of Haydn at a first hearing, but the ear which had never a chance of being trained would listen to chamber music at long intervals, usually under protest, and it seldom had the opportunity of hearing a quartet even twice.

In that first number I wrote an article on the practical utility of chamber music:

"I was reading the other day about some gramophone records that have been devised to help out physical exercises by setting them to catchy tunes, and it has struck me that the physical exercises might have been omitted and chamber music substituted for the catchy tunes.

"Incidentally, half the chamber music in existence has much more prehensile tunes than anything likely to be put on a gramophone record to help out physical exercises; although it seems impossible to eradicate from the waste ground of the popular mind the pernicious and weedy opinion that chamber music is dull."

Having collected fifteen more or less mutilated pieces of recorded chamber music, I drew up a programme of two for every day of the week with one extra for Sunday evening. The Schumann Piano Quintet in E flat, the Mozart Quintet in G minor (which was recorded during an air-raid), three Mozart quartets, two Mozart trios, the first three Beethoven quartets of Opus 18, Schumann's Quartet in A, Haydn's Quartet in B flat, Mendelssohn's Quartet in E flat and his Trio in D minor, and Schubert's Trio in B flat— that was the sum total of chamber music available for the gramophone in April 1923. Eight of these pieces had been recorded by Vocalion, six by Columbia. His Master's Voice had not yet ventured to put out more than a single movement, usually cut down to fit one side of a disc.

I commented:

" . . . The above 32 records will cost £12, and will provide 3 hours and 26 minutes' music, which comes to very nearly a shilling a minute, and sounds expensive. I do not know what the cost of a physical exerciser is, as I am happy to say I have never had occasion to use one, but I should imagine that it would be considerably cheaper than this. At the same time, if catchy tunes are to be invoked to help the physical exercises it will add greatly to their cost, and I am sure that my selection of chamber music will do a man much more good than plunging backwards and forwards from two stirrups, or whatever they are called, at the end of a yard of elastic. Personally, I should recommend taking one's musical exercises before getting up in the morning and before turning over at night; but I know that a great prejudice exists in England against lying in bed for any other purpose than sleep, and so I suggest that the morning music should accompany the shave. If you lather your face during the first two movements, you will get such a lather as only barbers know how to give; and if you start shaving to the third movement, you will find that the last movement will last long enough for you to put your shaving things neatly away. I still think that the best way for the soul's health would be to listen quietly in bed before getting up; perhaps this leisurely attention could be granted to the Mozart quintet on Sunday morning."

And I concluded:

"It is clear that the recording companies cannot go on offering music to the public at a dead loss, and I have written these few words in the hope that some of my highbrow friends will condescend to realize that *The Gramophone* has not been entirely devoted to propagating Saint-Saëns on the accordion. Music is something more than a drug; it can provoke an attitude toward life, but it must be approached with a certain humility and with a determination to gain from it what others have gained. I can promise those who will make this effort to circumvent the great bogey of dullness which guards the treasure that, if they will buy the fifteen pieces of chamber music recommended and play each piece once a week for a year, they will look back to their musical appreciation before they made this experiement with horror, shame, and remorse. I am not asking them to give themselves the trouble to acquire any technical appreciation, but merely to saturate themselves in melodious sound as they saturate themselves in warm baths. No appreciation of drainage is necessary for the appreciation of a warm bath."

When Yeomans had warned me how important it was to get the gramophone societies in our new paper I heard of gramophone societies for the first time.

Three and a half pages of that first number were devoted to gramophone societies. W. J. Rogers, the Honorary Secretary of the Glasgow and District G.S., provided valuable hints on starting a gramophone society, and we had reports on the activities of the Brixton Gramophone Society, the South-East London Music Society and the Tyneside Gramophone and Phonograph Society.

To-day, when I am President of the Scottish Federation of Gramophone Societies besides being Patron or Honorary President of more than a dozen gramophone societies all over Great Britain, and when the circulation of that paper which started like a school magazine thirty-two years ago will probably be nearly 70,000 monthly by the time these words are in print, I derive a sentimental satisfaction from recording the names of those four gramophone societies which helped to make up our first number.

In my review of the first quarter of 1923 I unwittingly imperilled the success of a great coup that Columbia were preparing for September when they intended to launch their new instrument called the Grafonola, the great feature of which was its apparent ability to eliminate the scratch. At this date the scratch was the arch enemy of the gramophone record. In fact the elimination of the scratch had nothing whatever to do with the instrument but was due to a new method of recording, which I lack the technical ability to explain. Obviously in order to have enough records with which to demonstrate this revolutionary instrument it was necessary to begin issuing them some months in advance. None of the musical critics in the Press who condescended occasionally, and that is the right verb, to mention gramophone records had passed any comment on the new Columbia method of pressing a record.

Completely unaware that I was behaving like an *enfant terrible* I wrote in that first number of *The Gramophone*:

"By far the most encouraging product of the first quarter of 1923 is the new wax that the Columbia Company is using for all its records. When played with the loudest needle there is less scratch on them than there used to be on old Columbia records with the softest needle in existence. Moreover, what scratch there is has no quality of harshness, and is less than the light crackle of a gently burning fire. The two records of the Léner Quartet of Budapest are really superb, apart from the almost noiseless wax the recording is magnificent and the interpretation of a linkèd sweetness."

Ridout got through at once on the telephone to ask for a reason he was not at liberty to disclose that I and our reviewers would abstain for the next four months from commenting on the scratch-lessness of the new Columbia records.

"I was going to suggest a rival to the H.M.V. dog," I told him. "A dear little kitten peeping out from every record with the motto, *I don't scratch*."

All was well in the end. In September the virtues of the new Grafonola were demonstrated at the Connaught Rooms to a gathering of the Press and 400 people. Sir Henry Wood proclaimed that the new instrument was the greatest contribution to the advance-ment of music since the original invention of the gramophone itself, and all the musical critics declared that the elimination of the scratch had saved the future of the gramophone.

Columbia shares were quoted at 5s. just before that first number of *The Gramophone*, but I had not the spare cash to take advantage of an offer to buy £400 worth. A pity. I should have made £40,000 if I had sold them three or four years later. Phew!

In that first quarterly review of records I wrote in *The Gramophone* I find I reviewed no less than seventy-two of one kind or another, and I reckon that I must have spent six hours a day listening to gramophone records, either to new ones or those I had already collected.

In addition to that the scanty chamber music available was being played to me night after night while I worked. Everybody on Herm took a turn at the job, and it *was* a turn in those days when the gramophone had to be wound up all the time and every disc had to be turned over. Herm was becoming a heavier financial burden all the time and I could not afford to stop writing. I managed to arrange for people to sit up playing every night until 3 a.m., but I myself often went on writing for another three or four hours.

One thing pleases me in that first quarterly review, and that is the recognition of Toscanini's genius as a conductor when he was unknown in Great Britain. I quote:

"I have two records of the Finale of the Fifth Symphony, con-ducted by Toscanini. These have been published in America and

Italy, but not in England. I think that Toscanini's small orchestra is the most effective of all on the gramophone. If a Beethoven fanatic will give himself the trouble to order these two discs, he will find them listed in the Italian catalogue. If he is content to wait for about six months while the French fool about with them in transit, and if he does not fear embarking on a long correspondence with the pompous buffoons who run the English Customs, and if he will pay the exorbitant duty of 33⅓% he will one day have his reward. If he is wealthy enough, patient enough, and fond enough of music, he might order at the same time a Gagliarda by Vincenzo Galilei, the Finale of Beethoven's First Symphony, and the Third Movement and Finale of Mozart's Symphony in E flat major."

Owing to the delay in our April number we could not get out a number for May, but there is no apology in the second number published in June for such casual behaviour. We had printed 6000 of our first number and during May unsold copies on sale or return were coming back from the newsagents. I decided to print only 3000 of the second number, hoping to obtain the advertisement of being sold out.

In this, chiefly on account of an admirable survey of all the Galli-Curci records by James Caskett, we were successful. I think it is true to say that Madame Galli-Curci was the first soprano to make it seem worth while acquiring a gramophone merely to hear her sing. She did as much to cultivate a taste for opera during the 'twenties as Caruso had done fifteen years earlier.

We missed bringing out a number in July, but in the third number which appeared in August I was able to announce that "our little venture had aroused more interest than we were prepared for and that we had found it necessary to open a London office at 25 Newman Street".

My wife went to London to live in *The Gramophone's* new premises, and I arranged that she and Christopher Stone and Hope-Johnstone should undertake a test of the leading instruments, sound-boxes and needles then on the market. This test was conducted in a heat-wave and Christopher Stone was writing in the September number:

"As these gramophone tests proceed, I seem to see the same set look of confirmed disillusionment forming upon the faces of my colleagues, as they sit in shirt sleeves, scribbling in note-books while the August sun makes and breaks its own records, and the closed windows of the room keep out the noise of Oxford Street traffic and convert the salon into an oven. . . ."

Meanwhile, I was hammering away at the recording companies to give us complete versions of string quartets and other chamber music.

"In the name of Orpheus and his lute I entreat, I beseech, I implore the Cerberus, not of Hades but of Hayes, to let the Flonzaley Quartet emerge into the light of day with anyhow one whole composition of a great master. Why has that sentimental fox-terrier such an objection to complete works of chamber music? Mr. Eugene Goossens and Mr. Lamond escaped his vigilance with the whole of the Emperor Concerto last year, and this very April Mr. Goossens eluded him with every single note of the Brandenburg Concerto in G. I am not going to say that with these records the problem of reproducing massed strings has been solved, but there is no doubt that they mark an advance."

The mention of Sir Eugene Goossens evokes from the past a picture of him at Newman Street listening to one of those brilliant records he had been making of old French light opera overtures for Columbia, *The Caliph of Baghdad* I think it was. He altered the time by a hair's breadth because he said that at 80 which was then the strict number of revolutions to the minute for Columbia recording (H.M.V. had by now stabilized at 78) the time was a fraction of an instant too fast. I was awed by an ear that could distinguish a difference mine was incapable of perceiving. I remember too that we played a record of *The Faery Song* from *The Immortal Hour* by Rutland Broughton.

"Ah," Goossens murmured, "if I could write one melody as good as that I would write an opera."

By August I was allowed to mention the new Columbia recording process.

"I should like to lay stress once more on the wonderful surface that the Columbia Company has secured, and I invite the other companies to concentrate upon securing a surface equally good. And I would plead once more for a cessation of the policy of reprisals, in other words of the duplication of records. This confuses and exasperates the general public, as I happen to know from the mass of correspondence I have received warmly approving my remarks about this in the first number. I know that in many cases the vanity of the artist is more to be blamed than the competition of the recording companies, but that does not mend matters for the poor buyer. We have not yet got on the gramophone one complete Mozart symphony, one complete Haydn symphony, or even one movement of a Brahms symphony. We have a negligible library of the great songs of the world. We have practically nothing but isolated movements of the great chamber music. Repetition may be the soul of wit, but it is the heel of Achilles in the gramophone world. For the sake of Orpheus and his lute give us the fourth symphony of Beethoven, the seventh symphony and the eighth symphony, before you give us two versions of *Don Juan* or the Siegfried Idyll or Ravel's *Mother Goose Suite*."

In October we were publishing our first article from the United States by Dr. F. S. Mead of San Diego, and the generous support we have received for over thirty years from phonograph enthusiasts in America enables me to boast that our circulation in the United States to-day is much larger than it was in Great Britain when *The Gramophone* started.

After Dr. Mead's article we recognized how much we owed to the United States, but at the same time his last paragraph was encouraging.

"For records of 'grand' opera, America and its Victor Co. undoubtedly lead the world. It cannot be said at present that there is a great demand here for complete string and orchestral music, which so happily is leading to the production of so many interesting records in England at the present time."

I used to argue with the late William Manson, the Manager of His Master's Voice in England. Manson was a charming and cautious man with a walrus moustache who took a pessimistic view of the commercial reward for issuing any orchestral records except a few popular hacks. When I mentioned chamber music he used to sound like the Walrus in *Alice in Wonderland*.

"I weep for you," the Walrus said,
"I deeply sympathize."

"Well, unless the gramophone builds up a catalogue of good music, the gramophone will vanish," I used to argue.

"But what support do we get from the public when we do issue records of classical stuff?"

F

"Not yet," I would agree, "because you have set yourselves to pander to the lowest taste for the last twenty years."

"Oh, come, come, that's rather strong. What about our celebrity list?"

"Yes, you've encouraged people to buy expensive vocal records because H.M.V. in England has been lucky enough in England to be able to benefit from the enterprise and financial strength of the Victor Company. But that won't last for ever. Already you've had to give up the single-sided discs and make your celebrity discs double-sided, or in other words halve the price. But singing isn't enough. And virtuoso fiddling isn't enough. Kreisler and the rest of them must realize that unless they give the public the best playing of the best music their vogue will pass. You're at the cross-roads and when the wireless begins to cultivate a taste for classical music you want to make sure that you take the right turning. In order to get a large public for good music you have to convince the musical people in this country that the gramophone is not a toy for tired, rich business men on the one side or on the other a toy for nitwits who like humming. A publisher has to build up a list of back sellers if he is going to last. He cannot live indefinitely on the books of a season."

Those words of mine seem strange to-day when every month brings from each company more long-playing records of good music than the sum total of recording companies could produce in a year at the date of which I am writing.

Chapter 9

IT may have been one day in the autumn of 1923 that Sir Edward
Elgar spoke to me suddenly, in the billiard-room of the old Savile
Club at 107 Piccadilly which was a beautiful bow-fronted house
looking over Green Park.

Looking more like a retired Colonel than ever he said:

"I suppose you people in this magazine of yours have discovered
that nothing I have written has the slightest value. However, you
can say what you like about my music, for I am no longer interested
in music. The only thing I am interested in nowadays is the microscope, and if you take my advice you will set to work to interest
yourself in the microscope in order to prepare yourself by the
contemplation of diatoms for the disillusionment which must come
to every artist nowadays after he has reached sixty."

He then told me that he was thinking of taking a steamer up
the Amazon as far as Manaos, but that he should not go unless he
could have a cabin entirely to himself. Among other remarks that
recur to me from our conversation are that Busoni had the greatest
musical mind of the time, that Schubert wrote too often in an exhausted key, and that when Elgar was young he had once told his
mother that he should feel he had done something in the world when
a postcard addressed to him as Edward Elgar without an address
reached him. Such a card had reached him from a South Sea island
and given him great pleasure.

Elgar, who at this date was about sixty-seven, provided an
example of the creative artist, overcome, overwhelmed, indeed, by
his sense of artistic futility in the face of the rapidly changing
world.

It has always seemed to me that his music was an expression of
the same state of mind as inspired Mr. Rudyard Kipling's poetry. I
should describe both as romantics who had attempted to classicize
their romance on the assumption that the British Empire, as revealed in all its outward glory in the Diamond Jubilee Procession
of 1897, had at least as long a future before it as the Roman Empire
in the reign of Augustus. Elgar was born and brought up a Catholic.
He lost his faith for a time, and it may be surmised that the British
Empire's development since 1897 proved a poor substitute. That is

the real failure of *The Dream of Gerontius*. It was an attempt to re-
create in himself something he had lost. Therefore, in the one
essential point it was as empty as Wagner's *Parsifal*. In spite of the
honours he received and the renown in which he was held, Elgar's
position as an artist was seeming tragic at this date. During his
rise to fame he had been treated by the academic English critics as
a vulgar innovator, and almost as soon as he had clearly established
himself as the superior of such composers as Parry or Stanford the
younger school of criticism began to treat him as a worn-out relic
of nineteenth-century romanticism. "I think I shall be among the
poets when I am dead," said Keats, dying, by favour of the gods,
young. Elgar, at any rate when I knew him, lacked this conviction
of his work's immortality. This is the supreme tragedy of a great
artist, and by any standards that we know we must call Elgar a
great artist. Himself an extremely simple man, his art was nourished
by the awareness and contemplation of grandeur. If the time
could have produced Jubilee Processions of increasing splendour,
pomp and circumstance, Elgar's genius would have thriven upon it.
It was the loss of this grandeur which drove him to the awareness
and contemplation of diatoms, and in the study of these lovely
minute algae to find the compensation of contrast. The British
Empire as understood by Elgar presented itself to those disillusioned
partially by the Boer War and completely by the First World War
as a romantic dream. Hence his classic bias is not evident to them,
and he appears like a musical echo of Tennyson, with whom indeed
he has much in common.

Warned by Elgar's ban upon the subject I never mentioned the
word "music" in his hearing in the course of any subsequent talks
we had at the Savile. However, one Saturday afternoon, probably
in the spring of 1924, I was sitting beside him on the dais opposite
the billiards-table when from the farther end of the long settee the
voice of the poet W. J. Turner said that he was going to Queen's
Hall to hear the Symphonie Fantastique of Berlioz.

Elgar turned to me abruptly and growled, "What's that about
the Symphonie Fantastique?"

When I told him it was being played that afternoon in Queen's
Hall, he asked me if I had ever heard it; on my telling him that I
had not, he asked me if I would like to hear it, and that, if I would,
he would take me with him to hear it, because it was a piece of music
which one ought to hear and appreciate for its importance in the
development of the art.

"Much of it is rubbish, but there is one thing which is really tremendous, and that is the March to the Guillotine. Go and tell the porter to ring through and reserve seats for me in the circle."

As we drove along Piccadilly in the taxi to Queen's Hall I was aware while I listened to Sir Edward talking about Berlioz's world of music that I was enjoying a momentous occasion in my life, but only one remark of Elgar's remains in my memory. He asked me if I realized that every time I passed my hand across my forehead when listening to music I missed two bars.

While Elgar was waiting in the vestibule I went over to the box-office to get the seats.

"I think you have two seats for Sir Edward Elgar?"

"Twenty-four shillings," said the clerk.

"But they are for Sir Edward Elgar," I reminded him.

He looked at me blankly, and repeated the price.

Not liking to tell Elgar that his name was apparently unknown to the box-office clerk, I paid for the seats myself. I remember being particularly struck by the clerk's crassness, because as it happened the vestibule was full of bills announcing a forthcoming Elgar concert at which the composer was to conduct.

Our seats were in the fourth row of the grand circle on the right-hand side. I do not remember who the conductor was that afternoon, but the concert opened with Strauss's *Don Juan*, by which Elgar seemed bored. When the Fantastic Symphony began, however, he sat up and took notice, and by the time the march to the gallows had been reached he was sweating profusely, mopping his forehead and muttering to himself, "Oh, my God! my God!" so loudly once or twice that some serious-minded young woman in front of us turned round and hushed him.

"Now, Mackenzie," he said, when the march began, "I am going to mark the rhythm for you on your knee."

As a matter of fact he marked it on my knee, my ribs, and on the arm of the stall, sweating more and more, and mopping his forehead with a large handkerchief. Then he got worried by the way the cymbals were being played. "Not like that!" he exclaimed, clapping his hands in the style of the cymbalist. "Like this, you fool!" putting his left arm over his right and playing on my right thigh the cymbals as he wanted them played. By this time most of the people in front were turning round to glare at us and hushes came from all along the line. They might as well have tried to hush Vesuvius in full eruption as Sir Edward Elgar that afternoon, for the merciless rhythm of that march was having such an effect upon him that I should not have been surprised if he had suddenly leapt from his seat, vaulted over the floppy young woman in front, and landed down on the conductor's dais in order to make that cymbal player handle his cymbals in the way he thought they ought to be handled.

At the end of the march there is a sudden stillness, and then the motto theme is played on a solo clarinet which is cut short by the fall of the knife of the guillotine. I think the clarinet player must suddenly have caught sight of Elgar and recognized him, for the expression on his face as he played that brief solo was that of a man who was about to be executed himself. Then the crashing separate chords marked the end. Elgar, still mopping his brow, rose.

"You are not going to stay to hear Rachmaninoff play his concerto?" I asked.

"No, no," he growled. "As I told you, I do not take the slightest interest in music any longer, but you'd better stay and hear it."

As the Witches' Sabbath began he plunged out up the stairs of the circle, the glances of the floppy young woman in front, who had come to Queen's Hall only to adore Rachmaninoff, following him indignantly.

With Elgar's departure the atmosphere became so ordinary as to seem heavy, and though Rachmaninoff himself was playing, and though I have no doubt he gave a splendid performance of his last concerto, I have never been bored so intensely by music, and I have never wished so much for a concerto to come to an end.

Elgar has been dead exactly twenty-one years to the day as I write these words and the doubts about his own enduring fame from which he was suffering in those topsy-turvy years immediately after the First World War have not been endorsed as yet by time. Fortunately, the musical public is much less at the mercy of criticism than the would-be literary public is nowadays.

If the tide of taste should turn against Elgar it will be a natural phenomenon and the musicologists will have had no influence upon it. Much musical criticism was hostile to him when he was in his prime, and inevitably during the decade after the First World War the febrile mood of the moment was inclined to dismiss him as the product of an envied and therefore in self-defence a derided period called "pre-war". The whirligig of time spun round more rapidly than usual, and the 'twenties had a very brief existence before they too became "pre-war".

We shall be celebrating the centenary of Elgar's birth in February 1957, and I feel that we shall still be following with him that elusive spirit of delight in the Second Symphony, that we shall ponder with him the sombre agony of the First World War in the Violoncello Concerto, that we shall seem to hear, nay, more than hear, to be a veritable part of the sea as he, most utterly English of composers, has let us hear, and be in his Sea Pictures, and that we shall still be trying to solve the lovely riddle of the Enigma Variations.

Percy Scholes, the music critic of the *Observer* at this date, did a great work for the gramophone, and his generosity to a jack-in-the-box amateur like myself never failed. Scholes's enthusiasm for the gramophone was not shared at this date by Ernest Newman, the musical critic of the *Sunday Times*, who had backed the piano-player as the medium for encouraging musical appreciation.

It must have been in that autumn of 1923 that I met Scholes for the first time and that soon afterwards he came to dinner with me at the Savile. I did not know that he was a strict vegetarian and I was upset as a host when he took his seat beside me at the long table and told me that there was nothing on the bill of fare that he could eat.

"But don't worry," he said. "A couple of carrots are all I want."

I pressed upon him the notion of some dish with rice as a basis, but he insisted upon the carrots.

Frank, the senior club waiter, who had been on the staff as a boy when Robert Louis Stevenson was frequenting the original home of the Savile in Savile Row, looked at me in mute reproach when I asked if he would see about getting two carrots for my guest. He obviously thought I had made a joke that was not in the best of taste.

"Mr. Scholes has asked for the carrots," I assured him.

"Just what I should like," said Scholes, smiling at Frank reassuringly.

Frank walked away gloomily to communicate to the kitchen what he considered was an order that broke every tradition of the Savile.

With the memory of those carrots and also, let me hasten to add, of a most profitable evening after dinner, spent in discussing the future of the gramophone, I quote from a review I was to write ten years later of a remarkable enterprise by Mr. Scholes:

"Just when I thought it was time to forbid myself the word 'romantic' for six months the fourth volume of the Columbia History of Music reaches me and with it some observations on Romanticism by Mr. Percy Scholes which leave me with no alternative but to return to the subject. I rather thought Mr. Scholes was looking for trouble in the near future when he included Beethoven and Schubert in the third volume. Let me say at once that the problem of dividing his history into albums which would fit in not merely with aesthetic theory, but also with the exigencies of recording, must have been a problem of the profoundest difficulty. Even to write a history of music for the printed page and preserve the due proportions between the volumes has been a task which has hitherto baffled authors and publishers and in saying that I am not forgetting the great Oxford History of Music. I wish to make it clear at the start that any criticism I utter is based entirely upon my admiration of what Mr. Scholes has done, and is not intended even faintly to depreciate the value of his remarkable achievement. The present volume is entitled *Music as Romance and as National Expression*. The three preceding volumes were given titles which merely indicated the passage of time and did not involve the historian in an aesthetic argument before the history began. In the case of the fourth volume, the definition of 'music as romance' involves a preliminary argument which cannot be avoided and is unlikely to be settled, and even the definition of 'Music as national expression' is not an absolutely clear definition of a fact accepted by everybody. Therefore we are not surprised to find that the accompanying booklet begins with the question 'What is romantic music?' and Carlyle's definition of music is quoted as an answer. 'A kind of inarticulate unfathomable speech, that leads us to the edge of the Infinite, and lets us for moments gaze into it.' That hardly takes us much nearer to a comprehension of music, does it? It would be just as sensible to say that it led you to the edge of the crater of Etna. Wordsworth could be nebulously polysyllabic on occasions; but his clouds were sometimes 'clouds of glory', whereas Carlyle's definition of music is no more than a damp fog exhaled by his own verbose perspiration.

"Mr. Scholes has allowed himself to be bewitched by that meaningless agglomeration of words when he says 'freed from the other arts' rather cumbersome necessity of expressing themselves through physical shapes and colours, or by words representing definite thoughts, music directly arouses in us just the feeling of which Carlyle speaks—the feeling that we are glimpsing infinity'. You will observe that Mr. Scholes has instinctively removed the capital letter from infinity, and by doing so he implies a doubt in his own mind of the adequacy of Carlyle's definition, which has, I may protest, considerably less value and beauty than an ordinary bubble of soap. Yet although he recognizes the responsibility laid upon words to represent definite thoughts, he nevertheless chooses for a wordy glimpse of infinity a sentence which as an expression of such a glimpse is hardly up to the intellectual or emotional level of a dog baying the moon. Let us remember, the next time we feel inclined to put a charge of small shot into such a dog, that the poor brute is only barking inarticulately and unfathomably on the edge of the Infinite.

"Confused by that clammy Scots mist of Carlyle's into which he plunged at the beginning, Mr. Scholes goes on to argue that the periods of Byrd and Beethoven are periods in which the spell of the infinite is stronger, and the period of Haydn and Mozart one when it is weaker. That steadies him. He escapes from the fog into comparatively clear air to contrast the 'periods when the constructional interest (the interest of beauty as such) with the more romantic periods when the emotional interest is uppermost'.

"Here we are back again with the old dualism of *classic* and *romantic*, and now that Mr. Scholes, to what must have been his relief, has discarded Carlyle's Infinite in favour of 'emotional interest', we can discard such highfalutin verbiage and agree with him that what we mean by romantic art is any art in which the direct expression of emotion is indulged at the expense of the design, the penalty of which when carried to extremes is a discordant eccentricity, as the penalty of extreme classicism is a sterile and academic formalism. The trouble with both *classic* and *romantic* is that neither word possesses an exclusive and unmistakable meaning. This drawback is well illustrated by Mr. Scholes when he calls Beethoven a Classic-Romantic because 'whilst the classic forms are still his almost invariable framework, the element of emotion often transcends the element of design'. There are far too many associative ideas evoked by *classic* and *romantic* to make them safe words to use in double harness like that. Among other things *romantic* cannot help suggesting an art preoccupied with, and to some extent inspired by, the Middle Ages. Yet the most superficial examination of Greek and Roman literature or medieval literature will reveal romanticism in the former and classicism in the latter. You could hardly find anything more romantic than the *Golden Ass* of Apuleius or anything more classic than the great work of St. Thomas Aquinas. Indeed, for the beginning of romanticism we shall have to go back to the Garden of Eden to find the realism of Eve spoiling, in conjunction with the romanticism of Adam, the Divine design. Equally we may discern in the Nativity Divine romance wrecking the dead classicism of Jewry. You would hardly call Euripides a romantic, but actually it was his romanticism which offended the admirers of the Sophoclean drama. And to which camp does realism belong? Are we to say that its ability to assume a design will make it classic, and its freedom from restraint romantic?

"In the current number of the *Fortnightly Review* Mr. Richard Church in an article on Maurice Hewlett proclaims the aesthetic intention of the younger generation as 'a large movement, romantic in its compulsion by rebellious faith, and classic in its demand for shape. Those two wretched words, *romantic* and *classic*, will in fact be thrown aside as symbols of an outworn dualism.' Yet Mr. Church could not avoid using those two wretched words to explain his aesthetic creed, which is hardly a hopeful sign of their successful elimination. As a matter of fact, romantics have always been just as much preoccupied with design as classicists. What they have always fought against is the limitation of design to one aspect of it. Nor should I say that composers like Haydn and Mozart sacrificed emotion so much to design as to manners. They considered art an unsuitable medium for certain emotions in the same way as the English public school forbids them in conversation. Shelley managed to survive Eton, but I doubt if even Shelley would have survived Winchester. An English public school and university education is probably the greatest handicap that can be imposed on a romantic artist, but in its day it has probably helped many a classical artist.

"In judging the poetry or music of any period we should always bear in mind how much of its expression is determined by external circumstances. Although it may sometimes appear that the supreme artists have defeated external circumstance and brought about a new period, I believe that in every case a deeper examination will show that they were the effect of a change already beginning, to which they may have given an added impetus, rather than the cause or inspiration of that change. When we contemplate with awe the revolution in music effected by Beethoven, the inclusion of his *Fidelio* overture in the third album was inappropriate. Perhaps the way out would have been to have ended volume three with an early composition of Beethoven and opened volume four with one of his later compositions.

"As it is, Mr. Scholes begins volume four with *Romeo's Reverie* and the *Capulets' Fête* from the *Romeo and Juliet* of Berlioz, whom he calls a realist romantic. But why realistic, unless realism is being used here in the sense of what is called programme music? There is no doubt about Berlioz being a romantic in the *popular* use of the word, from which, let me say, it was a great pity we ever departed. He looked like a romantic, he lived like a romantic, and he wrote like a romantic. But is Berlioz to be considered a romantic in the sense that involves being closer in touch with the Infinite than a Mozart or a Haydn? You see now where Carlyle's fog will land Mr. Scholes. Berlioz is followed by a nocturne of the Irish composer John Field. This was a felicitous choice followed as it is by a nocturne of Chopin, who owed the Irishman so much. Who plays John Field to-day. Mr. Scholes asks? Instead of endlessly reduplicating the performances of their rivals some of our recording pianists might give us an occasional taste of Field. And if anybody wants a good subject for a musical novel, why not try that queer association of Field and Clementi?

"Field and Chopin are followed in the album by songs of Schumann, Brahms and Hugo Wolf. Schumann was certainly a romantic; but I do not see how Brahms can be called a romantic in any sense of the word. I should have said that he was thoroughly scared by the wild course romanticism seemed to be taking, being by temperament a classicist. Certainly if you put Brahms next to Haydn he will seem an ultra-romantic in comparison. But is not that because by the time of Brahms the external circumstances of life were becoming immensely more complicated? The most fervid classicists of the future will never achieve the effects that Racine in literature and Bach in music were able to achieve. I see no possibility except in architecture of a comparable tranquillity. Brahms and Schumann are succeeded by the American composer MacDowell. Surely MacDowell is a sentimentalist, not a romantic? There is nothing in his life or in his work that justifies his presence in this album. In a history of literature on similar lines poets like Edgar Allan Poe and Walt Whitman might supply romantic illustrations in the same volume as Byron. But a MacDowell in the same album as Brahms! Field led to Chopin. MacDowell led nowhere.

"Dvořák with his First Slavonic Dance and Balakiref represent nationalism, and bring the album to a close. Mr. Scholes is right in considering the nationalist movement in music to be 'a definite and important phase of the romantic movement', but not for the reasons he gives. Nationalism so far from being 'a glimpse into the infinite (into depths of racial consciousness and racial ambition)' is exactly the reverse. Nationalism is the expression of the individual's acute and painful awareness of the finite vanishing in the infinite nebulosity of internationalism. Neither racial consciousness nor racial ambition has anything to do with the infinite, and to practical nationalists both present themselves as sentimental abstractions.

When nationalist music begins to proclaim the grandiosity of a self-conscious patriotism it ceases to be romantic. Well, if I have not been able to accept all Mr. Scholes' ideas about 'Music as Romance' I have at any rate enjoyed arguing with him. But that definition of music. Mr. Scholes splitting the Infinite with Carlyle! It would have been a subject for a painting by Watts."

A month later Percy Scholes, who by this time was living in Switzerland, sent an answer from which I quote some excerpts:

"Now what I said was not *quite* what I am quoted as saying. I did not give the Carlyle passage as an answer, but as an 'attempt' at an answer, and did not praise the passage as defining Romantic *Music*, but as defining '*the romantic on its more ideal side*'. . . .

"Returning, towards the end of his article, to his *bête noire*, the Carlyle quotation, Mr. Mackenzie asks: 'Is Berlioz to be considered a "romantic" in the sense that involves being closer in touch with the Infinite than a Mozart or Haydn?' The reply is neither a direct affirmative nor a direct negative. The point is not that Berlioz was 'closer in touch' with that 'Infinite', but that his touch with it was conscious and even deliberate. Look at the titles of Berlioz' major compositions. . . . They at once put Berlioz in a different pigeon-hole from that of Haydn and Mozart. Liszt was quite as literary as Berlioz, and also based instrumental compositions on frescoes of Orcagna and Kaulbach. In this interaction of the arts we have, as I have pointed out above, almost a new phenomenon of the Romantic Movement.

"Mr. Mackenzie raises the case of Brahms, whom he does not 'call a romantic in any sense'! To me there is no differentiation possible between the *general feeling* of the music of Brahms and that of the admittedly romantic Schumann, and so, though he was less 'literary', it is convenient to consider him as 'in the movement'. . . . That those composers of the twentieth century who are consciously and of set purpose reacting against the romantic nineteenth century and professing to produce a musical art 'free from romantic associations', put Brahms near the very head of their Index Expurgatorius."

I returned to the argument:

"Mr. Scholes definitely committed himself to the statement that the period of Haydn and Mozart was one in which the spell of the infinite was weaker, and in spite of his admirable defence, I still think that if he had never got involved with that hairy old bore from Ecclefechan he would have made his meaning much clearer. Surely the fundamental difference between what we call classic and what we call romantic in the arts lies in the amount of personal intrusion that the individual allows himself. I would claim that Catholicism and Buddhism were both classic, Protestantism and Mohammedanism romantic. I would even go so far as to claim that woman was classic and man romantic, and it seems to me highly significant that in centuries like the eighteenth and twentieth, when the influence of woman is predominant, art should show a tendency toward classicism.

"One might say that Catholicism was Aristotelian, objective, realistic, classic, conservative, epic and feminine; and that Protestantism was Platonic, subjective, idealistic, romantic, liberal, lyric and masculine.' Now, if one takes out the two religious systems, the antitheses of polarities suggested above can be applied to *classic* and *romantic*. One of the latest volumes of Dent's Everyman's Library includes Aristotle's *Rhetoric*, Demetrius *On Style*, and Horace's *Ars Poetica*. In this volume, not 300 pages long, he who wills may master for himself the whole theory of classic art. The most destructive piece of dramatic criticism I ever read was an article by A. B. Walkley in *The Times*, when by quotations from Aristotle's *Poetics* he shattered one of Mr. Bernard Shaw's plays. Mr. Bernard Shaw is a typical romantic. What we lack is any work on aesthetics which expounds the romantic canons with the clarity and assurance of an Aristotle. Some try to find such a work in Benedetto Croce, but to my mind the clarity is not there.

"Let us apply the test to Brahms. Mr. Scholes was evidently astonished at my refusal to call Brahms a romantic in any sense. We will begin by putting Brahms against Wagner. Brahms was realistic (or if it helps to make my meaning clear, let us substitute the word 'practical'): Wagner was idealistic. Brahms was always sternly conscious of what he supposed to be the limitations of music; Wagner would not admit these limitations. Both gained or lost accordingly, Brahms left music where he found it; Wagner indicated for it new territory which his successors have failed to develop. Brahms was certainly conservative. He regarded himself and he was regarded by his followers as the heir of a mighty tradition. His First Symphony was hailed as the Tenth with the implication that he was in the direct line with Beethoven, and he even went so far as to write a tune which recalled the tune with which Beethoven ended up the Ninth Symphony. It may be argued at this point that Beethoven himself was a romantic. I shall not contradict that. The romantic discoveries of the human soul having once been made will not allow any artist to treat life as if they had never been made. I find the nearest approach in literature to the musical achievement of Brahms in the work of Milton. Milton came at the end of a great romantic period, and an epic like *Paradise Lost* is really an attempt to 'classicize' that period. Milton and Brahms were both great eclectics. To put it crudely, they both robbed right and left from their predecessors, and in the case of Brahms one might add from his contemporaries. Throughout Brahms's music one comes across echoes of Schumann. I hesitate to say that what is called the 'Meistersinger' Sonata is a deliberate use of Wagner's Prize Song from the Opera, for I do not know which was composed first. This eclecticism is perfectly legitimate if we accept Milton and Brahms as classic writers. If we are going to call them romantics, such eclecticism would come perilously near a form of plagiarism. The late Professor Churton Collins once wrote a book to show where Tennyson had found many of his happiest inspirations. Collins had no intention of imputing plagiarism to the poet, but Tennyson, like his royal mistress, was not amused; in fact, he was so angry that he called Churton Collins a louse upon the locks of literature. Now Tennyson cannot by any standard be considered anything but a romantic poet, and he may have been justified by his own conscience in deploring Professor Churton Collins's inquisitive researches into his origins.

"To say that Brahms is epic and Wagner lyric offers obvious difficulties at first, because the antithesis between them is more evidently between the non-dramatic and the dramatic. And that is not quite the same thing. However, if one considers the lyric aspect of Brahms, as when he was writing his songs, the direct personal appeal is always subordinated to the form, and one might add to the capacity of the singer. If one compares Brahms's songs with those of Schubert or of Schumann they seem to possess a classic calm. Horace's lyrics have the same classic quality if we compare them with those of Catullus or Propertius.

"Mr. Scholes made a point in favour of Brahms's romanticism when he reminded us that the prophets of the twentieth-century reaction against nineteenth-century romanticism impeached Elgar for carrying on the romanticism of Brahms. The trouble with the twentieth-century reactionaries is their inability to recognize that one cannot eliminate entirely what has been added in the course of human progress. Ruskin was a great and in many respects a wise man, but he made the fatal mistake of trying to fight against the accomplished fact. Many of us might agree with him that the application of steam to motive power was a disaster for civilization; but it was as idle for him to fulminate against railway trains as it would be for a writer of to-day to fulminate against aeroplanes. Ruskin would have left behind him a more useful legacy if he had tried to show how to 'classicize' such romantic intruders as most mechanical inventions appear at first. The neo-classicists of the 1920's cannot survive because they lack spontaneity. They should take a lesson from the disrepute into which the Pre-Raphaelites have already fallen. What Fra Angelico or Botticelli painted with freshness of vision became an affectation when deliberately cultivated. The pictures of Millais were better pictures while he was a professing Pre-Raphaelite. When he discarded Pre-Raphaelitism and painted with his genuine self the kind of picture he produced was *Bubbles*. The insincerity of advanced art in every form at the present moment is demonstrated by the lack of an impulse common to all the arts.

"Take sculpture. The inspiration of the most modern sculpture is to be found in negro sculpture. Classic sculpture is anathema to the modern. On the other hand, the modern musician consciously aspires to produce music with the quality that Bach's music possessed. Inasmuch as the old gentleman had explored and, one might say, exploited every possible avenue for his kind of music, the modern has to aim at the equivalent effect by exploiting avenues which the old gentleman himself would have considered garbage-strewn and stinking blind-alleys. The modern architect is obsessed with the idea that, if he produces what he supposes to be a serviceable building, it will be beautiful by its utility or functional purpose. Many people consider a motor-car or a steamer *per se* a beautiful object, and I will agree that a modern car is more beautiful, or I should prefer to say less ugly, than a motor-car of the eighteen-nineties. Yet it would surely be absurd to pretend that either the Parthenon or the cathedral of Chartres was beautiful because it fulfilled a functional purpose. Surely both were expressions of the mind of man consciously aiming at producing what he considered to be a beautiful object? We may feel positive that if we possessed the whole of the great temple of Zeus at Athens we should consider it less beautiful than the Parthenon; but we can sympathize with the architect who, faced by the beauty of the Parthenon, was invited to produce another masterpiece. If one observes the decadence of any period it will always show itself in over-decoration, whether in literature or in painting or in music. Thus the form is seen to be exhausted, and a reaction sets in. The hope of the modernist critic is that the present manifestations of the arts are a spontaneous primitive impulse which will in due course develop into a grand period and ultimately into the accustomed decadence. My own belief is that the artistic impulse in Europe is slowly dying under the strain of material progress in every kind of direction, and that every artistic period will presently be so rapidly accelerated in consequence that the confusion of which we already see signs will increase.

"I have been listening to a great deal of Brahms lately, and an almost continuous playing of his music over many months has confirmed me in my belief that so far as it is possible for a man who sums up a romantic century to be classic, Brahms was classic; I stand by the comparison with Milton."

Chapter 10

IN the Editorial of the fourth number of *The Gramophone* I was writing:

"For some time past I have had in my head a scheme that requires much thought before it can be considered a practical scheme. Briefly, my ambition is to incorporate a number of enthusiasts for good music on the gramophone in a society which will aim at achieving for gramophone music what such societies as the Medici have done for the reproduction of paintings and for the printed book. In order to obtain the best music for the gramophone, it is only necessary to persuade the recording companies that there is an articulate body of potential buyers of records, clamouring for the best and willing to pay for it. . . .

"If I receive 500 postcards I will take the next step, which will be to start the society and give it a name. The main object of the society will be to find out by the votes of the members what works we require most urgently to be recorded; and I should hope that we could agree among ourselves upon one complete symphony, two complete works of chamber music, and one complete concerto a year. Supposing that this involved twenty records, we should then have to obtain a guarantee that every member would buy the records; and with this guarantee we could approach the recording companies and ask them to what extent and on what terms they would meet our wishes."

Eleven months later I was able to announce that the National Gramophonic Society had been successfully founded and that by the courtesy of the Aeolian Company we had secured the services of the Spencer Dyke Quartet. A year after I first put forward that hazy scheme we announced that Beethoven's Tenth (Harp) Quartet and Debussy's Quartet had been recorded and that the roll of members was being rapidly made up. Not more than twenty-four records were to be issued in twelve months and the liability of members would therefore be £6 a year to be paid in two instalments at Michaelmas and Lady Day.

In November 1924 I was writing:

"I may take this opportunity to thank very warmly those of our readers who with a really beautiful faith have joined the National Gramophonic Society without hearing one of its issues. I believe that they will feel themselves rewarded when they hear Beethoven's Harp Quartet and Debussy's Quartet complete. I have not yet heard the 'proof' of the Schönberg Sextet or Schubert's Trio in E, which will be the second issue. We are aiming to follow up these with the Franck Quartet and the Mozart Clarinet Quintet. I also want to thank the recording companies, who have helped us in the most generous way, not merely over the work of our society, but in every other direction connected with this paper."

One of the advisory committee of the N.G.S. was the late W. W. Cobbett, and it is time to speak of that remarkable man.

Walter Willson Cobbett was born in 1847 so that when the project of founding this society for recording chamber music was formed he was in his seventy-eighth year. He had been in commerce as promoter of the Scandinavian Belting Company Ltd., which later became known as the British Belting and Asbestos Company Ltd. During the First World War he made a great deal of money and unlike most men of business who make money he had an artistic passion to gratify. This was music, and in particular chamber music; he was himself a good amateur violinist. He presented gold medals as prizes for native composers of chamber music and makers of British violins. He founded the Cobbett Free Library of Chamber Music. He was President of the Haydn Society, Vice-President of the Musical Association and British Music Society, and he was a Master of the Worshipful Company of Musicians. Above all he was the Editor and Compiler of Cobbett's *Cyclopedic Survey of Chamber Music*, a standard work of reference, which remains as an enduring memorial to that pertinacious, indeed indomitable old man who would ride recklessly into any club conversation on his hobby-horse.

"Who is this old fellow, Cobbett, that's lately taken to using the Club?" members of the Savile used to ask.

In due course the time arrived for players to enter their names for the annual billiards handicap. The handicappers never having seen Cobbett play gave him 100.

I happened to be in the billiards-room when Cobbett was playing off his first heat—I think it was against Sir William Orpen, who was scratch—and he won by twice as much as his handicap.

I remember his turning to me after making two or three breaks of 30 and saying in that desiccated voice of his:

"You know, I think they've given me rather too big a start."

They certainly had, and Cobbett went on to win the handicap with ease.

The successful launching of the National Gramophonic Society gave the greatest pleasure to the old man, and in a spirit of generous patronage he presented to every member of the society a record made by his own string quartet in which he played first violin of a movement from Rubinstein's quartet and a movement from Raff's *Maid of the Mill* Suite. This would have cost him at that date at least £150. Later on he financed the recording of Schubert's Quintet in C major for the N.G.S. which none of the recording companies was willing to undertake. To-day we already have three recordings of that noble work on long-playing discs, and that demonstrates the progress that the gramophone has made in thirty years.

I am chary of seeming to exaggerate the influence that the National Gramophonic Society had upon the policy of the big recording companies, but I think the tangible evidence we were able to offer of the existence of enough people interested in chamber music to make it worth while to offer those people complete works instead of isolated movements or ruthless abbreviations did play a part in achieving the position in which the gramophone is to-day.

Besides the Spencer Dyke Quartet the N.G.S. recorded the Music Society Quartet of which André-Mangeot was the leader and John Barbirolli the violoncellist. Later on John Barbirolli[1] made his first records by conducting a chamber orchestra for the National Gramophonic Society. I had several wordy battles with the B.B.C. over chamber music in those early days. What to-day we should call a Third Programme attitude prevailed. When, rarely enough, chamber music was given a chance to be heard the musical people at Savoy Hill were determined with the best intentions to give listeners as much contemporary music as possible. The result was inimical to chamber music in general and to contemporary music in particular. The musically uneducated public heard chamber music being announced and this announcement seemed to their ears to be followed usually by trouble in an apiary. This menacing buzz from overturned bee-hives the general public came to associate not merely with modern chamber music but with

[1] Sir John Barbirolli.

all chamber music. Chamber music became a stock gag for comedians displacing the mother-in-law of once upon a time. There was no alternative programme in those days. Listeners were compelled to hear chamber music or nothing, and I used to argue that in such circumstances the B.B.C. should have broadcast nothing except trios, quartets and quintets capable of making an immediate appeal to the untrained ear.

The popular Press, which was always looking out for any stone to throw at what in Fleet Street was still believed to be a dangerous rival, was continually publishing letters from indignant nitwits protesting against the infliction of chamber music on their sensitive ears.

When I looked back to my own attitude even to Mozart and Haydn as an undergraduate I recognized that I was the last person to criticize the vulgar approach to chamber music. However, a convert is always anxious to share with others what he feels are the benefits of his conversion, and regarding myself as a perfect example of the man who did not know how much he loved music until he found out, as it might seem almost by accident, I was naturally fired with missionary zeal.

If somebody had prophesied at Oxford a mere two decades away from the time of which I am writing that I should be invited one day to contribute an article to a Cyclopaedic Survey of Chamber Music I should have considered him madder than the Mullah at his maddest. Yet, now here was Cobbett inviting me to do just that for his magnum opus which was to be published by the Oxford University Press in 1929.

I reprint here what I wrote then because, although to an enthusiast for chamber music on the gramophone over a quarter of a century later I shall seem to be severely restricted for my illustrations, that old article of mine manages to preserve the spirit of wonder at the precious gift which we were enjoying as a result of mechanical progress:

"Robert Louis Stevenson decided that the freedom it conferred upon a man to have his own string quartet and his own yacht was the chief, in fact the only real advantage attached to the possession of great wealth. Without claiming that the gramophone will soon discredit the utility of riches, it may be argued that with all the recent improvement on the technical side of recording and in the quality of the music recorded the gramophone is already a kind of rival of the private string quartet; and it is likely in the near future to become an almost completely adequate substitute. Of course, it will never be quite the same thing as the actual presence of the players, because not even with the aid of any cinematographic device that the future may provide could the purely external decorativeness of a string quartet be conveyed. Even should the gramophone ultimately succeed in deceiving the finest ear, it will always cheat the eye, for whether it be a woman seated at the piano or whether it be a full orchestra on the platform of a concert hall, the sight of instruments being played must surely add, even for the most austere lovers of music, some further magic to the sound. To watch a violin concerto and be reminded of a bird singing in a wood, to watch a piano concerto and perceive a boat at one with the waters on which it rides: I hope that those are not just the pictorial impressions of a literary temperament spoiling music with a pathetic fallacy, dishonest though it would be not to admit that some of those pictorial impressions are so vivid that I can recall the visual effect of music of which I should less easily recall the sound, as, for instance, the sight of the strings in the slow movement of Brahms's D minor concerto lapping against the piano and seeming almost to be rocking it gently beneath the green-shaded lamps of Queen's Hall.

"Now, the outward effect of a string quartet on my fancy is that I am perceiving a sublimation of all the domestic tasks that were ever undertaken, from that of the spider in weaving her web to those of spinsters knitting in the sun or old wives at their embroidery. In watching the combination of instruments I discern a pattern wrought in visible silver on the air, a pattern of not less exquisite complication and simplicity than that with which the frost may pattern a window-pane. Contrariwise, if I watch a spider at her task in the sunlight, I must be always straining my ears to hear the fine pattern of sound that seems to be directing her intricate path. All this external beauty of played music is denied us by the gramophone. Indeed, one of the great reproaches deservedly levelled against it is the utter lack of the reposeful beauty of sound in motion. The winding of it, the hiss of the needle, the interruptions caused by changing or turning of the discs, these would still be a detestable handicap, even if the reproduction of the music were perfect and the variety of it unlimited. Yet were the choice to lie between hearing all my chamber music in a concert room and being entirely dependent upon the gramophone, I should elect to rely upon the latter. I find the contact of strangers repulsive when I am listening to chamber music, and even if I sit between friends, with friends in front of me and with friends behind me, the discomfort of a concert-room stall and the odious system of sitting in rows combine to destroy the intimate delight of such music. I am not conscious of this malaise during the performance of an orchestra. Indeed, the presence of hundreds of other people adds much to my enjoyment, and were I rich enough to command the greatest orchestra in the world to perform for my solitary pleasure I should never claim the privilege. But chamber music for my contentment ought to be not so much something that is being performed as something that is happening, and if I cast my mind back to seek for an illustration of the extreme pleasure that chamber music has given, I find it in old days at the Oxford and Cambridge Musical Club, when, coming in about six o'clock of a foggy November evening from the murk and clatter of Leicester Square, one lounged in Joshua Reynolds' old studio and listened in the quiet, then contrived by double windows, to quartets of Haydn and Mozart, triumphing over time as one smoked and dreamed.

"Thus to insist upon the sensuous and the sentimental appeal of chamber music may appear to be treating it like a drug, and the danger of treating music as a drug should be kept in mind. I should be inclined to dread the perfect gramophone which never required winding, whose fibre needles were durable as teak, whose steel needles were velvet as cats' paws, whose discs changed themselves and never warped. In such circumstances, music for me might come to serve as poppies and mandragora indeed, for I believe that I should never listen to anything else except the first thrushes in February. Yet, without becoming slaves to music, we might make a better use of it than we do, now that we have the gramophone. In these days music always seems to partake too much of a ceremony. People sit down to enjoy it as they might sit down to eat dinner. In fact, the only occasional use that is made of music is to accompany a meal. And this inappropriate service has begotten a form of its own, so that we speak contemptuously of restaurant music where the clatter of dishes and the jingle of forks have entered into the very texture of the orchestration. But what occasions there are for music of which few avail themselves! It is easy to believe that he who has not heard a Mozart quartet played in the freshness of dawn has never enjoyed his music to the full, and since it might puzzle even a millionaire to rouse his private quartet at such an hour and make the players sit in the dews beneath his bedroom window, the gramophone becomes indispensable for such an occasion. The fatigue of turning discs may be more than usually tiresome when one has to cross a cold floor to get at them; but for compensation one hardly misses the visible grace of the players, because the changing sky above the tree tops or the chimney stacks is enough for the eye, and in so many of Mozart's quartets the pattern of the music is the pattern of the dayspring itself.

"Nor must Brahms be forgotten for this hour: particularly those two quartets of Opus 51, both of which we possess in recorded form. There are times when they seem to express better than anything else the business of the new day, for there is nobody like Brahms for meditating deliberately upon what seems at first such a commonplace little phrase until patiently and lovingly, as some old weaver of the Middle Ages, he has decorated it with the grave and gay design of his romantic common sense.[1] There is nobody who can more gently clarify a mind made turbid by the stir of worry or darkened by the shadow of looming complications. His music has the dignity of a trusted family doctor, who by his confidence not merely drives away our physical ills, but in doing so affects us with his own spiritual calm. Brahms has that perfect sanity which touches holiness, and the more often I listen to his chamber music the more profound becomes my reverence for him. One may turn to Mozart or Haydn for relief, gaining from their music an illusion that care will be as easily overcome as the sweet sadness of their own andantes by minuets and tripping measures. We may take refuge in Beethoven and feel that our small displeasures are much ado about nothing; but Brahms is able to seize our pettiest moods and direct them as wisely as he will use his first violin. There is nobody like him for suppressing the individual instrument in his chamber music except when he writes for the clarinet, to which he allows the freedom of a spoilt child. Where did I read of Brahms at table emptying the oil out of the bottom of a tin of sardines into his mouth? Almost one feels sometimes that he is allowing his favourite instrument to behave as greedily. No other composer has allowed the clarinet to gobble quite so lusciously, and no other composer, not even Weber, has with those gobbles rivalled the nightingale herself.

"There are two composers whose chamber music is unworthily represented on the gramophone, and it happens that these two composers—Schumann and Mendelssohn—are sadly out of favour all round at the moment. This being so, it would be impertinent to occupy space with an argument which would neither correct those who suppose that they have outlived such falsifiers of what a

[1] I think my use of 'romantic' here is one up to Mr. Percy Scholes.

fashion chooses to call reality nor edify those who feel themselves secure against the ebb and flow of taste. I cannot refrain, however, from expressing a fervent wish that young people could be given a chance to know and love as much of Mendelssohn and Schumann as, thanks to the gramophone, they can know and love of Haydn and Mozart. Distrusting as I do the short-cuts to perfect taste which are a feature of this 'get rich quick' age, I feel convinced that the owl-eyed young man of the moment who has never been thrilled by Tennyson's *Maud* has missed as authentic an emotion of youth as if he had never loved before he was twenty; equally I am sure that to pass in one jump from a self-conscious and literary enjoyment of Mozart to horn spectacles and Stravinsky leaves that young man as callow in taste and as aesthetically raw as if because he had always travelled by aeroplane he should claim to despise the beauty of meadows and forests and the sound of bees in small gardens.

"Among my letters from strangers I receive many musical confidences, but none was ever more welcome than a letter from an Eton boy who wrote to beg my influence for the recording of a complete work of chamber music by Mendelssohn. This request filled me with hope that the generation now on the road to manhood was turning back to the more familiar ways of youth and to 'such sights as youthful poets dream on summer eves by haunted stream'. I heard, faintly indeed and dim as Oberon's horn, the first tremulous fanfare of a romantic revival. At any rate, whether it portends a change in fashion or not, it is reassuring to know that young people still exist who can enjoy sweets without being ashamed of their taste.

"However, in wanting more Mendelssohn to be recorded for the gramophone I am equally concerned for those thousands who can enjoy so much of music but who are still cut off by a wide gulf from the pleasures of chamber music. We want more bridges, and Mendelssohn is one of the bridges. Knowing as I do how many people cross the gulf by means of Schubert and turn back because Brahms repels them, I want more Schumann, because it seems to me that Brahms is more easily reached by way of Schumann. Yet beyond two mutilated versions of the piano quintet, a mutilated and badly recorded version of the quartet in A, two snippets from the quartets in A minor and F, and a snippet from the *Phantasiestücke*, we have nothing in England. I had hoped that members of the National Gramophonic Society would have voted for the recording of some of Schumann's chamber music that has been proposed; but the response was cold. I suppose he is paying the penalty for allowing cerebration to interfere with simple emotion, for every period has its peculiar cerebration which is often apt to seem superficial or insincere to other periods. Moreover, the mixture of it with intense emotion, as in the case of Schumann, may produce an effect of sentimentality just because the artist is well aware of the danger and is trying to avoid it. Schumann sought too much inspiration from art instead of life. Did he not lock himself up for a year to study Beethoven's quartets before he wrote his own? Perhaps nothing dates an artist so mercilessly as self-consciousness, because that self being what he supposes himself to be rather than what he genuinely is, he will reflect for the future only the illusions of his period and personality. Schumann thought too much about what he was doing. He was one of the precursors of the present self-conscious age and he has paid the penalty, for the present age is too profoundly occupied with itself to listen to him. Without suggesting the least parallel between him and R. L. Stevenson I could use the latter as an example of what I mean in literature. Had Stevenson never written a word about his craft, he would probably have avoided the disrepute into which he has fallen among our contemporary intellectuals.

"Schubert, who, as far as I know, was never hampered by theories, has survived the malice of time as a piece of natural scenery might survive new main roads and the traffic of charabancs. Of his chamber music we already have recorded the octet, two quintets, two quartets, two trios, and a number of snippets, and I can safely assert that just as the *Unfinished Symphony* is the most popular of all symphonies, possibly of all orchestral works, so by one or other of his compositions in chamber music more people have entered that charmed highway of art than by any other; for chamber music is a highway, though, like the Via Appia, it may have all the amenities of a by-way. I find that I am always inclined to play Schubert's chamber music at twilight; and that not because he appeals to the sentimental mood which arrives so easily when the day's work is done, for to say truth my day is lazier than my night, so that about twilight I am more likely to be feeling tense than relaxed. But Schubert suits the twilight, distilling his melodies as the flowers their scents at such an hour. His tunes come in successive gusts of perfume as when one passes from border to border of the garden at the shutting-in of a long June day. Now it is a cluster of stocks, now the 'homely cottage smell' of sweet williams, then suddenly a melody rich as lilies, but threaded by a brief and exquisite poignancy as of crushed thyme or sprig of rosemary plucked in passing and lightly tossed away.

"It may be objected that to surrender oneself to such a purely sensuous enjoyment of music is in fact to become its slave. That is the difficulty of trying to communicate in words what except by music is incommunicable. It would appear from reading what I have just written that I deliberately set myself to procure from music a series of sensations; but that is not so. With the aid of the gramophone I obtain for myself as much music as from a Medici print of the *Primavera* I can obtain of painting. What, after all, is the reason of hanging any picture upon our walls? Not that we should sit down and deliberately use it to evoke a sensation, but that it should beautifully haunt the background of our minds. In these days the man of most fastidious taste is a prey to ugliness. However earnestly he may strive to preserve his immediate surroundings from any taint of that ugliness, he will hardly resist the temptation of reading the daily paper. That is quite enough to corrupt his style, even should he forswear all but the noblest literature for the rest of his reading. I cannot help feeling that to read one's daily paper in the presence of a great picture, even though that picture be present only in the form of reproduction, and to the accompaniment of great music, even though that music be played only on a mechanical instrument like the gramophone, is to provide oneself with a prophylactic against some of the ugliness that is perpetually being pumped into the mind. Were the gramophone a much less efficient machine than it is, the privilege of putting one's mind in order by what surely at its best is the most orderly medium of art in existence—a string quartet—would be of inestimable value. The reason why I have made a habit of working to the accompaniment of chamber music is not due to any desire on my side to procure an appropriate state of emotion; but every writer, whatever his capacity for concentration, is peculiarly exposed to attacks of the irrelevant and trivial when he is most fain to be free of them. And these petty assaults are somehow warded off much more successfully when the background of my mind is occupied by great music. I do not intend to convey by that phrase the subconscious mind. It is more imperative that the subconscious mind should be concentrated on the business in hand than any other function, because finally it will be the subconscious mind which will produce the material. It is the background of the conscious mind for which I crave an occupation. The music is playing the same part as the beads of a rosary. Usually, in spite of working I am able to follow the music intelligently enough to know when the wrong side of a disc has been placed on the turntable, but there are times, rare, alas, but all the more wonderful for their rarity—when the determination to hammer some sentence into shape is so tremendous that a long quartet can be played from beginning to end without my being consciously aware of it. And this is really a surprising and delicious experience, because I shall have heard the whole composition as it were in a moment of time, so swiftly will time have swept past, and the impression of the whole work on my imagination will have been faintly comparable to the original conception of the composer, since I shall have heard the essence of his inspiration as he must have heard it in a moment of time. I should be inclined to make a positive claim that the only way for the average man to listen to music for more than a very short while is as an accompaniment to some occupation. All honest people will admit that the trivial and the irrelevant are most aggressive when they are deliberately listening to music, and one of my objections to programme music has always been that perpetual intervention of the trivial and irrelevant between myself and the composer's mood. Moreover, I am inclined to resent his assumption that he is capable of inducing in me the state of mind and the experience round which he is writing, just as, were I a musician, I should resent being told by a poet that words strung meaninglessly but musically together were a substitute for music itself. I am so jealous of music's potency that I hate to see it shackled with fetters of which poets and painters would only be too happy to disembarrass themselves, could they but do so. Nothing is more hostile to programme music than the gramophone, because, as it seems to me, the possibility of frequent repetition is fatal to such a convention; for either the composer's programme is so realistically conveyed that the composition becomes a short story, in which case, however subtly wrought, familiarity must breed contempt at last, or the programme is so vaguely conveyed that it is not worth affixing. Take, for instance, Schönberg's sextet, *Verklärte Nacht*, to which is attached a tiresome and sentimental piece of Teutonic narrative. By all the rules of the game, frequent repetition should gradually inure us to its beauties. Does this follow? On the contrary, the frequent repetition of what is only saved from complete amorphousness by the illustrations in words that accompany it, may become finally more exasperating than the first performance might have seemed to the most conservative ear.

"And here is a problem for the gramophone to solve. One is so continually hearing it asserted that modern music only fails to attract

because it is unfamiliar, that one is anxious to take advantage of
the gramophone as one might take advantage of the printing press
to remove this handicap. An important object of the National
Gramophonic Society was to give modern works of chamber music
a chance to compete with the classics. Yet since the society was
founded, the majority of the members have voted more and more
emphatically every time against modern works. This may be only a
very small straw, but it may be taken as a good enough indication
of the wind's direction; amongst the members of such a society we
might expect to find a large proportion of modernists. The older
lovers of chamber music most of whom for a long time regarded the
gramophone as a vulgar and inadequate machine to supply them
with music, are in fact a small minority. Moreover, contemporary
composers, who have taken the existence of the gramophone for
granted, surely ought not to be more heavily handicapped by it
than Haydn and Mozart.

"Yet there are times when one is grateful for a label. A case in
point is the Spring Sonata of Beethoven, which, perhaps because
the name was not affixed by the composer himself, seems to possess
a better descriptive value, for inasmuch as we are not obliged to
accept it, we can accept it more easily. I never hear it played but I
become aware beyond the music of the sharp young green of the
budding quickset, of deep and luminous April dusks in which
lingers the frore breath of winter, of the bitter-sweet perfume of
primroses and the waking fern. It is not spring as we look forward
to spring in winter, thinking to stand again in the sun's eye, but
the shy spring we remember in the plenitude of July, such a spring
as Keats wrote of on St. Mark's Eve. There is a sonata of Mozart's
for violin and piano which we are lucky enough to possess in recorded form also—Op. 18, No. 1, in A—to give it the only title it
ever had—and this does suggest the spring to which we look
forward, poignant indeed, but only as all youth is poignant and as
every spring is poignant with a delicate and faint apprehension of
what might be, but pure of all regret for what might have been.

"There is a further charm which the so frequent playing of
chamber music to oneself can cast, and that is the way snatches of
melody and brief phrases will come unbidden to provide the music
that some exquisite moment demands. It is easy enough at such
times to beguile oneself with the fancy that the secret meaning of
that andante of Mozart's or that rondo of Beethoven's has been
revealed, or why should it return thus as free of one's bidding as a
butterfly? Nor is it necessarily one's own mind that is illuminated

by the echo of a tune. Sometimes a companion by whistling or humming it will make the revelation. The fourth movement of César Franck's sonata, so beautifully played and recorded for the gramophone by Cortot and Thibaud, will always be associated in my memory with going downhill through thickets of broom and myrtle, past crimson cyclamens in the glinting shade of the big arbutus bushes that overhung the fragrant path; for once, when by such a path I was descending a gorge to the blue Tyrrhenian sea fifteen hundred feet below, my companions a few yards ahead were whistling the melody of that fourth movement. If for nothing else, I should hold the gramophone justified by making us free of César Franck's sonata and quartet and sublime quintet. He, perhaps, more than any other composer, requires the right mood for his music, and how seldom shall we find it in a concert hall! I do not care to hear that quartet in a crowd but in my own room with my own books and pictures round me, I am beside him in his organ loft, and I have heard the 'seraphim whose footfalls tinkled on the tufted floor'. Surely, if ever the Holy Angels walked beside a human being, they walked beside César Franck up there in the organ loft of Ste. Clotilde. Like Blake, he never lost his childish vision; and of all sublunary delights, I know of few that can compare to reading to oneself the *Songs of Innocence* late on a winter night and then playing to oneself the quartet. That, indeed, is to hold eternity in an hour.

"I am not forgetting Palestrina when I lament that the age of faith never really expressed itself in music. When we hear what a César Franck with the vision of a Van Eyck can do in music, we look but in vain for a composer who might be set beside Dante. Not even to Beethoven can we grant that eminence of the human mind. When I heard the later quartets occasionally I used to think that Beethoven had passed beyond the reach of a mortal, but now that I have been able to play these quartets over and over again, and listen to the Ninth Symphony over and over again, I have realized that he never for an instant transcended mortality as in the *Paradiso* Dante transcended it. The finale of the Ninth Symphony is a descent to earth from those flutterings in the first movement on the brink of life's secret. Not that I would have Beethoven shed one trace of his common humanity with ourselves. I glory in his sublime failure to voice the ineffable, and I love him as I could never love Dante; but there are moments when I long for him to be able to soar undismayed and never to groan, as he inevitably will somewhere in his greatest compositions, that life is after all nought but a wry joke. Prometheus bound was a greater poetic conception than

Prometheus unbound, and it is significant that since Shelley we have had no cosmic great poet. Prometheus was unbound and poetry died. And now, though we know that it was nothing but a titanic delusion from which Shelley and Beethoven suffered, and though we have proved its falsity on many battlefields, poetry does not come to life again, and even music gasps.

"This is one of the pleasures of the gramophone, this continual company of music which enables one to speculate upon it in various moods, which makes one independent of other people's programmes and which turns half one's library into records of music. Those gifted and fortunate beings who can take a miniature score to bed with them as I might take a volume of Propertius are often too musical to be able to convey even to themselves what music means to them. In any case it must be a very long while before the average intelligent man will be able to read a score as he will read a book.

"Although we owners of gramophones possess the privilege of familiarity hitherto denied to all but the most musical, it would be unduly sanguine to expect from us any aesthetic speculations of much value. People like myself, who find music an illustration of life rather than life an illustration of music, are so apt to attach an undue importance to those illustrations. Still, in being able to listen with all our attention to music on the gramophone, as we can in the solitude and comfort of our own rooms, we are gaining more from music than by listening to it in a concert hall with a mind distracted by the impertinence of the surroundings or buzzing with the trivialities of everyday existence. Yet perhaps it is too much to claim that we do actually listen with a more genuine concentration. Perhaps the habit of thinking about music is set up by the sheer amount of it that percolates through the mind when, as by the aid of the gramophone, it becomes the normal accompaniment of one's daily life. The old way of educating by endless repetition had more to be said for it than most people in these days are ready to admit. The abandonment of that system for what seems a more enlightened way of teaching Latin and Greek is what the Americans did many years ago. Yet, knowingness does not entirely take the place of knowledge, and the knowledge that directs taste can only be acquired by a process of exhaustion. Repetition effects a kind of catalysis of the mind, and no substance demonstrates this more clearly than music. Habituated as we are to the chemical action of reading a book over and over again, we take for granted that only the best books, as we call them, will bear frequent re-reading. I do not find, however, that the ability to be often re-read necessarily endows a book with 'goodness' as a work of art. Some of the worst books ever written will sustain repetition more easily than some of the best, and I find this even more definitely the case with music. The early and middle period quartets of Beethoven bear reiteration —I mean extensive reiteration, not a mere half a dozen performances—more satisfactorily than the late quartets. The chamber music of Haydn and Mozart can be played night after night without the least wearisomeness. In the earlier days of the gramophone, when some fifty records making a total of six hours' music were all that I could collect, I have played the same isolated and often much shortened movement every night for two months at a stretch without even a momentary desire for a change. Indeed, nowadays when my shelves are crammed with a variety of chamber music that makes it unnecessary to repeat a whole quartet more than once in three months, I sometimes find myself looking back with something very near regret to those restricted programmes. Asking myself now what was the precise quality in the music that made it not merely endurable but equally delightful every time it was repeated, I have come to the conclusion that it was the predominant gaiety of the excerpts to which we were treated. Mirth set out in a pattern eases the heart more surely than any other kind, and I believe it is fair to say of all chamber music that the outstanding quality is its *allegria*:

> 'Thou Goddess fair and free,
> In heaven yclept Euphrosyne,
> And by men, heart-easing Mirth,
> Who lovely Venus at a birth,
> With two sister graces more,
> To ivy-crowned Bacchus bore.'

"So much does this tradition persist that even Tchaikovsky allowed himself a happy ending in his major D quartet; it is not until we reach contemporary writers that we are liable to find a complete elimination of *allegria* from their chamber music. We are inclined to talk about the externality of Haydn's and Mozart's music, and by that epithet impute to them a lack of depth. I think we assume too easily their innocence of life's profundities. It is true that progress has added so much to the complication of existence that numbers of people have sought from music the expression of an inward emotion and an assurance of something permanent behind the rapid shifting of external circumstance; but really it is the contemporary composer of chamber music who scarcely ever does reach beyond external circumstances. His music, in fact, is far more truly external than that of Haydn. It is far more the illustration of a state of affairs than the expression of a mental or emotional attitude. Ugliness is nothing new; but the self-consciousness of the modern artist causes him to be overwhelmed by it, and with a desperate optimism he strives to perceive beauty in that ugliness and to extract beauty from it. His art is a kind of homoeopathy or inoculation; the art of Haydn and Mozart was an antidote. Not that I would suggest for a moment any deliberate attempt to uplift poor humanity or soothe its ills. Such an express determination would have appeared presumptuous to composers whose music glows and blushes with a beautiful modesty. It is a commonplace of criticism to say that Mozart's music reflects none of the trials of his workaday existence; and if this means that his music is never a defiant ex-ploitation of himself it may pass unchallenged. Yet I cannot believe that anybody like myself, who has rarely allowed a day to pass without turning to trio or quartet of Mozart as he might turn to a crystalline spring for refreshment, could be content to perceive no more in that music than the bright hours of a sun-dial. It is true that the pointer marks only the sunny hours, but it marks them with a moving shadow. And for me, Mozart's music is like that shadow travelling over the dial of our life.

"As I have been writing these words and thinking about Mozart, the gramophone has been playing the G minor quintet. I happen to know that these three discs were recorded by the players during one of the daylight air-raids of the war. They played the quintet under the stress of the nervous tension that such conditions would naturally create, and the music, turning all that tension to the service of beauty, is so compact of grace and courage that all the debonair sacrifice of youth flowers in that quintet as a world may flower in four lines from the Greek anthology. The least imaginative creature could hardly fail to respond to these old-fashioned discs which perpetuate, in the guise of sounds emitted according to a pattern of two violins, two violas, and a violoncello, yet hardly recognizable as such and almost drowned by the hiss of the needle, half an hour in the emotion of our national life. No doubt with improved methods of recording we shall soon have another version of the quintet, but some of these early discs of chamber music will have a charm quite independent of any adventitious help from air-raids, a charm that greater realism will never succeed in dis-pelling. The fluty tones of the strings may sound grotesquely false, the scratch may exacerbate a sensitive ear; but if these discs are played with a fibre needle on a good machine in the intimacy of their own rooms, all who are not the slaves of realism will surrender to the spell this elfin music casts upon the firelit air—surrender so completely, perhaps, as not to miss the outward beauty of the players about their business and to accept the motion of the shadows on the walls and ceiling as a perfect substitute for the flickering bows and the way the 'cello seems to be reading with its master the music. There are two trios of Mozart arranged for piano, violin and viola which make the very books of my shelves appear to dance. There is a quartet in E flat by Haydn (Opus 64, No. 6) which, played to the accompaniment of Siamese cats and kittens at their sport, confounds sorrow. Purists may object, and reasonably, that the antics of kittens have nothing to do with Haydn's chamber music. I can but reply that with the help of the gramophone I have convinced myself that everything which enhances the beauty of the interior scene gains something from the performance of chamber music and in its turn adds something to it. Sweet peas in a bowl look more beautiful if looked at through an invisible web of sweet sounds. So much, indeed, is my library impregnated with music that I have almost reached the stage of believing that the music is made by the room itself, and I can hardly listen to the gramophone in a strange interior without being discouraged by its mechanical aspect. But then I am quite unable even to read a borrowed book with the least pleasure, and I have denied myself a sight of many of the earth's beautiful places merely because I should have to stay in an hotel to enjoy them. Yes, I suppose I were wise to admit that my chamber music on the gramophone is nothing but self-indulgence. Let it be. I shall not defend myself, but find my justification in Milton:

'Lap me in soft Lydian airs,
Married to immortal verse
Such as the meeting soul may pierce,
In notes, with many a winding bout
Of linked sweetness long drawn out,
With wanton heed and giddy cunning,
The melting voice through mazes running,
Untwisting all the chains that tie
The hidden soul of harmony.

These delights if thou canst give
Mirth, with thee I mean to live.' "

H

That article was written early in 1925 before the introduction of electric recording, and in 1928 I wrote a brief addendum which will fit in better to the chapter dealing with that revolution. Cobbett himself did not die until 1937 at the age of ninety. His services to music were recognized rather tardily with a C.B.E. when he was eighty-six.

My last glimpse of him was in that year, driving in a taxi-cab with three violoncellos. A wonderful and indefatigable old man.

Chapter 11

IN December 1923 I made the following announcement:

"I am most anxious to devote some space to the player-piano in
the New Year. This new feature will not rob the gramophone of a
single page; but it will mean a slight increase in our size. The
devotees of the player-piano and the gramophone are apt, each of
them, to regard the other's instrument as hostile to his own. I cannot
help recognizing that for many people the path of appreciation has
been cut by the player-piano, and for the benefit of music I am eager
to secure the support of player-pianists for the gramophone. In other
words, my main reason for adding this section to our paper is to
make proselytes and enlist the support of a potentially large body of
enthusiastic converts. I have no doubt that some of the bigoted and
exclusive upholders of the gramophone will reproach me for making
overtures instead of playing them; but I have thought it over very
carefully, and I believe that an alliance between the gramophone
and the player-piano is essential to the security of music."

For a year and a month we fought hard, well supported by
Blüthner's and Steinway's in particular. Blüthner's went so far as
to send me a Carola instrument to the tiny isle of Jethou where by
now I was living, having disengaged myself from the financial strain
of the Isle of Herm. However, at last we had to face the fact that
a player-piano supplement was not wanted by readers of *The
Gramophone*.

In March 1925 I was writing:

"In the last number a simple question was put to the readers of
The Gramophone. They were asked to declare whether they read the
Player-Piano Supplement, which has now been issued gratis to them
for more than a year. The answer has been direct and unequivocal.
The vast majority of them do not read it; a certain number confess
to a mild interest in it; a very few welcome it keenly, and quite a
fair number as keenly resent its existence.

"In deference to this counsel the Player-Piano Supplement
appears for the last time with this issue of *The Gramophone*. Since

December 1923 when the objects for adding the section to our paper were set forth, those objects have largely been achieved or rendered unnecessary. On the one hand nearly all player-pianists have been persuaded to buy gramophones, as we can judge from the small number who subscribe exclusively for the Supplement; on the other hand the progressive policy of the record-making Companies and the stagnant policy of the roll-making Companies have done away with the complaint—justified a year ago—that in order to become acquainted with the great works of classical music it was advisable to have recourse to the catalogues of piano-rolls.''

I ought to have realized that my disappointment with the catalogue of aeolian rolls which led to my acquiring a gramophone was a warning about the vitality of the piano-player as well as of the aeolian organ. Some years later I should make the mistake of being too soon instead of too late in starting a paper of radio programme criticism before even the daily press had begun to criticize wireless programmes.

In May of that year *The Radio Times* published the article I had promised to the Managing Director of the British Broadcasting Company two or three months earlier.

"Yesterday afternoon (I write these words in mid-April) I was sitting on a terrace that overhung the Mediterranean. A gentle wind slipped in and out of the Aleppo pines, and from the water far below the voices of the swimmers came up with a sound of summer in their mirth. We had endured four days of Easter travelling. Every train and boat and hotel had been packed. It was pleasant to sit here, warm and idle, after all that confusion of noisy tourists and changing weather.

"In the course of conversation I told my host that early in June I should be broadcasting some remarks about gramophone records, and to my amazement he asked me to let him know the exact time and date so that here in Capri he might listen. My mind travelled back across the Bay of Naples, drove along the clangorous Naples streets to the railway station, crashed up in the train through Campania to Rome, dealt with the complication of changing trains, settled down to the long journey from Rome to Paris in the *wagon-lit*, puffed up through Italy into the Mont Cenis tunnel, puffed out of the tunnel and up through France, drove across Paris in a taxi-cab, grappled with the dirt and crowds of the Gare du Nord, rattled along the dreary track between Paris and Calais, savoured the immemorial odour of the Channel boat, beheld the white cliffs of England strung across the horizon like distant washing hung out to dry, puffed on through Kent until it reached Victoria, swept along the Embankment in a taxi-cab to the Savoy, and ended its last journey in the studio of the British Broadcasting Company.

"There in a quiet room, even the windows of which were hidden by grey draperies to deaden the echoes, I should stand and speak about a yard away from the kind of instrument that one sees in an optician's shop; here in Capri on this terrace overhanging the Mediterranean, pine-shadowed, warm, murmurous with the mirth of swimmers far below, my friends would hear what I had to say.

"Of course, there is nothing more miraculous in being heard on Capri when one speaks from London than in being heard at Aberdeen; and, if mere mileage is to count, it is much less miraculous than sitting up until three in the morning to hear a man talking at ten o'clock in America. But, somehow or other, this was the first time that the miracle was really brought home to my imagination. We have come to take so much for granted during this last quarter of a century into which has been packed more human ingenuity than into all the many millions of years before it. We have become like the children of rich parents, and are no longer capable of appreciating the marvellous toys that are showered upon us.

"I feel that, if I read in to-morrow's paper of a distinguished Czecho-Slovakian engineer who had invented a rug like the rug in the Arabian Nights, on which one would sit and be instantly transported wherever one wanted to go, I should not be at all astonished. I should just mention that somebody had invented a rug for going anywhere at once and say how strange it was that such an invention had taken so long to perfect and that I must get one as soon as the price was at all reasonable.

"When I read the diaries or the letters of our grandparents and note what an amount of stupefaction they lavished upon such an edifice as Paddington railway-station, and when I remember how the sight of a bone-shaking safety-bicycle drew every little boy and girl to stare at it wide-eyed, and how the first pneumatic tyres induced other little boys and girls to run along the kerb shouting 'Pneumatic tyres! Pneumatic tyres!' as though the rider had descended from another planet, I feel ashamed of the nonchalance of our modern imagination. Yet for the future of the human race broadcasting is as heavily fraught with potentialities as the discovery of printing.

"I suppose that at the end of the fifteenth century a number of people asked themselves what was going to happen to literature under the influence of the strange new monster of print that threatened individual expression. And certainly at the present moment many people are asking what will be the effect on literature of broadcasting. In a way, of course, it is a return to the more primitive method of publicity when the bard stood up and recited his own epic. But it is a return with a difference; whereas formerly the audience was limited to a few hundred listeners, the audience of the contemporary bard may be several hundreds of thousands, and within the next few years it may easily be several millions.

"Personally, I view such a prospect with complete optimism. Poetry has been slowly expiring under the influence of the printed page; but, though I fear it may be too late, it is just conceivable that the spur of recitation by the poet himself may yet recover it. Poetry was never meant to be read; it was meant to be heard. The recitations by the poets of their own verses will test them more severely than the best hand-made paper; and while broadcasting will provide them with a larger audience than they have ever dreamed of, it will act as a check on over-production.

"Any extension of the facilities for obtaining literature is, in the long run, an advantage to literature. At first, the tendency is to help what is second-rate; but a public whose mind has been more nicely nourished will soon become surfeited with bad food. Yes, I look forward with confidence to getting rid of a lot of worthless printed matter with the growth of broadcasting; and indeed the publishing trade now badly needs a Malthus or a Marie Stopes.

"Young women and young men produce books in these times as a hen lays eggs in spring. It is true that comparatively few people read their works, but I am hoping that with the growth of broadcasting nobody will read them. And when we examine the case of music we have grounds for optimism, for even within one year we can already see the tremendous improvement in the quality of music that is being issued by the gramophone companies.

"Whatever may be the effect on literature, there is no question at all that the effect on music is going to be entirely beneficial. For my own part, I believe that we are moving toward a point of human development when it will only be possible to express in music the complicacy of modern emotion. The great obstacle in the way of music has always been the difficulty of obtaining it.

"It is pathetic to think that an inadequate instrument like the piano should have represented practically the whole of the mechanical facilities which music received during a hundred years of mechanical progress in every direction.

"And when, finally, the gramophone arrived, it was allowed to remain perfectly unprogressive by those who exploited it. As usual, the public was blamed, and we were told that the public did not want good music and that they would not buy good records. It is hardly necessary to point out that this was all nonsense, for as soon as the gramophone companies began to provide good music in sufficient quantity, they found not merely that Wireless, their mighty new competitor, was not going to ruin them, but that it was actually going to help them.

"I had occasion last year to deplore what I thought was the rubbish that the British Broadcasting Company was offering the public in the way of music. It seemed to me lamentable that such opportunities for education should be neglected. All that is changed now, and I affirm with respect and gratitude that no great financial corporation has ever shown itself so eager and so willing to help the cause of art.

"Many listeners write from all over Great Britain protesting against what they consider is the highbrow music that is being offered them. Presumably some of the malcontents will read these words of mine, and if any of them are so far honouring me, I beg them to pause when next they want to grumble at being given a performance of good music and to ask themselves if they really are anxious to remain in a state of barbarism. I beg them to doubt their own perfections and to bring themselves to wonder if they are not still capable of learning. Let me assure them that their fellow men who derive a sharper pleasure from a symphony of Beethoven than from some silly little tune of the day (which is, after all, only attractive because it is a repetition of a hundred and more catchy little tunes before it) are enjoying an infinitely greater pleasure than they themselves have ever experienced in their lives.

"Such men would probably write and protest with equal vigour if they were compelled to listen to nothing but nursemaids' novelettes. Yet, musically, they are in the condition of the nursemaid. Wireless has given these men an opportunity to raise themselves if they will only have the humility to realize that they want raising. People like them gain the general public a bad reputation; and yet the general public has the only really infallible taste, for it must never be forgotten that a work of art becomes what is called a classic not by the verdict of a few dank-haired critics, but by the capacity for enjoyment it can give to the general public in every generation.

"I doubt if *Yes, We Have No Bananas* would have been the success it was if the public ear had not been prepared for its rhythm by Handel's Hallelujah Chorus. And what about the success of *Lilac Time*, in spite of the fact that before it was used for a musical comedy every tune in it was Schubert's Op. something or other?

"Complacency is the great foe of Art, just as it is the enemy of Religion and the destroyer of Love."

Neither broadcasting nor television has had any contraceptive effect on the publication of books and this overproduction threatens the future of literature by stifling it with mediocrity. There is no justification for publishing three-quarters of the novels, three-quarters of the travel books and half the autobiographies which are being published to-day. If only the promising first syllable of penicillin meant that it was a reliable cure for *cacoethes scribendi*.

I was paid ten guineas for that article and wrote to point out that such a fee was below my current rate. The Editor in his reply said ten guineas was the most *The Radio Times* could afford for a page and consoled me with the information that H. G. Wells, Bernard Shaw and Arnold Bennett had all been satisfied with ten guineas.

Payment by the B.B.C. in those days was low for everything. I was offered three guineas to do a commentary of an hour on some gramophone records of my own choice. That was in June 1924. The time chosen was one o'clock—there was no one o'clock news bulletin in those days at Savoy Hill which was then known as 2LO—and broadcasting was still being done in a single large studio with lots of people moving about in it from whom silence was demanded when the microphone was 'live'.

The microphone itself was suspended above the back of an empty arm-chair, rather like the spider that came to sit down beside Miss Muffet.

"Where's your script?" asked whoever it was that was producing the broadcast. I told him I had not got a script. "But you can't broadcast without a script. You'll dry up. People get microphone fright."

I said I was used to talking without notes and did not think I should be nervous.

"Oh, well," said the director, "we must hope for the best. Anyway, it won't matter much if you do dry up because the only people listening at one o'clock will be the women washing up."

"Now, it's quite simple really," I was assured. "Don't be nervous. Just imagine that an old friend of yours is sitting in that arm-chair and talk to this imaginary friend in exactly the same voice you would use if a friend was really sitting there. Don't bother about the gramophone. You'll hand me the record you want played when you're ready for it."

Just before the broadcast was going to start, a Sunday-school treat escorted by a clergyman arrived in the studio to be shown how broadcasting was done.

"Do you mind very much if these children sit at the other end of the studio while you're doing your broadcast?" I was asked. "You'll have your back to them."

I said I thought the sense of an audience actually present would be welcome, and the broadcast started. I hope the women washing up enjoyed those old records more than the men washing up to-day enjoy the one o'clock news.

I was not in the least nervous as I chatted away about each record in turn before I handed it to the producer to put on the gramophone, and I was glad to detect in myself as much sensitiveness to an audience as if I were standing on a platform and saw it in front of me.

Just before putting on an old Vocalion record of Lionel Tertis I said, "A new record by Lionel Tertis always gives me particular pleasure because apart from his being the greatest living viola player, he and I were both born . . ." I was on the point of saying "in that rather grubby old town" and then I pulled myself before a vision in the mind's eye of the men of West Hartlepool watching their wives washing up after dinner . . . "both born," I went on, "in that old town beside the North Sea which the German fleet bombarded in the war."

Soon 2LO became a cherished memory of jolly amateurs. The old all-in studio vanished and talkers were housed in small studios, one or two of which were lined with the backs of books to give them a suitable scholarly background and encourage the talker to feel the solemnity of his job. At first the speaker always had the clock behind him, which meant cricking the neck as one looked rapidly round to see if one's broadcast was lagging behind the time allowed for it.

In those days the announcers had to wear dinner jackets and look the part as well as speak it. One evening I said to one of these

grave and impressive figures, "I suppose there's a technical reason
for putting the clock behind the speaker?"

"No, I don't think it matters where the clock is," he replied.

"It doesn't? Well, wouldn't it be better if the talker could see the
clock without cricking his neck?"

"Oh, that's a very good idea."

And soon after this the clocks were moved within sight of the
broadcaster. I like to believe I was responsible for that change.

Then there was compèring in those days. The compère of to-day,
comfortably isolated from the orchestra in front of his own microphone, does not know what an ordeal it used to be for the pioneers.
The compère had to sit among the members of the orchestra, from
which he emerged to bend over and speak into a microphone hung
about eighteen inches above the floor. I remember I was once
compèring a performance of old Alhambra ballet-tunes, seated
among the violoncellos and trying to get out of the way of their
ardent bowing. Before each new tune I would have to come out and
say something like this:

"And now here is a melody that will bring back to many older
listeners wonderful evenings at the Alhambra once upon a time when
they leant back in those gloriously comfortable fauteuils with a good
cigar and watched that great ballerina . . ." and so on. You know the
kind of thing. Well, as the programme went on, it became more and
more difficult to bend down to within eighteen inches of the floor
and in that position suggest the luxury and ease of the Edwardian
decade.

"I suppose there's a technical reason why the microphone is
only eighteen inches above the floor?" I asked.

"No, I don't think so," said the announcer.

"Then wouldn't it be easier for the speaker if it was level with
his mouth?"

That too was considered a good idea.

In April 1924 I was writing in *The Gramophone*:

"One of the most moving things I have read in recent literature
is Mr. Lloyd Osbourne's account of how his stepfather, Robert Louis
Stevenson, used to pick out for himself on a flageolet scraps of music
and how he wished that R.L.S. could have had the joy of a gramophone or a piano-player in Samoa. I do not know how Sir Sidney
Colvin and Mr. Gosse[1] would have liked sending him out records
instead of books and receiving despairing appeals to know where

[1] Sir Edmund Gosse.

they were. I am sure my friend Mr. Gosse would not have liked it, for he hates music, and when I told him last autumn that I had started a gramophone review he looked at me with puzzled compassion. Mr. Lloyd Osbourne says that his stepfather was really starved of music. When I think of the pleasure the gramophone has given to people all over the world I grow a little impatient of remarks such as this from Mr. Ramsay MacDonald:

" 'There is too much over-indulgence in recreation to-day—an incapacity to spend a quiet Sunday. I am amazed that there should be so many people who can do nothing but be amused and entertained by a gramophone, and who have no capacity to spend time profitably with themselves.'

"To be sure, we know the kind of gramophone he meant and the kind of music that was being listened to, but I can never help feeling a little annoyed by remarks like these, which are rather like the stale old jokes about spring poets. My revenge for them is always to convert another person to the gramophone. I go to my club, fix on somebody, lure him round to Newman Street, and when he leaves me the light of faith is shining in his eyes, and I know that before a week is out his bank balance will be considerably lower. I have not yet succeeded in converting a bishop, but I am looking out now for a suitable one."

Chapter 12

IN the last number of our first volume I wrote an article which I called "The Search for the Absolute", and although the sound-boxes and instruments mentioned are all museum pieces now I think some of it is worth preserving as a prologue to the test of instruments we had arranged to hold a month later in June 1924 at the Steinway Hall.

"I find an increasing tendency among our correspondents to ask what is the best machine, what is the best record, what is the best needle, what is the best sound-box, when what they should really ask me is the best attitude of mind in which to try to discover what is the best machine, etc., for *them*? Time after time I have expressed my conviction that the absolute in the gramophone and its accessories is not attainable. One correspondent writes that he is bewildered by the claims of our advertisers. Let me assure him that he cannot be half as much bewildered by them as I am. Fortunately, I have been granted an exceptional rapidity of assimilation, and so I never suffer from mental indigestion with its unpleasant con-comitants—the heartburn of jealousy, the acidity of disappointment, and the flatulence of so much critical opinion. Not only have I been granted rapidity, but I have also been granted normality of experience. It may be that in a certain number of months I shall accomplish in the adventures of taste what the average man accom-plishes in the same number of years, but he and I are going to reach the same goal ultimately, and the only difference between us will be that I get there first. By living alone as I do the speed of mental experience is considerably accelerated. It is only when I come to London that I find my opinion veering to every point of the compass in turn like the cowl of a London chimney.

"All this is by way of preface to my having realized that, like everything else in nature and art and life and society and politics, we must, before going any further, split the gramophone world into two broad divisions. We will put on one side for a moment the various machines and confine ourselves to a consideration of the sound-box. What is the best sound-box? Like autumn leaves that strew the brooks in Vallombrosa, like swallows gathering in October, like bees swarming, like ants, like midges, like stars in the heavens, that question reaches me from every part of the world. The highest Andes have echoed it; it has floated on the yellow waters of the Yangtse-kiang; it has rustled the gum-trees of Australia and ruffled the lagoons of the Pacific. My answer must take the form of a counter-question. Are you male or female? Are you Liberal or Conservative? Are you a Platonist or an Aristotelian? A romantic or a realist? A Catholic or a Protestant? A Buddhist or a Mahommedan? What do you really believe that the gramophone is for? And when you try to answer this last question do not forget that the gramophone is one of the many rivulets into which the great main stream of artistic expression has been broken up by the complications of modern existence.

"The gramophone has passed safely through the conjuring-trick stage; we are no longer amazed at the miracle of recorded sound. In other words we have all of us passed beyond the state of savages. It took a long time for the recording companies to discover that the standard of intelligence in the British nation was beyond the standard of intelligence of primitive races, and in America the recording companies are still inclined to cater for their clients as an old-fashioned explorer catered with beads for the cannibals he encountered. But what neither the public nor the makers of gramophones have yet realized is that the appreciation of the music they provide (I am talking now about the quality of sound, not the merit of the compositions) depends on the temperamental prejudices of the various individuals who patronize it. I fancy that we have most of us begun (or at any rate most of us who are out of our twenties) by thinking of the gramophone in terms of a rather bad instrument with a mica sound-box, which was either worn or improperly adjusted or merely clumsily thought out. The result is that when we first hear a composition sound-box giving that mellow tone and generally softening the asperities of an imperfect instrument, we are led into a romantic passion for the novelty, which lasts in the case of those of us who are not true romantics only so long as the novelty, but which in the case of those who are confirmed romantics may last for ever. Now I, who am not a confirmed romantic, am obviously incapable of advising those who are what is the best sound-box. Romantics stand or fall by subjective standards. Half the confusion existing in the minds of my correspondents is due to their not perceiving this. I most earnestly beg that nobody will ask me to commit myself to an opinion on the respective merits of any, for instance, of the following romantic sound-boxes—the Astra, the Tremusa, the Ultone. They are all good, and it is open to the champions of any one of them to claim that it conveys better the impression of real music being played than any mica sound-box on the market. Besides these, however, there are a number of romantic sound-boxes, of which I might instance the Peridulce and the Pianina, which in my opinion achieve their romantic effect illegitimately by a deliberate falsification of life. I do not like to illustrate my points from the works of a fellow novelist, but we have to do these things, and I cannot find a better comparison for the Peridulce sound-box than the novels of Mr. W. J. Locke. I am open to wager that if any of you like the novels of Mr. Locke (and it is clear that many more readers will than won't) you will like the Peridulce and the Pianina. Both these sound-boxes are mica, which in my opinion makes their influence all the more dangerous, because they don't look like romantic sound-boxes. They are dressed like ordinary English gentleman sound-boxes, without the sombrero of the Astra, or the dark, dank locks of the Ultone, or the silvery draperies of the Tremusa.

"Captain Barnett[1] came to see me the other day, and he had the nerve to pretend that he was not a romanticist. You know how unromantic it is to have a cold in the head? Well, that is what these sound-boxes feel about the oboe, and I accused Captain Barnett of wanting to turn the oboe into a flute. He blenched at the accusation and protested his innocence of any designs upon the oboe; but I was not to be shaken from my opinion. I should accuse the inventor of the Ultone (if I knew him) of trying to turn the violin into a violoncello. Yes, these sound-boxes are the warm baths of the gramophone; they are the poppies and mandragora of the gramophone. The hearts of those who play upon them ache and a drowsy numbness pains their senses. They want feathers burnt under their noses or drops of sal volatile sprinkled upon their foreheads. In other words they want a small brilliantly tuned mica sound-box. They want an objective standard of reality. I believe that devotees of the Exhibition sound-box[2] are nearer to the truth than any others, but here again we must be careful of excess of realism. We know that Galli-Curci is inclined to be nasal, but we must beware of letting that nasality be over-accentuated.

"Like all realists, the small mica sound-boxes are apt to insist unduly on the unpleasant things in life. Realists are always more

[1] One of our regular contributors.
[2] This was the sound-box used by His Master's Voice and Victor.

honest than romanticists, who when reduced to their least common multiple are merely liars, and they have suffered a great deal from the recurrent attempts to blur literature. I might say that the whole of the Victorian age is to be found in the Astra sound-box—its solemnity, its massiveness and its majesty, its breadth and its profundity. And now we are beginning to ask ourselves if some of these qualities were not acquired by a certain deliberate dishonesty, by a certain cowardice and snobbishness and insensibility. The result has been a reaction, and our modern writers in their endeavour not to shirk the unpleasant facts of life have nearly succeeded in persuading us that life consists of nothing else but unpleasant facts. I am glad to think, if I may be egotistical for a moment, that contemporary critics have called me in turn realist, romanticist, and sentimentalist, for it seems to me clear that a novel which pretends to be an abstract of the times must contain all these qualities, any one of which will seem to predominate according to the personal opinions of the critic. Unfortunately at the present moment English criticism is at a very low ebb. Unanimity is no substitute for an objective standard. Too many of our critics are fly-papers on whose sticky minds a mass of ephemeral flies buzz for awhile and then expire.

"*The Gramophone* should try to set up an objective standard; but the readers of *The Gramophone* must realize that the pursuit of the perfect sound-box can only be carried on by the very severest testing of their individual tastes. They must learn to distrust first impressions; they must ask themselves what they really want. At present most of my correspondents are content to ask *me* what they want. I want them to decide if they believe in the perfectibility of the gramophone, and not merely in the perfectibility of the gramophone, but in its ultimate absorption into the Nirvana of pure music. I notice with alarm a tendency to widen the gulf between gramophonic music and played music, and to say that inasmuch as it is obvious that we cannot reproduce the music of the orchestra, or the chamber, or the concert platform, or the opera house, we must develop the gramophone along musical lines of its own. I view with regret the existence of a Platonic idea of music that is at once beyond both gramophonic music and played music. These gramophonic Platonists hope to approach the ideal music by an entirely different road from that of played music. While sweetening the sound of the gramophone they are really substituting it for played music. Even a book is in many ways only a substitute for a personality, but it is probably as far as that personality can go toward expressing itself. Devotees of the gramophone should desire to make the gramophone a more perfect expression of the music we have rather than despair of its imperfections and try to turn it into another kind of musical instrument. Indeed, I am going to refuse to allow the gramophone to be called an instrument any longer. It is a machine. Let us face that fact. It is a machine invented to reproduce played music. So long as we keep its mechanical character before us we shall not be led away into worshipping a falsification of music.

"I am assuming that few readers of this paper do not already own a gramophone; but if any reader is intending to invest in a gramophone for the first time and wants my advice about the purchase of a machine, let him please answer the following questions when he writes:

"Who is your favourite poet?

"Who is your favourite novelist?

"Who is your favourite composer?

"Who is your favourite painter?

"Do you prefer English or Italian singing?

"Do you like the viola as an instrument better than the violoncello?

"Do you like the oboe or the cor anglais better?

"Are you interested in the occult?

"What kind of scenery do you like best?

"Which do you hate worse, a liar or a thief?

"Do you like dogs or cats better?

"Do you think it is easier to shock a man or a woman?

"If you are going to take a patent medicine, do you order it in liquid form or in pills?

"I am not joking. Any correspondent wanting my advice must give himself the trouble to give me the answers to these questions, knowing which I shall be able to advise him much more usefully than in ignorance of everything except his handwriting."

I look back as to some incredible dream in 1924 and see the Steinway Hall filled by seven o'clock of a warm June evening with 400 enthusiasts who had booked every available seat days before. The records to be played in Class I limited to instruments of 25 guineas or less were the Adagio from Beethoven's *Spring Sonata*, the second half of *L'Après-midi d'un Faune* and the Quintet from *The Mastersingers*.

The records for Class II open to any instrument were the first movement of Mendelssohn's Trio in D minor and the great duet between Brunnhilde and Siegfried sung by Florence Austral and Tudor Davies. Seven instruments were entered in Class I and eight in Class II, each of which in turn played the set piece, through a gauze-covered aperture, the stage being hidden from the audience by screens. The judges were Miss Marie Novello, Mr. Alfred Kalisch, Mr. Percy Scholes, Mr. Peter Latham, Mr. Alec Robertson (who has been reviewing for us on *The Gramophone* ever since it started) and my old friend the late Francis Brett Young who, besides being a poet and a novelist, was a musician of exquisite taste and considerable accomplishment. Apart from the marking of the judges the audience were given cards and that considerably more than half of these were filled up testifies to the endurance and enthusiasm displayed in this musical Marathon. It was a pity that neither His Master's Voice nor Columbia felt justified in competing but obviously neither of them could afford to be beaten by the other in such a contest.

There is no point in chronicling the result of these battles long ago, but it will interest many to know that the world-famous E.M.G. instrument made its début at this test and tied for a silver medal with an instrument called the Algraphone. The E.M.G. named after its original designer E. M. Ginn appeared first as the Magnaphone, but the designer was notified that this was a copyright title and it became E.M.G. In the knocked-about Residency at Imphal I saw a great E.M.G. horn in 1947 and for many years an E.M.G. was my standard gramophone in the Hebrides.

I recall with a faint melancholy those tussles between "romantic" sound-boxes and "realistic" sound-boxes, between fibre needles and steel needles, between a dozen different accessories and constituent parts of the gramophone.

None of us would go back to those days of acoustic recording if we could. Nevertheless, those who have known nothing else except electrical recording have missed something.

A superlative radiogram like the H.M.V. Electrogram de Luxe or the Decola with abundance of long-playing records is now taken for granted. Nobody as far as I am aware is at any rate at present speculating upon improving the gramophone still further. No doubt the future holds some miracle of reproduction that will make the gramophone the exact equivalent of music heard from the concert platform but that is a long way off yet and meanwhile we sink back contented with what we have. Not so thirty years ago. We suffered from a divine exasperation with our beloved machine. We were perpetually on the alert for the faintest improvement. I shall recall a typical example of our search for the elixir of life.

I

In May 1925 I was writing in a spirit of something uncomfortably like bravado:

"I will not rest until I hear an orchestra from the corridor of Queen's Hall when I listen to an orchestral record in the next room. And let me tell you as I write these words that I am nearer to that achievement than I have ever been. And if I am not more enthusiastic about the Flex diaphragm it is because there is danger in any device that tends to satisfy gramophonists. It *is* very good, but it is an improvement that leads nowhere. With regard to the tension device I feel the same thing. A fibre needle is a realist's counsel of despair. When a gramophonist settles down to fibre, it is a sign of gramophonic sclerosis. It means to say that he has run the gamut of his gramophonic adventures and has surrendered to what he thinks is the inevitable imperfection of his instrument. This week I have listened to the gramophone playing 600 double-sided records or at a modest calculation to 4200 minutes of music, which works out at listening steadily for ten hours a day to a very loud needle playing every kind of record.

"The device which enabled me to perform this feat of concentration is occupying my mind to such an extent that I cannot do justice to anything that seems to me to partake of a makeshift. For long fibres the Dawes-Clarke tension device is excellent, but it is an experiment that leads from my point of view nowhere. That does not detract from its ability to do what it sets out to do. But it does not set out to do enough. The same applies to doped fibres. I cannot hear that there's any improvement in tone from the use of doped fibres, and I think that Mr. Dawes-Clarke may claim with justice that ordinary fibre played with his tension is likely to last just as long as a doped fibre. Fibres are as uncertain as the bamboos from which they are cut. You never know when a bamboo will flower and die, and if one bamboo in the neighbourhood begins, the rest usually follow suit. So it befalls with a box of fibres. No, I say as the King of Assyria said to Hezekiah, 'Now, behold, thou trustest upon the staff of this bruised reed.' Will you see a reed not merely shaken, but broken by the wind? Then dope your fibres with all the drowsy syrups of the world and try to play the Parlophone record of the *Pique Dame* Overture."

This hint of being in sight of Eldorado sent a shiver of excitement through what was still the very small world of gramophone enthusiasts. Indeed, such was the excitement that I got complaints of a falling off in the sales of instruments and I had to issue a caution in the following month.

"Now about the happy combination of which I wrote last month. This is how matters stand at present. I am getting at Jethou, with the help of an apparently simple gadget, on my Balmain machine far better results than I have ever dreamed of getting from the gramophone; but my helpers and myself cannot yet obtain equal results anywhere else. We are working hard to see if we can not only get them ourselves but guarantee them to others. As soon as possible I shall publish an account of our struggles. The gadget itself is no novelty, although I cannot believe that its potential importance has ever been fully realized. What I want to make perfectly clear, however, is that nobody need have the least hesitation about buying any existing gramophone, because, if the principle is as sound as I think, it can be applied to any gramophone at a merely nominal cost. It is not a new sound-box. It is not a new amplifier. It is not a new tone-arm. It will render obsolete nothing that is at present on the market."

It was in that same number of *The Gramophone* that I was able to refer to an announcement by His Master's Voice of a new method of recording electrically. No sooner were these words in print than what we now call the public relations staffs of H.M.V. and Columbia were asking me not to allow the term "electric recording" to be used anywhere in *The Gramophone*. The operative words were to be "new recording". The bar on the use of electric recording lasted for quite a year. When the first electrical records did appear they were published in the regular monthly issues without telling the public that they were the products of the new recording. The Victor people in the United States were well ahead of the more conservative rulers at Hayes. Certainly all the first records issued were American. Not a single musical critic in the daily Press spotted the new recording. A secret mark was impressed on the discs but even those unaware of that mark should have been able to recognize at once that a profound change was at work in the recording studios.

Some of those first electrical recordings were ghastly. There was one of Goldmark's Rustic Symphony which I remember with a shudder. Even the best of the new issues were often deplorable in reproduction because many of the sound-boxes in use were not able to deal with them. His Master's Voice, perhaps with the advantage of the Victor Company's experience with the new method, brought out a new instrument in the autumn of 1925 designed to give the new method a fair chance.

In that November I published a full account of the new gadget to which I had alluded, and at the same time my first impression of the new H.M.V. instrument.

"Last spring the Rev. L. D. Griffith, Rector of Silvington, wrote to me to say that he had discovered a device which had greatly improved the tone of his gramophone and for which he had applied for a patent. Would I advise him what to do with it? Now many people write to me in that strain, and I had begun to think that the spring of my hope was growing a little weak under the demands that are made upon it. However, I asked him to let me try his invention if it was not too bulky for transport. In due course came a letter to say that he had sent it to me. I summoned all hands to the beach to help land the device when the boat arrived that morning, but the precaution turned out to be unnecessary, because the device was small enough to be carried in a waistcoat pocket. In fact, it was nothing but a little piece of indiarubber tubing apparently cut off a garden hose and enclosed in two curtain rings. I felt a little discouraged, for it did not look as if it would improve a broken teapot, much less a gramophone. I turned my attention to the directions for use that accompanied it and read that Mr. Griffith's theory was that the reproduction of recorded music was immensely improved by a flexible tone-arm. My Peridulce is the easiest machine for this kind of experiment, and on the Peridulce my first experiment was made. But, from the record's point of view, just how much flexibility was desirable? I looked round for a record to spoil, and I had no hesitation in choosing . . . no, let charity stay my pen. I harnessed the sound-box to the tone-arm with the tube as directed and not only could not perceive the slightest improvement, but actually fancied a definite inferiority. I tried again by adjusting the curtain rings to achieve the miracle that Mr. Griffith had promised. It was no good. I tried it on the H.M.V. horizontal grand. Worse. I tried it on the Balmain. No good at all. The Orchorsol does not lend herself to these experiments. I tried the Jewel Portable. This time I fancied that there was a slight improvement, but not enough to bother about. In the end I decided that here was another case of auto-hypnotism, produced this time by life in a solitary country parish.

"Then the next morning two more tubes arrived, more workman-like affairs, which Mr. Griffith recommended as much better than his own hand-made article. I took the same bad record and tried it

on the Peridulce again. The improvement was astonishing. I tried
the H.M.V. horizontal grand, but the tube did not fit the gooseneck
tone-arm well and, though there was a distinct improvement, it
was nothing remarkable. Then I tried the Balmain with the No. 2
sound-box, and it was a clear case of 'Eureka!' I had no longer the
least hesitation about using my best records, and I opened with the
H.M.V. *Entry of the Gods*. This was really marvellous. Never before
had the cymbals clashed or the timpani rolled so realistically. I went
on through record after record—orchestras, bands, sopranos, violins,
pianos, chamber music—and in no case was the experiment anything
but remarkable. So far as I could make out, the flexibility gave a
genuine mellowness, not the meretricious mellowness of a composition
diaphragm; it did not diminish, but it certainly sweetened the
scratch; it helped definition; and it produced increased resonance.
I could not believe the last for a long time, but I satisfied myself
by experiments of listening in remote rooms through closed doors
that there was increased resonance. With a Columbia No. 7 on the
Peridulce I had splendid results; but the H.M.V. horizontal was
obstinate, and I failed to effect the same improvement there. With
regard to records, those that benfited most were Columbias, both
old and new. In fact at this moment I am positive that the finest
performances of Columbia records can be heard at Jethou. The
records which benefited next were Vocalions, Parlophones, and the
older H.M.V.'s .The newer H.M.V.'s (I don't mean the very newest
recordings; I shall come to them presently) were much improved, but
not to the same extent.

"What to do next? In my excitement I could not resist hinting
at my happy combination, and I was rather taken aback to find that
half the readers of my paper were prepared to go nap on the
announcement. The sale of records fell off through fear of a new
process, the sale of instruments was more static than it should have
been; altogether it was essential to quieten people down, because,
after all, it was only a rubber tube, and I was not yet convinced of
its general applicability. Moreover there was the question of the
patent, and then—horrid thought!—had I been hynotizing myself
in Jethou? I determined to call to my aid a case-hardened dis-
believer in new inventions, and enthusiastic cynic. Need I say to
readers of this paper that I chose Mr. P. Wilson?[1] I knew that he
would come down to Jethou with a firm determination not to believe
in what I had by now come to call the Lifebelt. Moreover, as likely
as not, he would arrive feeling very squeamish after the night

[1] Who, thirty years later, is still our principal expert adviser for *The Gramophone*.

voyage (he did!), and if a partially sea-sick man with the sceptical mind of a mathematician could come straight from the Board of Education and be converted at 11 o'clock in the morning, I felt that I should not need to worry any more about auto-hypnotism.

"The first thing Mr. Wilson did on arrival was to argue with me that the Balmain machine was not better than his own horned H.M.V.

" 'Wait a bit. You've only heard the office Balmain, which is badly placed and the horn of which is not nearly so well designed as mine.'

" 'Are you going to use an H.M.V. Exhibition No. 2?'

"This question put contemptuously.

" 'My H.M.V. No. 2 gives on my Balmain the best reproduction I've heard.'

" 'I've brought a Virtz sound-box with me, and I'm perfectly sure that your No. 2 can't possibly give what my Virtz gives me.'

" 'Well, what record shall I put on first?'

" 'Try the beginning of the Columbia Beethoven Seventh.'

"I demurred.

" 'Why choose a record that can never be a really good one?'

"However, I put it on.

" 'Yes, it's very good,' Wilson allowed. 'But it's no better than my Virtz,' etc., etc. 'Try the Columbia Beethoven Third. There's some soft timpani work there which I've never heard except on my Virtz,' etc., etc.

"We heard those shy timpani on my Balmain-cum-Lifebelt all right. Then Wilson wanted to hear an oboe that couldn't be heard unless you got up on a May morning and bathed your face with dew, unless, of course, you had Wilson's Virtz sound-box, etc., etc., etc., etc., etc.

"Well, he heard that oboe so clearly that he didn't recognize at first that it *was* the elusive oboe, and went on looking for it until I got the score and proved that it must be the same.

"That finished Wilson, and for two days and two nights we played through record after record, going to bed tired but triumphant in the not so wee sma' hours. . . .

"As soon as I found that Mr. Wilson was as perfectly satisfied as I was that on all 'forward' machines, or shall I say on all machines with an internal or external horn, and not a rectangular amplifier, the improvement was incontestable, I told him that I intended to give the public the benefit of Mr. Griffith's discovery immediately the patent was through. Mr. Wilson, however, felt convinced that he would never be able to patent a device. He pointed out that anybody could acquire a piece of rubber tubing and that anybody could sell a piece of rubber tubing. I agreed with this, but I argued that our experience had proved conclusively that *any* piece of rubber tubing was *not* enough. It required to be of exactly the right resiliency to do its work, and I considered that any sensible gramophonist would not, for the sake of a paltry 5*s.*, deny himself the advantage of our experience. My plan was to get a variety of types of the Lifebelt and when we had definitely decided which was the best to issue them to the public at that price. I added that I did not much mind if the patent failed to go through. I was anxious that Mr. Griffith should have some material benefit from his discovery and I said that I was sure that if I backed his Lifebelt, I could count on our readers not bothering about anybody else's. The only thing that really did worry me was the comparative lack of improvement with the H.M.V. machine. Would Mr. Wilson make a few experiments on his own account at home, and see if it could not be brought into line with the rest? I gave him *carte blanche* to get any moulds made that he considered necessary, and I also asked him to obtain the opinions of one or two people whose opinions would be worth while. I particularly wanted to know what Mr. Balmain thought about it.

"Mr. Wilson went home, and a day or two later I had a letter from Mr. Balmain to say that he had been using a piece of rubber-tubing himself for years and that many other gramophonists did the same. With the letter he sent from his museum an old Pathé sound-box with a piece of rubber tubing attached. He sent at the same time an article on the principle of flexibility. This did not look much like any patent going through. By the same post Mr. Wilson wrote me an account of his talk with Mr. Balmain and enclosed a piece of rubber tubing that Mr. Balmain used—a beer-connector. But when I tried this, which was very flabby, I found that it merely gave a kind of mellowness to the music while taking out of it all the 'bite'. In other words the Balmain beer-connector was merely another method of romanticizing the record.

"This encouraged me, because it too seemed to prove that any piece of rubber tubing was not good enough. That rubber tubing had to possess the right amount of resiliency to make it a genuine Lifebelt. The next item of news was that another patent method of achieving flexibility had been filed at the Patent Office. This was encouraging, because it seemed to indicate that other people were on the track of this desirable quality. Then Mr. Virtz sent me one of his sound-boxes, and I found that he had achieved a measure of flexibility by the free use of rubber. On top of this Mr. Griffith wrote to say that his patent had been accepted, and that I could make the announcement when I chose."

The Lifebelt had a great vogue until the development of electrical recording, pick-ups, and all the improvements that to-day we half fancy were always with us made it no longer necessary.

I find that as early as 1925 I realized that women offered a strong sales resistance to the gramophone and particularly to the purchase of records by their husbands. I once said to Mr. Arthur Rank that one of his problems was to persuade men to frequent the cinema because they wanted to see a film, not because their wives or sweethearts wanted to see it. "And my great problem," I added, "is to overcome the hostility women feel for records." That hostility lasted until the introduction of the long-playing record assuaged the housewife's hatred of seeing valuable shelf space occupied by her husband's collection. Without doubt the removal of this feminine prejudice has been of enormous benefit to the sale of records, comparable, on a much smaller scale of course, to the enormous benefit reaped by the tobacco people when women took to smoking on a grand scale. In that summer of 1925 I was writing:

"I am glad and thankful to be able to say that our circulation rises steadily every month, both at home and overseas; but a paper like this, which stands alone without the support of other publications, must stand all the more firmly on its own feet in consequence. It cannot have capital lavished upon it, because a specialist's paper cannot obtain an unlimited circulation. It is because we feel that we have not yet nearly reached that possible circulation that we are making this strenuous effort. For instance, not a single copy of *The Gramophone* is sold in the City of Norwich from the London office. (I am not talking of copies sold by the big distributing agents like W. H. Smith.) Not one is sent by us to Lichfield, Durham, Exeter, Chester or Gloucester. In fact, episcopal sees are apparently all anti-gramophonic, with notable exceptions like Canterbury, and, of course, great cities like Liverpool and Manchester. I wish we could convert a few ecclesiastical dignitaries. I have not much hope from bishops, because bishops are naturally fidgety people and also much overworked. But deans are not overworked, and they are rarely fidgety. Can none of our readers convert a dean? Dr. Inge would benefit enormously from a steady course of Haydn and Mozart. He should be tried with a fibre needle and an exceptionally mellow and romantic sound-box. Judges, too, might be angled for. I should have made an attempt to convert Sir Henry McCardie the other night when we were fellow-guests of the Whitefriars Club, because, in proposing the Ladies, he emphasized the fact that he was himself a bachelor. So one of the great objections to owning a gramophone did not exist in his case. This brings me to an awkward topic, which is the indifference, nay, the positive hostility, of the fair sex to gramophones. I suppose I have received some two or three thousand letters about my books, of which at least half have come from women. I should not care to guess how many letters we have received about the gramophone; but not one in twenty comes from a woman. We have only one feminine contributor to this paper, and that is my own wife writing as 'F Sharp'."

Two women heaped coals of fire on my head by winning our next competition, but for many years the gramophone remained as much of a masculine hobby as bowls.

My remark about judges was also contradicted when the late Mr. Justice Charles tackled me at the Club and revealed that he was a passionate devotee.

"And I'm teaching the man and wife who look after me to develop a really impeccable taste in chamber music, particularly for Mozart."

We held a Gramophone Congress in July 1925 at the Central Hall, Westminster, which was attended by 2000 enthusiasts and went on from 10 a.m. to 10 p.m., tests being held in the Caxton Hall. The National Gramophonic Society was flourishing. We were getting subscribers all over the world.

And now to leave the gramophone for a while and meet two singers who did more for its popularity than any except Caruso.

Chapter 13

IN August 1924 I was invited by the Government of the Irish Free State to be their guest during the celebration in Dublin of the Tailteann Games. The Games were a revival of an ancient gathering and in effect the famous old Dublin Horse Show was being given Celtic trappings. Oliver Gogarty who was a Senator had been entrusted with the job of assembling various British representatives of the Arts who had not hesitated during the bitter years of strife to plead for the justice of the Irish case. Painting was represented by Augustus John, architecture by Sir Edwin Lutyens, literature by G. K. Chesterton and myself, and music by Sir Henry Hadow, who had been Gogarty's tutor at Worcester College, Oxford. Arnold Bax would have represented music more effectively on an occasion like this; although at this date Hadow was Vice-Chancellor of Sheffield University he still looked lost outside a Senior Common Room in Oxford. I could fancy him standing on a rock and murmuring to himself:

> "Roll on, thou deep and dark blue ocean, roll,
> A thousand fleets sweep over thee in vain."

"Why was Hadow invited?" I asked Gogarty. "I don't recall his speaking up for Ireland."

"No, no, but he's a charming fellow," Gogarty urged. "And he was always very decent to me at Worcester."

I had the pleasure of crossing the Irish Channel with Augustus John. We left from Birkenhead to arrive at London Wall close to where the bowler-hatted aproned porters of Guinness were rolling the great barrels of that noble liquid down to the Liffey for transportation overseas.

Gogarty was on the quay to tell us that John was to stay with Lord Dunsany, and that I was to be the guest of Tim Healy, the Governor-General, at Viceregal Lodge.

The first function was a banquet given by the Lord Mayor and Corporation of Dublin to the visitors, at which I was happy to find I should be sitting next to John. When he arrived at the preliminary reception I was faintly surprised to find that he was wearing the upper half of evening dress with a pair of brown tweed trousers.

"I left my evening trousers on the boat," he told me.

John was completely unperturbed by his mixed costume, and of course as we were in Ireland nobody else was perturbed. I did not observe one sidelong look of eyes asking if they have been deceived. O blessed country where criticism is constant and sharp enough but does not bother about brown tweed trousers with evening dress!

Among the guests at the high table who would be called upon to speak was the late Jam Saheb of Nawanagar, the immortal Ranjitsinhji, with two slim shy young nephews in attendance. One became the present Jam Saheb and the other was K. S. Duleepsinhji whom health robbed of parity with his mighty uncle in the annals of cricket. As well as the nephews C. B. Fry was present who, as I write these words, is still on the edge of eighty-three, one of the finest figures of manhood in the world.

The Jam Saheb was dressed, as I remember, in rich robes of light blue silk with many great pearls in his turban, and when this majestic figure rose to speak I had a sudden vision of summer at Hove and Ranji sending the ball to the boundary with a flick of that consummate wrist. He spoke of his pleasure in having acquired an estate in Galway and of his pleasure in the company of the peasantry who had the same dignified approach to life as his own Rajputs in far away Kathiawar.

As the Jam Saheb sat down and General Mulcahy, the Minister of Defence, rose to reply, the banqueting hall was plunged into absolute darkness. The employees of the Dublin Municipality engaged upon electricity and gas had decided to have a two-minutes' strike to protest against something or other. Through the darkness sounded the light tenor voice of General Mulcahy addressing the Jam Saheb and the asembled guests in Irish.

"What on earth is happening?" Augustus John asked me, from a pit in Erebus.

"It's a Free State General replying in Irish to the toast of Ranjitsinhji," I told him.

"Thank God," John muttered. "I thought I'd gone mad. I'm only drunk."

In fact he was perfectly sober.

And a minute later the lights came on again.

Gogarty had told John that his host, Lord Dunsany, had a horror of alcohol and begged him not to drink anything while he was staying in Dunsany Castle. At the same time he had told Dunsany that Augustus John was anxious to drink nothing during his stay in Ireland and therefore to avoid asking him to drink.

John used to escape surreptitiously from the Castle to a local pub but he found it a strain, and finally one night after his host had been talking to him about the great Irish harp John had left the Castle and walked the fourteen miles or so to Dublin. It happened that I was to breakfast next morning with Gogarty in Ely Place, in that enchanting house with the enchanting garden where George Moore had lived. After breakfast Gogarty went up to his bedroom and presently came down.

"Who do you think is in my bed? Augustus! He left Dunsany Castle in the night, arrived here while we were at breakfast and got right into my bed."

At the Governor-General's state banquet a miscalculation led to their being an excess of men, and about half-a-dozen of us enjoyed the atmosphere of a club, all except one, and that was Baron Palmstierna, the Swedish Minister to the Court of St. James's.

After dinner he was observed by Edwin Lutyens to be looking solitary and disgruntled.

"What's the matter with you?" Ned Lutyens enquired in that high-pitched voice of his, his eyes in a twinkle.

"I am rather displeased, Sir Edwin. I have had a most unpleasant experience. I know that this is a young nation and that they do not appreciate yet the protocol, and when for instance the sentry pays no attention at all when I come and when to that Afghan there . . ." the Swedish Minister looked furiously across to where Prince M—— K——, the Court Poet of the Shah, in an astrakhan fez was listening politely to somebody . . ."

"That's the Persian poet," said Sir Edwin.

"It is of no importance. To him every sentry presents arms. Click-click! But to me they pay no attention at all. I understand it is just the ignorance of protocol. This evening, however, before dinner I find I am to take in the Marchioness MacSwiney. I am pleased because the Marchioness is a very handsome and extremely intelligent woman. And then just before we go in to dinner Mr. Doyle . . ." Mr. Doyle, a very popular Dublin hotelkeeper, was the Controller of the Household . . . "Mr. Doyle takes away the Marchioness and she went in to dinner with that Afghan, Persian, anything you like, and I the senior diplomatic representative present am left to go in to dinner by myself."

"Never mind," said Ned Lutyens, tapping the disgruntled diplomat lightly on the shoulder to console him, "never mind. You're still our greatest little Swede. In fact I shall call you little Mangelwurzel."

Once at the luncheon table of the late Lady Colefax I found myself sitting next to Walter de la Mare. Lutyens, who was sitting opposite on the other side of the table, suddenly leaned across and said:

"May I ask you something, de la Mare?"

The poet nodded a shy assent.

"Why do you poets always write such nonsense?"

The Persian Prince and poet gave me an amusing experience that evening. When the ladies led by Miss Healy, Lady Lavery and Mrs. G. K. Chesterton retired from the table to the furthest drawing-room from the banqueting-room Prince M—— K—— went pattering after them.

Presently in the door of that drawing-room about thirty or forty yards away appeared Miss Healy, waving.

"Mr. Doyle," called the Governor-General, looking up over his beard.

The Controller of the Household approached.

"Miss Healy seems to be making signals of distress. Will you kindly go along, Mr. Doyle, and find out what's the matter?"

The Controller went along and presently returned with a baffled expression.

"It's His Highness, Your Excellency."

"His Highness?" the Governor-General echoed.

"His Highness is sitting in the drawing-room with the ladies and embarrassing them very much, Your Excellency."

"Did you not tell him I wanted to have a word with him?"

"I did that, Your Excellency, but he wouldn't budge an inch."

Tim Healy looked across to me.

"Mackenzie, you're a young man of tact and address. Will you be good enough to go along and rescue the ladies from the Prince?"

So along I went to find the Persian prince and poet sitting in the middle of the drawing-room, some twenty ladies round the room all looking coldly disapproving except Hazel Lavery who winked at me.

"Altesse," I began, "Son Excellence m'a envoyé pour exprimer son espoir que vous lui donnerez le plaisir——"

The Prince interrupted me sharply and in the tinniest of Levantine French snapped:

"Non, non. Je ne viens pas. Toujours chez moi après le diner je reste avec mes femmes, en leur lisant la poésie. Alors, maintenant, je commence à lire. Bon soir, monsieur," and with this he took out of his pocket a volume, as cool as Omar Khayyám himself.

I have no business to be telling these stories in a record of music, but going back in memory to those delightful days in Dublin thirty-one years ago I could not resist them.

We drove down from the Viceregal Lodge to Croke Park for the opening of the Tailteann Games. Relics of the bitterness of the civil war were conspicuous in the shape of slogans painted in green on the walls of the Dublin gardens. DEATH TO THE MURDER GANG and that sort of thing.

"They'll probably take a shot at us on the way," said Tim, his voice grave and deep, his eyes twinkling.

"I'm quite safe, sir," I said. "I'm driving in the same car as G.K., and no bullet will have a chance of hitting me."

And indeed that was true, for Chesterton in his voluminous inverness filled the car. Mrs. G. K. and I had perfect cover.

A big round of applause greeted the arrival of the Governor-General, and then soon afterwards there was another equally big round of applause. That was for John McCormack. I recorded my impression of that first meeting with him at the time:

"One of the keenest pleasures in an artist's life is to be able to tell another artist sincerely that he admires his work. 'Yes, but I expect you think I sing a great deal of rubbish,' said McCormack to me. I agreed, and suggested that for this side of the Atlantic he had sung enough. 'Yes, but I'm going to sing Wolf and Brahms now, and all sorts of songs that I really want to sing.' 'That's the best gramophone news I've heard for a long time,' I assured him.

"And it is, because it means that the greatest living tenor is going to bequeath to posterity a treasure of music whose infinite variety age will not wither nor custom stale. Besides one hopes that the good example will be infectious and that Kreisler, who is a great friend of McCormack's, will decide to leave behind him something better than radiant shreds and patches of music.

"Not that I want readers to run away with the idea that McCormack has sung nothing but rubbish. Nor do I want them to suppose that rubbish cannot be thoroughly enjoyable when it is sung by a master. Moreover, the enjoyment of rubbish without knowing that it is rubbish is an important stage in the development of taste. There are no short cuts in art. I should like to print that sentence in letters of fire. No man can appreciate good poetry who has not at some time in his life been moved by bad poetry. And this applies equally to music. There is no such birth in taste as that of Pallas Athene who sprang fully armed from the head of Zeus. Distrust good taste that has not grown out of bad taste. It is like one of those palms that cinema producers stick into an English beach to represent the scenery of a tropical island. You must believe me when I tell you that *you* will enjoy chamber music, just because there *was* a time when I could not stand it. I have already alluded to the inconvenience, to use a mild term, of too exquisite taste, and I should advise everybody for his own pleasure to preserve his capacity for what may be called immature enjoyment.

"I am glad to confess that some of the greatest rubbish sung by John McCormack still gives me in certain moods a genuine delight. That is because, whatever the words, whatever the indulgence in what Ernest Newman called 'greasy chromatics', the singing is the singing of a master, and the character behind it is a simple and beautiful character. McCormack would tell you that he has sung a great deal of his rubbish because he could not resist the money it brought him. Good luck to him, for let it be remembered that he has sung that rubbish as well as he knew how, and I venture to think that there was a time when he was not nearly as sure as he is now that it was rubbish. His own taste has been growing all this time just like the taste of his listeners, and, good actor though he is, I wonder whether if he were to record again some of those ballads he could imbue them with so much sincerity. After all, every entertainer of the public has a right to earn as much money as he can, and let it be remembered that the more he can make the more he can give. As an entertainer, which is what a novelist ought to be but sometimes out of snobbishness or incapacity fails to be, I get reproved by critics for not always writing as solemnly as I ought, but what they don't grasp is that an entertainer will cease to be an entertainer if he is not entertaining himself as well as the public. For my part, I would sooner earn my living by writing nothing but light novels than earn it like serious critics by purging all amusement with however bubbling a wit. In other words, I would rather be a bottle of champagne than a bottle of Eno's fruit salts.

"After meeting McCormack I heard him sing at one of the two concerts he gave for the benefit of the Tailteann Games. The Theatre Royal was packed, and there must have been three hundred people sitting on the stage behind him—an ordeal for any artist. He sang perhaps sixteen songs, each one in its own way perfectly. I rejoiced that when the gallery shouted for *Kathleen Mavourneen* I could be as deeply moved by the old song as the gallery was, and I am sorry for anybody whom it cannot move. His diction is little less than miraculous. Test it in *Come into the Garden, Maud.* I cannot believe that Sims Reeves at his best sang this song better. It is significant that of the two contemporary singers with the clearest English diction one is an Irishman, and the other, Sir Harry Lauder, a Scot. I have heard people take exception to McCormack's pronunciation, and to choose one instance, his pronunciation of 'brook' in *Ben Bolt*. But the singer is right, and we who pronounce it 'bruk' are wrong. The fact is that he has taken advantage of his Italian training to acquire an ability to distinguish between close and open vowels. His own Italian is marvellous. I have known several Italians who, listening to his records, absolutely refused to believe that he was not an Italian himself. The truth of it is that he does not merely pronounce Italian well; but that when he sings in Italian he is Italian. He is a genuinely creative singer.

"In order to write this article I have played through 150 songs, many of them twice over, in three days. Yet I have clear recollection of every song. I know why I liked it more or why I liked it less. I can tell you that in *Drink To Me Only With Thine Eyes* he sings 'love's nectar' when he ought to sing 'Jove's nectar', and 'could not withered be' when he ought to sing 'might not withered be'. I can tell you that in a tiresome song called *Eileen Alanna* 'Ireland' is made to rhyme with 'my land' and 'shillelagh' with 'daily' (not by the singer). I venture to think that without jotting down a single note I could not have concentrated like this unless the singer were getting something different out of each number good or bad, extraordinary or commonplace, and not only getting it himself but giving it to his audience. Versatility is one of the hall-marks of a major artist, whether he be singer or painter or writer.

"McCormack can sing *Il Mio Tesoro* on one side of a record as if he had never sung anything but Mozart in his life, and on the other *Una Furtiva lagrima* as if he had been entirely devoted to Donizetti. He can sing *Carmela* like a Neapolitan, and *Oh, Cease Thy Singing Maiden Fair* like a Slav. His *Molly Brannigan* is as rich a piece of *genre* as some of Lauder's. He sings *Take, Oh Take Those Lips Away* as the very ghost of him who wrote the divine words might haunt this green earth and sing it. Nobody can give Tom Moore's Irish songs like him; that is not surprising. But when he gives us something more ancient and more truly Irish than anything Moore ever wrote, like *The Snowy-Breasted Pearl*, it is equally unparagoned. His *Che gelida manina* is the best of the lot, and on the other side *Il fior che avevi* as near the best as makes no matter. If we put on one side the clarity of his diction and forget the chiaroscuro of his voice (comparable to Correggio's in colour), and merely pause for a moment to wonder at its sweetness and strength and ease, it is the capacity for *being* the

When *The Gramophone* was thirty years old

song he is singing that gives him the right to be called the world's greatest living tenor.

"I heard him at Dublin sing a song about a fairy behind a hedge, and, confound it, his voice actually seemed to go behind the hedge. He might have been a ventriloquist, and yet of course he was doing nothing in the least ventriloquial; he was just being the fairy behind the hedge, and by the intensity with which he was being that fairy he bewitched his audience into thinking that the fairy was there all the time. Two of his failures in records are *The Lost Chord* and Tosti's *Good-Bye*, and I believe that it is just this capacity for being the song he is singing that makes them failures. He cannot help being an organ in *The Lost Chord*, and wonderfully near as he gets he does not quite convince us. The song is not good enough really to help the illusion that we are listening to a tenor more robust than Tamagno."

That meeting in Dublin led to a friendship the memory of which I dearly cherish. In the autumn John McCormack was to make his first appearance on an English concert-platform since the war. He had become an American citizen in 1919. He had been getting anonymous letters accusing him of treachery, ingratitude and threatening him with a demonstration if he ever dared to sing again in England. On the morning of the concert John had gone to church and had remained in church until it was time to present himself at Queen's Hall. He had asked me to go with Countess McCormack— she was still Mrs. McCormack then—and their daughter. The hall was packed and we were sitting in the middle of the front row of the circle. I kept muttering: "I'm sure that there's not going to be any disturbance. I'm sure John will get a tremendous welcome." I seized Lily McCormack's hand as John, white as paper, entered for his first song. The audience was silent for a moment and then there was a spontaneous outburst of applause from all over the hall, succeeded by a breathless silence as the singer opened with that high note of *O Sleep, Why Dost Thou Leave Me?* from Handel's *Semele*.

By a coincidence as I started to record this first appearance of John McCormack after the war I tuned in to the Third Programme on the Radio just as the soprano was singing that very aria. Then I began to wonder whether my memory had played me false and whether in fact the great tenor did begin his concert with a soprano aria. Anyway, the concert was a triumph, and a much relieved John McCormack gave a marvellous supper party at the Carlton where he was staying. John and I shared one particular taste and that was

K

champagne. We drank a lot of champagne that night, and I had Madge Titherage next to me, which meant the best of company.

On the committee of students who fought the Glasgow Rectorial to get me elected Rector in 1931 was a young man called Sydney MacEwan. He used to sing as a barytone in those days but presently discovered that his voice was a tenor. And what a tenor! I did not think I was mistaken in its quality, but I determined to take advantage of John McCormack's good nature and ask him to hear Sydney MacEwan sing. I was delighted when John endorsed my judgment, and advised the young man to make singing his career. He won a scholarship at the Royal Academy of Music and I asked my old friend Harry Plunket Greene to give him lessons in diction if he agreed about the merit of the voice. Plunket Greene's voice was recorded when he was past his prime and in pre-electric days his bass lacked the resonance to conquer the old horn into which in those days singers had to sing for the gramophone. He was, however, incomparably the best English bass I ever heard and his mastery of style was complete.

Plunket Greene agreed with me about the quality of Sydney MacEwan's voice and undertook to give him all the help he could with diction. Then came the day when the young tenor set out for a concert tour in Australia where he had a great success and then he discovered in himself a vocation for the priesthood, gave up his professional career, and went to the Scots College in Rome, to be ordained in due course.

I did not think that such a voice and such a singer should be lost to the world, and I urged Mr. Preuss, the imaginative artistic director of the Parlophone Company in England, to make records of him. These were highly successful, and to-day he is being recorded by the Columbia Company in America. Moreover, the ecclesiastical authorities allowed him to make two more tours to Australia where he enjoyed a triumph and whence he was able to bring back a very large sum of money which was devoted to finishing the tower of the beautiful Catholic Cathedral in Oban. In 1954 he went for a month to the United States for the first time and had an immense success there, but of course eleven months of every year is taken up by his work as priest of the mission at Lochgilphead in Argyll.

John McCormack's generous encouragement of that young aspirant was typical of him. He once greeted Caruso as the greatest tenor in the world. "You are being very modest, John," said Caruso. We hear a great deal about the jealousy of artists but within my experience the best of them lack jealousy; I have seen more signs of jealousy among soldiers and politicians and even sailors. Of the professions I give the palm to barristers for generosity about their rivals.

I went with John and Lily McCormack to a performance of *La Traviata* at Covent Garden just before the Second War. Beniamino Gigli was Alfredo; I forget who was playing Violetta. We were sitting in a box in the middle of the grand tier, and when in the second act Alfredo dressed in the Latin conception of a sportsman's attire was singing *I miei bollenti spiriti* John began to fidget, then to sing *sotto voce* the way he thought the aria should go. At last his own *bollenti spiriti* boiled over and he sang one phrase right out. There was an indignant admonitory rapping from the boxes on the other side, and presently an usher came along to say that the people on either side of us were complaining. John shook his head and withdrew to the back of the box; this was not *La Traviata* as it should be.

I heard Gigli again that summer as the Count in *Rigoletto*, and decided that however beautiful the voice, the really great opera singer must be an actor as well as a singer. He was overweighted by his Gilda, not vocally but physically. I went behind the scenes to pay my respects to the singer and I longed to ask him why he and Gilda in the love duets leant over toward one another like a couple of trees over a stream.

John McCormack gave up singing in opera because he did not consider himself a good enough actor and took exclusively to the concert platform. It is a pity that he was not encouraged to continue with *lieder*.

After that concert in London he played over to me the records he had made of songs by Brahms and Hugo Wolf. However, the public did not respond by buying them and when to that was added the condescending attitude of the musical critics he was fed up and went back to popular fare.

During the Second War McCormack wore himself out giving concerts in aid of the national effort. He had a plan for him and me to talk to Italy over the Radio in Italian, for both of us thought that the propaganda to Italy during those first months of the war was contemptible. He had rooms in Grosvenor House and we used to sit late into the night in a gloom over Europe that was lightened occasionally by champagne. And then in 1945 he left us too soon: he was eighteen months younger than myself.

I remember that late one night we were sitting with him, myself in a good deal of pain from the end of a sciatic attack, and that suddenly John dived over and slapped me on the knee, exclaiming, "Oh God, I love this man."

I winced at the time, but glad would I be to feel that hefty slap on the knee again, in whatever pain I was in, for I loved that man.

The other great singer I met in Dublin, Amelita Galli-Curci, did for the soprano voice on the gramophone what Enrico Caruso fifteen years earlier had done for tenors. The Theatre Royal was packed out for her concert, but she was not a success. Fresh from triumphant concerts at the Royal Albert Hall and in Glasgow she was a puzzled and unhappy little soprano when I went round to pay my respects at her hotel after the concert.

"Che popolo apatico!" (What an apathetic people!) she exclaimed to me, and when I assured her that the Dublin audience was considered the warmest and most appreciative in Great Britain and Ireland she evidently did not believe me. And when I suggested that her programme had been badly chosen, she apparently understood me to mean that it should have been more popular, whereas she had offended the audience by singing *Just A Song At Twilight* for an encore. She opened her programme with some of the stock old English songs like *My Lovely Celia*, all of which it must be confessed she sang dully. Then she sang a Wolf song, movingly I thought, though I fancy that a Wolf expert would have had none of it. At last she sang one of her familiar arias, the Polonaise from *Mignon*, for which as an encore she gave *Viene, Carmé*, which was silly of her, because in the first place it is not a soprano song, and in addition to that she sang it very badly. In fact it was not until her last item, when she gave the *Shadow Song* from *Dinorah* that the audience really believed it was Galli-Curci at all, as you might say. This was the first genuine encore she had, and all she gained she took away by singing *Just A Song At Twilight* to celebrate it.

She wore a lovely cloth of gold dress and looked perfectly charming with her big Spanish comb, but nobody seemed to have taught her how to take the stage. You were aware of something bright that began to sing before the audience had time to realize who had entered and give her the reception to which her fame entitled her. It was that bad entrance which started the whole concert wrong, on top of which came the old English songs with which she opened so dully.

Her husband, whose name was Homer, as I recollect, was a solemn-looking young man and appeared worried when I told the Prima Donna that she should make sure they knew how to pull back the curtains for her entrance.

"Madame was quite disgusted with the audience," he kept saying. "She will never come to Dublin again."

I went on to talk to her about her gramophone records and asked which of them was the most popular. "*Lo, Here The Gentle Lark*" was the answer. I then asked her why she had never sung for the gramophone the great aria from *Norma, Casta Diva*. This seemed to strike her as a happy idea, and she said she should do it when she got back to America.

Madame Galli-Curci expressed her great appreciation of the London audience and rather took me aback by alluding to its *raffiinatezza* (refinement of taste), a quality which I had not hitherto associated with an Albert Hall audience. I kept off the subject of the London critics who had indulged at her expense in one of those splendid bursts of unanimity with which from time to time they bolster up their timid individual judgments, and reassure themselves that they really do know what they are talking about. Word had gone round that Galli-Curci sang flat, and for several days after her first concert I was astonished to find what wonderful ears for music all the paragraphists had, though that was a talent of which I should never have suspected them.

While we were talking the *diva's* maid had been packing her last dress in one of the big American trunks that stood about the hotel sitting-room like the ruins of an old abbey. Madame Galli-Curci kept saying how much she was dreading the crossing and just as much the prospect of travelling in the smoky jolting train the few miles to Dun Laoghaire.

"But aren't you going to drive down to the harbour by car?" I exclaimed in surprise.

"An automobile would be so expensive," both the *diva* and her husband protested.

Considering that the concert had brought in about £1,000 I was awed by such austere economy. The idea of a seasick nightingale was painful to me. So I begged the *diva* to send out at once before the shops closed to procure a box of Mothersill's remedy for *mal de mer*. I guaranteed its efficiency and proclaimed myself to have been the worst sailor in the world until the virtue of Mothersill's was revealed to me.

Madame Galli-Curci's dark eyes grew bright with the reflection of my enthusiasm for the talisman. She began to hope that the crossing would not be so bad as she feared, and as I closed the door behind me I carried away a memory of a delicately carved piece of ivory.

The much greater success that Madame Galli-Curci achieved on gramophone records than either in opera or on the concert platform is a conspicuous example of the effect on art of the changing mediums in which artists have been called upon to express themselves during this century.

I doubt if the public realizes that a good actor or actress on the stage can be bad on the films and vice versa, or that a good actor or actress in sound broadcasting can be hopeless on television. People have already forgotten how many stars of the silent films were extinguished by the talkies. And if television should succeed in destroying sound broadcasting many a favourite will be faded out from popular esteem.

The singers and instrumentalists recorded by the microphone have an immensely easier job than their predecessors who had to sing or play into a large horn. Yet without doubt that old horn was better able to reveal the great artist than any microphone.

I remember that great violinist Madame Renée Chemet saying to me once at Hayes after she had made a record for His Master's Voice: "But you know, I miss my old horn. I was so fond of it."

And rightly, because she was a great enough artist to overcome the handicap. Violinists without half her accomplishment and without a quarter of her passion, fire, genius, vitality, call it what you will, have, thanks to the microphone, achieved a reputation that they could never have achieved by playing into that discouraging horn.

Tamagno, Caruso, McCormack, that incomparable basso cantante Pol Plançon, Battistini and a dozen more singers I could name were greater than any contemporary singers in this year of 1955 when I write these words. Listen to an old record of Tamagno singing Othello's aria *Ora e per sempre addio* made at least fifty years ago, and in spite of its scratch and in spite of its ghostly accompaniment you will think that every Othello you have heard sing that aria since is just nowhere.

Galli-Curci was a superb soprano for the gramophone and no doubt we shall have others equally good, but they will not be great singers unless they can bewitch an audience of flesh and blood.

There may be some significance in what I was writing about Galli-Curci two and a half years later when electric recording had made the horn obsolete.

"It seems to me clear that her voice and her style have deteriorated, and it is unfortunate that electric recording should have coincided with this deterioration. I regret more than ever that she did not record *Casta Diva* four years ago in her prime. I really cannot believe that those discs of *Come per me sereno* or *Ah non credea* deceived us. I play them now, and they seem as lovely as ever. Surely they would still be as lovely had they been recorded electrically."

So let us hope that the competition of mechanical performance in the future will not render the opera obsolete for lack of support.

The domination of the drama by the films to the detriment of the stage is a grave warning. Galli-Curci was able to win world-wide renown as a soprano because her exquisite voice was nearly always recorded in perfection after any tendency to sing flat had been corrected and because to the vast majority of those who heard that exquisite voice her personality on the stage or the concert-platform was unknown.

American readers may dispute that statement and argue that her début with the Chicago Opera Company in November 1916 was an outstanding triumph, and that the verdict of Chicago was confirmed by New York in January 1918. Nevertheless, I shall maintain that without the gramophone she would never have attained the height of renown as a singer which she reached.

Chapter 14

IT was plain to all except a few old-fashioned musical critics who had decided once upon a time that the gramophone was the enemy of music and regarded it as evil ever since that electrical recording was going to enhance its value and widen its potentiality immeasurably. Nevertheless, progress was so slow at first that for a year with very few exceptions (happy flukes we believed them) electrical recordings were intolerable. Probably, as in the case of long-playing records more recently, the revolution broke out prematurely. It would have been better to wait for at least another year before offering electrical records to the public. Two years after electrical recording had been introduced I wrote a postscript to my article on the gramophone and chamber music for Cobbett's *Cyclopedic Survey of Chamber Music* which was published in 1929:

"Electric recording has brought the gramophone much nearer to perfect reproduction. We are not actually near it yet, but we can imagine the possibility which with old methods had ceased to be even a dream. The first electrical recordings of chamber music were a great disappointment. What was gained in balance and spatial sense was lost in tone. The violins sounded metallic, the viola watery, and though the 'cello played its part more conspicuously, it seemed sometimes to be performing a solo accompanied by Jews' harps. By the use of fibre needles some of this metallic effect was damped down, but such early electrical recordings as that of the Debussy quartet by H.M.V. or the Mendelssohn trio in C minor by Columbia are already as much out of date in a couple of years as old acoustical recordings became in ten. After a year the improvement was astonishingly rapid, and within a few months the recorders showed a realization of their new powers that deserves the highest praise. The Beethoven centenary in 1927 gave the recording companies an opportunity to publish a large amount of chamber music, and the twelve quartets of Beethoven played by the Léner Quartet and published by Columbia did more to familiarize the ordinary public with chamber music than any musical enterprise yet undertaken.

"It would be tedious to enumerate the additions made lately to the gramophone's repertory of chamber music, and if special attention be called to such performances as that of Casals, Thibaud, and Cortôt in Schubert's trio in B flat major or Mendelssohn's trio in D minor, it is not merely because of the unusual splendour of the ensemble, but also because of the really remarkable technical triumph of the recorders. Nor should the publications of the National Gramophonic Society be passed over. Many works of chamber music for which the popular demand would have been too small have been published for a limited and appreciative public of amateurs, and among these works have been several of contemporary British composers.

"The next few years are likely to see even greater improvements both in recording and in methods of reproduction, and with the repertory being steadily enlarged almost every month, the future for lovers of chamber music is debonair."

Could I have written that footnote in 1929 I should have been able to claim much more for electrical recording which had been advancing rapidly throughout 1927 and 1928.

We were so disappointed by it at first that we did not use it at once for the records issued to members by the National Gramophonic Society. This now seemed established and we had subscribers all over the world. Nevertheless, we were disappointed that the new readers of our paper were not supporting the Society proportionately. Without doubt it performed the useful service of letting the big recording companies know what a much larger demand there was for chamber music than they had supposed.

Mr. Ernest Newman with all his authority had failed to convince the musical public that the player-piano was the next best thing when he wrote:

"To have absolutely perfect technique at one's command is, as every artist knows, the indispensable prerequisite for artistic playing, only when you can forget your fingers can your brain be perfectly free. It surely stands to reason, then, that the ready-made technique of the player-piano sets the musician's brain free to attend to the purely artistic side of the performance."

I had a respect amounting to veneration for the great critic, but presently I was involved in a duel with him. In April 1926 I had written:

"The issue of a compendium of Beethoven's letters edited by Dr. Eaglefield-Hull may be valuable for students of music, but my own feelings are so tremendously hostile to the publication of anything that enables the hyena biographers of the present to nose in the entrails of dead lions, that I open a work like this in trepidation. I don't really believe that a study of these letters will help anybody to appreciate the Ninth Symphony better; but at any rate, the selection has not been made for the apparent purpose of belittling a mighty genius, and that is something for which to be grateful. I was shocked to read Mr. Ernest Newman's defence of the publication of passages in Mozart's letters which a pious hand thought to have erased for ever, but which with the help of micro-photography have now been deciphered. Mr. Newman thinks that it is a laudable achievement to destroy the legend of Mozart built up by his admirers, and he seems to exult in the publication of 'priapic passages' from letters to his wife. Is it really so important to grasp the fact that Mozart was not a saint? Whether the quintet in G minor was written by a eunuch or a satyr signifies nothing. We all know the gossip who has heard that the celebrated X goes to bed drunk every night, and we are most of us guilty of having derived some pleasure from the thought that X, however greatly celebrated, is prone to the common weaknesses of humanity. But now this ghoul gossip must violate the tomb. *De mortuis nil nisi malum.* Our democratic mind is so much afraid of any inequality that we grudge the very dead the legend of the least virtue that was theirs on earth."

This upset the great critic, and commenting on my remarks rather like a headmaster of the old style commenting on a stupid schoolboy's essay he wound up by asking what it was I had the temerity to be shocked by.

I replied:

"My remark last month about 'hyenas nosing in the entrails of dead lions' provoked such a loud roaring from Mr. Ernest Newman in response, unaccompanied by the least suggestion of laughter, that I am bound to suppose he was anxious to convince me, once and for all, of his own zoological status. He really need not have put himself to such an expense of breath. Readers of *The Gramophone* know that I have always regarded Mr. Newman as a lion and invited them to regard him as one, so that it never occurred to me that he could possibly confuse himself in his own mind with an hyena. In justice to myself, it seems advisable to point out that I have never defended idealized portraits of great men. My contention is that the present fashion in biography lays an undue emphasis on what is base or petty or ridiculous in genius. There is a mean between sentimental glozing and this monotonous denigration, and the truth is as much maltreated by the one method as the other. So far as Wagner is concerned I make no protest. He left his own body to the dissecting room when he wrote that autobiography, and the surgeons are entitled to claim him. At the same time, when I read such a sentence as this: 'Let us hope that in the disturbance Wagner's first and only thought was for Minna, and that, with his arm round her dainty waist, he had taken her for cover and for safety into the orchestra, possibly behind the big drum', I ask myself if some of these surgeons are not merely facetious quacks. That is an extract from the latest life of Wagner by William Wallace. The vulgarity of such writing may seem incredible to those who know Mr. William Wallace's other work, but it can be matched on many other pages of this lamentable little book, which is a typical product of the contemporary fashion.

"Mr. Newman thinks that our appreciation of the G minor Quintet will be heightened by listening at the keyhole of Mozart's bedroom. I think that the relations between a man and his wife may be taken for granted. There are, however, plenty of people to agree with Mr. Newman, and with a certain amount of malicious pleasure I will quote one of his supporters who, commenting in *The Clarion* on the argument between him and myself, says: 'Mozart's "purity of thought and style" has been drummed into us so often that it comes as a relief to know that he was capable of writing letters to his young wife of so outspoken a nature that feverish attempts were made to erase certain passages for ever. When listening to *The Marriage of the* [sic] *Figaro* and the *G minor Symphony* in future, with our thoughts fixed as usual on "angelic beauty", we shall find this information distinctly useful. It is comforting to know that when next we hear Mozart we need not strive so energetically to push our heads into the clouds, and that our feet will be quite in order if they do not show a desire to clink [sic] tenaciously to good solid earth. As with Mozart so with Beethoven and others. And when we find ourselves in the "religious" atmosphere of *Parsifal*, with its absurd accompaniment of bated breath, awed silence, and prohibited applause, we can keep our balance, and gain a great deal of amusement, by reminding ourselves that Wagner was an awful little liar with (as Mr. Newman so drastically puts it) "the morals of a monkey" '."

Mr. Newman then fired a heavy broadside, to which I replied:

"Where is he living, clipp'd in with the sea
That chides the banks of England, Scotland, Wales
Which calls me pupil, or hath read to me
And bring him out that is but woman's son
Can teach me in the tedious ways of art
And hold me pace in deep experiments.

"Thus Owen Glendower in the play, not, as you might suppose, Mr. Newman in the *Sunday Times*. But let me quote his actual words:

'The undeveloped state of English criticism may be gauged from the pontifical assurance with which our men of letters, and especially the minor novelists, deliver their opinion upon music. They, like other men, are, as I have said, entitled to their likes and dislikes. But music is, in the first place, a highly technical art, and, in the second place, there is not a critical problem connected with it that does not require to be seen against a vast background of history and aesthetics. It is no reproach against our men of letters that they have neither this technique nor this background. Our only reproach against them is that they will meddle with complex musical questions that they do not understand, instead of keeping to the writing of novels or some other equally easy form of manual labour. That these cobblers will persist in neglecting their own last in order to bring light into the darkness of musical criticism is, at bottom, simply another phase of the eternal ambition of an amateur to play Hamlet.'

"We have passed from the *argumentum ad hominem* to the *argumentum ad homines*, unless we are to suppose that Mr. Newman is playing Falstaff in the same play:
" 'If I fought not with fifty of them, call me a radish: if there were not two or three and fifty upon poor old Jack, then am I no two-legged creature.'
"No, it won't do, Mr. Newman, and without a moment's hesitation I *do* call you a radish.
"Whatever the faults of men of letters and minor novelists, they are as a class quite unaccustomed to pontificate on the subject of music. In fact, as Mr. Newman himself was inclined to complain not so long ago, novelists are singularly shy of the subject, and he was actually expressing surprise that some of these manual workers did not try their horny hands on the life of a composer. I am not quite clear what Mr. Newman intends to convey by his remark about

Hamlet. If he knew anything about acting, which his recent criticisms of the opera convince me he does not, he would know that Hamlet is probably the easiest big part in the whole of drama—not to play supremely well, of course, but to play at least well enough to make any amateur appear a much better actor than he really is. If, on the other hand, as I suspect, he intends to convey that Hamlet is the most difficult part for an amateur, I presume that he wishes us to suppose that musical criticism is something above the reach of any creative artist in any medium. Yet he begins his article by saying that musical criticism is as yet hardly out of its infancy. In saying that, Mr. Newman does himself less than justice, for some of his recent writing about music savours of the fretful curiosity of puberty, and it is only when he writes in King Cambyses' vein about men of letters that he relapses into the infantile.

"We have now had Mr. Newman's justification of the patient Teuton who, with the help of micro-photography, restored the erasures in Mozart's correspondence, and practically all he tells us in two very long articles is that there was a daemonic element in Mozart (which a drunken clown would discover for himself), and that like musical criticism he remained sexually undeveloped longer than usual. If Mr. Newman knew as much as he claims of the vast historical and aesthetic background against which he places his criticism, he would know that a tardy sexual development is widely spread among men of creative genius. I will go so far as to say that if Mr. Newman himself had not extinguished for the moment his own spark of critical genius he could have deduced this fact from Mozart's music without the help of the microscope. The manual labour of novel-writing may not compare with the cerebral travail of musical criticism; but a D minor novelist with an ear for music might have divined that fact. However, I suppose that with the emergence of musical criticism from the swaddling-clothes of academic decency (and in using that word I am thinking more of manners than of morals) we must expect a good deal of schoolboy knowingness. I suggest a little Aristotle as a corrective: yes a little Aristotle and a fortnight in the sun, that is my prescription for the growing-pains of musical criticism."

What I felt thirty years ago about digging out the details in the life of a great artist in order to bring down to the monotonous level of mediocrity for which the egalitarian fashion of our time hungers, I feel even more strongly to-day. We have been given page upon page of late about Charles Dickens and his love-affair. To what end?

To gratify prurient curiosity, and perhaps provide an Eng. Lit. exponent at this or that university with blood for his dryasdust brains. Not content with scornfully dismissing the social pretensions of the past we must somehow or other reduce the intellectual giants to the level of the little man. I heard one of these Eng. Lit. fellows indulging recently in some intellectual crooning on the Third Programme in the course of which he assured his listeners that to-day criticism was more important than creative writing.

I owe it to Mr. Ernest Newman and certainly to myself to say that our exchange of discourtesies over Mozart's married life was no more than a passing squall. My veneration for him as a critic of music remains profound; he on his side has always been gracious in any reference to myself.

It may be of interest to recall how conductors stood in regard to the gramophone in 1926:

"Since the new recording the question of the right conductor has become of really vital importance for an orchestral record. It is evidently not enough to have musicians of taste, discretion and conscientiousness. I might almost add that dignity and a certain nobility of manner which we associate with some conductors are a hindrance rather than a help to the recording of orchestral works for the gramophone. I can understand, and in some moods sympathize with, the listener who does not care to see the conductor sweating like a stoker, and I admit that it may easily induce in the audience a sense of fatigue which is far removed from the highest of aesthetic pleasure. At the same time I must avow that the two conductors I know who sweat most profusely and whose collars at the end of a symphony are wetter than the inside of the horns do happen to be the very two conductors who galvanize their orchestra into what seems a veritably daemonic condition; and I feel convinced that an orchestra stimulated to this extent is the one in the most suitable condition to be recorded. It is no use talking about the phlegm of British orchestras. The British orchestra with the right conductor can give as inspiring a performance of a great orchestral work as it is possible to hear anywhere else in the world. But we are not getting daemonic performances on the gramophone when they are most required, and however authoritative the conducting by a man like Weingartner of the Ninth Symphony of Beethoven may be, the ineluctable fact remains that life is absent from it. At present on the gramophone there are two conductors who have unmistakably known how to transfer their own life to a machine—Toscanini and

Albert Coates; and I do not think that I am prejudiced by friendship if I add the name of Eugene Goossens.[1] A conductor who I am
convinced would have the same power, but who has not yet been
recorded, is Koussevitsky. One might expect this life-breathing spirit
from Sir Henry Wood, but Sir Henry Wood is really overworked.
He achieves one miracle of energy every year with the Promenade
concerts, and it is not reasonable to expect him to supply another
miracle for the gramophone. It is significant that one of his earliest
recordings, which was a shortened version of the Eroica Symphony,
remained his most vital performance. I am not alluding to technique
now. No doubt other recordings of his have been technically
superior; but whatever their technical superiority they lack the
precious breath of life.

"I read in the October number of *The Phonograph* (which is the
first number of a monthly review designed to be the counterpart in
America of *The Gramophone*, and on the appearance and contents of
which I venture to congratulate warmly everybody concerned) a
most enthusiastic notice of a Brunswick record in which as guest-
conductor Toscanini takes the New York Philharmonic Orchestra
in the Scherzo and Nocturne of Mendelssohn's *Midsummer Night's
Dream*. I can well imagine the triumph that genius of conducting
must have achieved. Now then, which company is going to get
Koussevitsky?

"I liked the Scherzo of the Ninth Symphony best in the Columbia
recording under Weingartner, though even there I wished for
double the vigour, particularly with the timpani, just as in the third
movement I should have welcomed double the emotion, or rather
not so much double the emotion, as that ecstasy of the human soul;
and again in that advance of double-basses I longed for some expression of the dauntless humanity they stand for. If you could but see
Koussevitsky charming his double-basses in this movement. It is
Orpheus over again. Those sombre and sullen instruments turn to
melodious nymphs at his bidding. He could make love-sick schoolgirls of them. In writing like this I expose myself to the charge of
literary rather than musical appreciation, but after all the Ninth
Symphony *is* a drama, and even though that drama be played
without adventitious help from other arts in terms of purest music,
it demands life, and from this recording life is absent. For this I
blame most of all the conductor. Let me hasten to make it perfectly
clear that I am not impugning the interpretation of Weingartner

[1] Sir Thomas Beecham had not decided to galvanize orchestral recording when I
wrote these words.

in a concert-hall, but what I do assert is that he is not capable of transferring himself and his orchestra to a record."

I had just written that when there came from the Victor Company a record of Leopold Stokowski conducting the Philharmonic Symphony Orchestra in the *Danse Macabre* of Saint-Saëns; and I added:

"I must now add Stokowski's name to the list of conductors who have expressed their personality through the gramophone. This *Danse Macabre* is more like the orchestra as one hears it in a full hall than anything we have been given yet."

When I think of the conductors whose work is being recorded to-day I feel as if those words of mine were written in a dream.

And if three years earlier I had announced a symposium in our Christmas number such as I propose to dig out of the past now I should have been sure I was dreaming. I marvel now at the kindness with which thirty-four distinguished men and women answered my questions about their favourite song, their favourite composer, their favourite tune, and their favourite singer, from the answers of whom I choose a selection:

Max Beerbohm:

"I think my favourite song is 'Voi Che Sapete'; and I would call Mozart my favourite composer (thus making a very chaste impression on your readers) but for the fact that on the Mozartian heights I have never felt quite so much at home and so happy as on heights less exalted. The tunes made later by Lionel Monckton and Paul Rubens for the Musical Comedies, and the tunes made by Mr. Herman Finck for the Revues, are what I have been and am most really and truly thankful for. Adelina Patti, though she was old when I was young, remains my favourite singer. I never heard such limpidity, or art 'so natural' as hers. Had she made any gramophone records of her voice, I should certainly buy a gramophone, and Jenny Lind would become my favourite singer."

Hilaire Belloc:

"For a song, the love-song in 'Don Juan', Mozart's. For a composer, Mozart. For a tune, why that of the song. For a singer, I can't judge; but the one I liked best was a man who sang tenor in

the puppet show in Rome in '21, the show called 'The Little Ones';
or else Mignon Nevada.

Lord Berners:

"My favourite song is 'The Last Rose of Summer'; my favourite
composer, Bach; my favourite tune is the third of Schönberg's six
pieces for pianoforte, because it is so obscure that one is never likely
to grow tired of it (which you must admit is as good a reason for
preferring a tune as any other); and if by 'singer' you mean any
kind of singer then the one I prefer is Little Tich. But, on the other
hand, if you mean merely concert singers, please substitute Clara
Butt."

G. K. Chesterton:

"My taste in songs wavers among somewhat different examples;
but I think it would probably be between the noble Scottish song,
'Caller Herrin', which seems to me full of the Scottish sense of
human dignity for the poor, and some specimen of the broader and
more genial English spirit, such as the beautiful lyric that goes:

> Father's got the sack from the waterworks
>   For smoking of his old cherry briar,
> He, said Foreman Joe, would bloody well have to go,
>   As he'd probably set the waterworks on fire."

Noel Coward:

"My favourite song is 'L'Heure Exquise'. My favourite composer is George Gershwin. My favourite tune is 'Mountain Greenery'
by Laurenz Hart and Richard Rodgers. My favourite singer is
Yvonne Printemps.

"I am doing this during a rehearsal, so it may sound rather
peculiar."

Walter de la Mare:

"Yours would be a difficult catechism even for an expert, so you
can imagine what it must be for a mere amateur.

"In spite of many efforts, I cannot decide on my 'favourite' song.
But if, at pain of being jazzed to death, I was compelled to come to a
conclusion, I think I should find myself at the last still hesitating
between a song of the 'folk' kind and one of Brahms's or Schubert's.
Among the records I know, one of the most successful, I think, is

Hahn's 'L'Heure Exquise'; but my range is limited. I suppose a list of records of quiet 'parlour' renderings of good songs long since appeared in *The Gramophone*, and by 'quiet' I mean, chiefly, not of operatic technique.

"For 'composer', though 'favourite' sounds both a feeble and arrogant term in relation to such a name, my choice would be Bach, and for 'tune' the aria 'Have Mercy Upon Me, O Lord', in the St. Matthew Passion Music. After him, I think, Mozart; but after the apex, difficulty of choice increases like the width of a pyramid.

"Singers are even more difficult to choose between—by one, that is, who is nothing of an expert. So, much as I admire and delight in many singers, may mine be an abstraction? He or she would be an artist with a voice so delicately and sagaciously trained that at hearing of it one would not suppose that it had been trained at all. It would be a voice as responsive to the 'meaning' of the mind and the imagination making use of it as a beautiful face is; and so lovely in itself that you would hardly be able to distinguish between it and its music—because the form (the singing) and the content (the thing sung) would be so perfectly at poise and at peace together. This sounds exceedingly vague as well as hopelessly negative, but it is the nearest I can get."

Norman Douglas:

"Impossible for me to tell you the name of my favourite song, tune, composer, etc., for the simple reason that I don't go in for favourites—not in the department of music, at least.

"Sometimes I like one of them best, sometimes another; it all depends upon the state of my mind, the state of my stomach, and endless other contingencies.

"Feed me properly, and I can stand anything.

"Now if you asked me the name of my favourite toothpaste . . ."

John Galsworthy:

"I'm not a good hand at symposiums, but since it's you who asks, here goes:

"My favourite song (well sung), 'Che farò', from Gluck's 'Orfeo'.

"My favourite composers Bach, Chopin, dead heat, with Gluck beaten half a length, Stravinsky beaten off, and Wagner left at the post.

"My favourite tune depends on my mood and varies from 'The Marseillaise' to 'The Bens of Jura'.

"My favourite singer. At the moment, I would rather hear Chaliapine sing 'The Volga Boat Song' than any one else sing any other song."

General Sir Ian Hamilton:

"You are quite right—I hate, from the bottom of my heart, a symposium. Still, as an old Gallipoli comrade, here you are:

"Favourite song: Whatever my best girl sings.

"Favourite composer: Mozart—by long chalks.

"Favourite tune: 'The Dinner Call'. Known in the Army as 'Officers' Wives Get Puddings And Pies, But Soldiers' Wives Get Skilly'.

"Favourite singer: My old friend, Nellie Melba."

T. M. Healy:

"Your letter reached me in a time of tragedy, when the mind is not attuned to the questions you submit. I will, therefore, shortly give you my opinion.

"It is that Scotch folk-song is the best as regards words: and that Irish melody is the best as regards airs. I think 'Old Robin Gray' one of the most powerful of ballads.

"As regards Irish songs, I think, in spite of the modern contempt cultivated for Moore, that he will never be surpassed. True, he had to stretch on the rack Gaelic music to English words—of which Bunting complained so bitterly:

"What can beat such lines as begin with

> Oh, who would not welcome that moment returning,
>   When passion first gave a new life to our frame;
> And the soul, like the wood that grows precious in burning,
>   Gave forth all its sweets at love's exquisite flame.

"N.B.—I am now over seventy-one."

Sir John Lavery:

"How dreadful. I don't like music. When I was quite young I was told that music and poetry were essential to the painter, and that he could not possibly be an artist if he did not revel in both. Well, I tried hard for years without success, all the time pretending that I loved and understood them, till I married Hazel—late in life—when I confessed to her the deception I had been practising by having concerts in my studio, attending all sorts of musical festivals, and all the time being bored to tears.

"She gave the show away, since when I have had the moral courage to make the above statement."

D. H. Lawrence:

"My favourite song is, I think, 'Kishmul's Galley', from the Hebridean Songs, and my favourite composer, if one must be so selective, Mozart; and singer, a Red Indian singing to a drum, which sounds pretty stupid."

W. J. Locke:

"You appeal to a man by no means unmusical who, however, has passed his life outside the sphere of music as the word is now understood of the cognoscenti. But it means a bit more to me than I can express by mentioning my favourite anything.

"My favourite song? I have heard thousands of beautiful songs. When the world was young, and my place in that world was the gallery of the Albert Hall, I heard Christine Nillson sing 'The Sands of Dee', and after, it seems a hundred years, the elfin notes still haunt my ears. Dame Clara Butt, in my own house on New Year's Eve, a year or so ago, sang 'The Swanee River', and made me weep like a cow.

"Under your apparent guilelessness, you really demand an essay; for, from the multitudinous musical associations of a longish life, how can one pick and choose? How can one declare a choice, say, between the plaint of the woodwind in 'Tristan', and the immortal waltz motif in Weber's 'Invitation'? Between the Toreador music in 'Carmen' and 'Le Jardin sous la pluie' of Debussy?

"A sensitive being is one of many moods. Suppose I were dying. What music would I like to hear, as my last consciousness was merging into infinite oblivion? I can imagine a mood in which the splendour of chords in Beethoven's 'Funeral March' would befit the majesty of my dissolution; but, on the other hand, I can readily imagine another mood in which I could ask nothing better than that Gounod's 'Marche Funèbre d'une Marionette' should dance my spirit humoresquely across the dreaded frontier.

"And that, in a few words, *mon cher confrère*, is all I can say about it."

W. S. Maugham:

"What a devilish fellow you are to ask a harmless and respectable gentleman like myself to answer such questions; but here they are:
"Favourite song: 'The Prize Song.'
"Favourite composer: Wagner.
"Favourite tune: 'The Fire Music.'
"Favourite singer: Lotte Lehmann.
"Curses on your head."

Ivor Novello:

"My favourite song is 'Morgen' by Richard Strauss; my favourite composer, Wagner; my favourite tune (I presume you mean of the modern variety), 'By the Lake'; and the singer I most admire is Emmy Bettendorf, who you know records for Parlophone. I choose her not only for the exquisite quality of her voice, but for her astonishing versatility. She seems to be able to sing anything."

Sir Landon Ronald:

"I can answer all your questions easily excepting the question of which is my favourite song.
"I love so many of Schumann, Strauss, Grieg, the Sea Songs of Edward Elgar, songs by Roger Quilter and Vaughan Williams, and many, many others, that it is quite impossible for me to say that I have a favourite.
"(Perhaps I should add that I forgot to mention Schubert, Liszt, Wolf and Brahms.)
"My favourite composer is undoubtedly Wagner, and my favourite tune, without doubt, is the 'Marseillaise' ".

George Bernard Shaw:

"Only people in a deplorably elementary stage of musical culture have favourite tunes and so forth. I consider the question a monstrous insult."

Hugh Walpole:

"As you rightly remark, these questions are a damn bore, but if it gives you any pleasure to know it, I would say that certainly Brahms is my favourite composer, and the singer I most admire, Van Rooy; but he is singing no longer, so perhaps I should say in general, Eleanor Gerhardt and, for Scandinavian things, a pal of mine, Lauritz Melchior. As to a tune I can think of thousands; two of the best, if you call them tunes, are Desdemona's song in the last act of 'Otello', and the Orestes music in 'Elektra'. They are melodies anyway."

Alas, only four of those who wrote the replies quoted above are still with us.

Chapter 15

THE circulation of our paper was rising steadily every month and the National Gramophonic Society was continuously getting new members from all over the world except Great Britain. We owed much to the enlightened attitude of the great recording companies. I venture to wonder whether the history of British journalism can show an example of ruthlessly frank criticism being accepted by great business interests with comparable equanimity and attention.

From over the Atlantic a tribute to the work of the N.G.S. was paid by Axel B. Johnson who in Boston had launched a magazine on the same lines as *The Gramophone* called *The Phonograph*.

This generous and discerning tribute was a reproach to the English musical journals which, however much in sympathy with the objects of the society, could not bring themselves to support it in print.

We were also the subject of a leading article in the huge *Talking Machine World* of New York. In this the sympathy of the British recording companies with the objects of the N.G.S. was held up for admiration as an example of shrewd business foresight. "The phonograph industry over there had the wisdom to see that a new lode of ore had been tapped by an independent prospector. They did not try to run the discoverer out of town. On the contrary they called him in and asked him what they could do for him. And consequently all of them have flourished."

Sir Louis Sterling, the Managing Director of Columbia, himself an American, should have been pleased by that comment, for it was he who at a time when his company was almost literally hard pressed by their own work gave orders that the recording and pressing of the National Gramophonic Society was to be undertaken.

Yes, all was rosy in the gramophone outlook, but the B.B.C. which was trying hard to fulfil its duties to music was being seriously assailed by the popular Press for upsetting the little man with symphonies and chamber music. I felt it was time to hit out, and in February 1927 I wrote:

"I do not profess to understand what lies behind the present campaign of the popular Press against the B.B.C.; I presume that, like most outbursts of moral indignation, it arises from jealousy. It is the duty of every reader of this paper to use any influence he may possess to combat the barbarian attack which has suddenly been launched all along the line. Here is a hee-haw from a jackass with exceptionally long ears who calls himself 'A Listener' and whose brays are published on the chief page of the *Daily Mirror* of January 15th:

> " 'Instead of bright musical comedy selections that always appeal we are treated to an excess of the symphonic, and modern English composers have been crowded out by ancient Germans, Austrians, and Russians . . . if the B.B.C. can regain the intimate human touch it had when broadcasting began and make our evenings bright with English songs and melodies, instead of the excessively intricate compositions of ancient foreigners, a boom in wireless will come again.'

"Quite what a boom in wireless means I am not sure, but probably it means that a hundred thousand cretins like the author of this article will waste their money in buying new gadgets to deal with the selections from modern English musical comedy, which are to fill the ether when dance music is not being played. The action of the popular Press in arming these criminal lunatics to help them in a campaign against the B.B.C. is, with the exception of the vile personal attack on Venizelos in 1922, the most cynical abuse of power in which it has hitherto indulged itself. The B.B.C. has had to contend with hostility on all sides and that at the present moment it is able to offer every day a programme of such remarkable variety, interest, and utility must be regarded as an unqualified triumph. I have hardly ever read in the Press a tribute to what it has achieved, outside, of course, the pages of the *Radio Times*, and even there the B.B.C. has shown itself extremely sparing of self-praise. . . .

"I hope that I am voicing the opinion of *all* our wireless readers when I say to the B.B.C. that we are watching with an immense disgust and a profound uneasiness the savage attacks upon it from all sides, that we hope it will pay no attention whatever to these Choctaw war-cries, and that we recognize with gratitude its high sense of responsibility and its unmistakable devotion to high ideals. *Floreat!*"

It is commonly believed that when a writer attacks the popular Press he is thenceforward the mark for a vendetta. I have never hesitated to attack the popular Press when I believed it ought to be attacked, but I have always received from the popular Press fair, indeed generous, treatment for forty-four years. A short time after those remarks about the *Daily Mirror* I was asked by the *Sunday Pictorial* to write a weekly review of gramophone records which I only gave up, after not missing a single week for five years, when I became the literary critic of the *Daily Mail*.

During convalescence from the worst attack of influenza I had ever had, the effect of leaving my island to dash about London, the *Daily Mail* held a plebiscite over broadcast programmes. The result nearly caused a relapse.

"I am suffering from the humiliation of the *Daily Mail's* plebiscite over broadcasting programmes. I feel that I have gone on a spiritual strike to protest against the respect given to a quarter of a million trousers and skirts. In another column the *Daily Mail* was expressing anxiety for the future of English singers. It was wondering why English singers are driven abroad. Personally I don't feel that it very much matters whether many of the English singers I have heard on the gramophone are driven abroad or not; but I cannot stand these clammy crocodile's tears. If the British public is encouraged to suppose that its opinion expressed en masse has any greater value than the similarly expressed opinion of Hottentots, we may as well give up pretending to be anything else but one of the less prosperous colonies of the United States. This washing of our aesthetic dirty linen in public is the greatest disservice that can be rendered. I have no animus against the man in the street provided that he remains a man in the street, or sticks to his strap in the Tube, and does not pretend to be the man in the studio or the library or the concert-hall; but when we are asked to time the intellectual progress of the race by this heavy, stolid, costive creature, who cannot even get as far as his office without a dose of Kruschen salts every morning, the time has come to protest. It is not that any reasonable being objects to what with a pathetic euphemism are known as variety entertainments, though usually the last quality they achieve is the slightest variety. What one does object to is the deadly monotony of the mediocrity or drabness. There are not enough good performers of this class of entertainment to supply either the radio or the gramophone. When the King attends the Victoria Palace it is possible to secure an excellent two hours' entertainment by ransacking the United Kingdom and the Dominions; but ask even these first-rate entertainers to perform to the same audience every week for a year and it is obvious that everybody would be sick of them in a month. How many comic records stand playing half a dozen times?

"It is not the fault of the recording companies; they can't make bricks without straw. When these trousers and skirts vote in their thousands for variety entertainments on the Radio, they are thinking how much they have enjoyed such an excellent performance as that at the Victoria Palace. If I were the B.B.C. I should feel strongly tempted to give the British public variety entertainments all day and night for three months with nothing except an occasional solo on the mouth-organ to relieve the monotony. Then perhaps we should hear a little common sense talked. Yet, twenty-seven thousand people did vote for chamber music, and although this is a miserable fraction of the civilized population, it is a larger number than one might have expected.

"Some two thousand people voted for recitations and readings, and I must confess I was surprised that twenty of them had done so. The reading of their own works by English poets for the Radio has been sufficiently execrable to give the quietus to English poetry for good and all. Why a man should think Keats' *Ode to a Nightingale* (or whatever he reads) will sound better if he puts his head in a soup-tureen I do not know.

"Anybody who had the privilege of hearing Sir Edmund Gosse read Wordsworth's *Ode on the Intimations of Immortality* will wish that Sir Edmund might start a reading class for budding and full-blown English poets. I am enlarging on this subject because a number of our readers have written to beg the companies to give us authoritative recordings of contemporary writers reading their work. This may sound a delightful idea to anybody who has not heard English poets on the Radio, but that anybody who has should want to perpetuate these intestinal moans and groans is incredible. Why spend money on a record when you can get the same effect by running the water out of your bath? It is nothing to do with being nervous. Numbers of poets genuinely believe that this is the right way to read verse. Numbers of clergymen suffer from a similar delusion. It's a kind of Pharisaic blight—an attempt to express a caste."

The year 1927 was the centenary of the death of Beethoven.

"Warned by the example of several distinguished literary men whose recent eulogies of Beethoven have sounded more like tributes to Pelmanism, I shall not venture to add one word to what has already been written about the great man himself. During this last month I have drawn nearer to him through those talks of Sir Walford Davies on the Radio than ever before, and I confess that when, the other night, he turned from the piano and put on a marvellous disc of Kreisler playing the Violin Concerto, I was not far from tears of gratitude for the way that sudden burst of divine music might be sounding in some of those little houses whose aerials I always count from the train and for whose inmates I always beg in passing the grace of joy in beauty. In 1827, when Beethoven died, the children of England who in 1927 were listening at a concert to the Prometheus Overture might have been starved and naked slaves in mines, and I do not think that I shall be sentimental in claiming that without Beethoven men might have been even less merciful than they are.

"In spite of the fact that London is unable to support Queen's Hall, the nation is apparently able to support more good music in gramophonic form than any other in the world. The threatened closing of Queen's Hall is attributed to the competition of Radio. There was never a more unworthy lie uttered.

"What has made Queen's Hall unprosperous is the increase in the cost of upkeep, of which one of the most conspicuous items is the increased expense of the Orchestra itself. The only possible effect of Radio can be to add to concert audiences as many new lovers of music as it has added to the gramophone. The Metropolitan Opera House of New York is not a sign of musical taste: it is an advertisement of material well-being. The departure of Eugene Goossens to America is not a sign that he is better appreciated there: he is imported like caviare or any other obviously expensive luxury. Read the Wireless programmes of the rest of the world (Germany excepted) if you suppose that other countries can support music. In spite of the musical superiority of America, an English messenger-boy last month took over for Columbia as personal luggage more records of good music in a few days than America has produced in twenty-five years. Whatever our ignoble deficiencies in other directions our recording companies cannot be accused of any failure to do their duty by this centenary. They must have spent an enormous sum of money, for which they cannot possibly expect to recoup themselves, at any rate for a very long time. They have engaged the finest performers and given those performers the best possible reproductions. The performers themselves have played as if they believed Beethoven himself could hear them, as indeed, pray God, he can."

About this time we were being told that a record of the *Londonderry Air* made by Felix Salmond the great violoncellist was the most popular of all the records on the American market.

"I hope I may be allowed to say, without offence, that such an item of news is of no more interest to music lovers over here than a similar item of news about an English record would be to music lovers in America. What would be a good testimonial for a safety razor is not necessarily a good testimonial for a gramophone record. What it does tell us is that the same tunes are as popular in America as over here, and after the failure of the Naval Conference at Geneva that is encouraging politically. One of the most significant comments on the relations between France and England is that the two nations do not like the same tunes. The *Marseillaise* may find a place in every Englishman's list of best tunes, but the tune of *God Save the King* is used not only in England as an expression of solemn national emotion but in America and in Germany as well. It seems to express something that all these nations wish to express emotionally about themselves, whereas the *Marseillaise* is admired objectively. It is a tune which elates, and I fancy that when the English, American and Germans go to war they require to be fed with sentimental assurances rather than romantic excitement. I should imagine that if one made a collection of the various songs sung by the Southerners and the Northerners in the American Civil War one might find the same contrast, sentiment in the North, romance in the South. America at present, with the exception of the progressive or reactionary minority (whichever way you regard it), is devoted to an outpouring of sentimentality in art (I must use the great word for a small thing) which has met with an immediate response from England. The sentimental ballad which for so long held pride of place has been dispossessed, in spite of the efforts of lachrymose tenors to throw rose-buds on its grave, but it is becoming every day more difficult to write sentimental ballads of the old style about the young woman of the new style, and at first one is thankful to shingles and short skirts for killing the pernicious thing. But one is not so thankful when one considers the substitute that America has provided. The tired business man over there has to be titillated by endless songs about little blondines and cuties and Hoosier sweethearts, and the tired business man over here evidently finds that such titillation is just what he requires too. It is a kind of how to be naughty without tears.

"I read from time to time in the daily Press that the modern girl is not sentimental. Well, she may not be, but she seems to be able to evoke as much sentiment in the male as ever. I imagine that few of my readers have not read that masterpiece, *Gentlemen Prefer Blondes*; but in spite of its warning to every man, gentlemen continue to prefer blondes and to marry brunettes, and that is the key to the slushy philosophy which runs through most of the songs of these whispering basses, murmurous tenors, and confidential barytones. A lot of people make a fuss about the Americanization of England which is being sedulously carried on by means of records, plays, films, and books, but why bother about it? The eagerness with which England welcomes its Americanization proves that it is just what it was waiting for. 'Ain't she cunning, ain't she sweet? Everybody speaks well of her', exclaims the hero of one of the recent songs in a whine of fatuous complacency. In other words he seeks the approval of democracy for his marriage. 'Everybody in the world speaks well of him,' says Sir Peter Teazle to Sir Oliver Surface. 'Everybody speaks well of him!' retorts Sir Oliver. 'Psha! then he has bowed as low to knaves and fools as to the honest dignity of genius and virtue.'

"Sheridan wrote *The School for Scandal* before the world had completely surrendered to democratic tyranny. We have entered the Ford Age. We can look forward to a world of comfortable slaves, all speaking American, with no birds but sparrows, with no fish but plaice, with no god but the chiefs of departments, and to console humanity for the loss of its Homers and Shakespeares an infallible method of birth control to prevent the overcrowding of char-à-bancs, and in that comfortable standardized world there may not be a single individual left to lament that what began with the *Marseillaise* ended in the *Frothblowers' Anthem*."

I quote again:

"The Balalaika records and Spanish dance records are a relief from the monotony of fox-trots. Evidently the paso doble and the tango are never going to conquer the English. What amazes me is how the deuce the waltz ever got hold of them. It was apparently an instantaneous success when it came in about a hundred years ago, but how on earth did the young Englishman of the day in his tight pantaloons manage to lose his self-consciousness sufficiently to dance it? Another puzzle is why the Charleston has been able to do what the tango failed to do. It may be laziness. The Charleston can be improvised but the tango cannot; you have got to learn the steps of the tango. I can understand the Blues being popular in

England. The rhythm is eminently suited to the English temperament in a dance room. But why not the tango? Perhaps it is that most Englishmen think of dancing as a form of exercise primarily; it is an evening substitute for golf. All except the very best English dancers, however well cut their evening clothes, seem to be dancing in plus fours."

The Beethoven Centenary was soon to be followed by the Schubert Centenary, and the Columbia Company offered a prize for the completion of the Unfinished Symphony.

"The prize is a large one—£2000; but in addition to this the Company is offering thirty other prizes of considerable sums to be competed for by the musicians of national groups, from the winners of which the £2000 man will be finally chosen. The co-operation of various musical societies has been sought and obtained. The Viennese Society of Friends of Music is one of them. The Regia Academia di Santa Cecilia is another, and in almost every country societies of equal eminence have agreed to help. Whatever we may think about the value of the scheme from an artistic point of view, the enterprise and generosity of the Columbia Company must be saluted. It is a pleasure to find a great commercial business so sensitive to its obligations, and I confess to being astonished and not a little distressed at the manner in which the announcement of this competition has been received in this country. I make haste to admit that the case against any encouragement to finish the Unfinished Symphony is a strong one, and from a purely academic point of view even unanswerable. But though I may be sceptical of the value of the completion as a work of art, I have no doubt at all about the value of the completing. The analogy Sir H. Walford Davies drew between that completing and restoring her arms to the Venus of Milo is clearly shown by Professor Donald Tovey in an admirable letter to *The Times* to be a false analogy. The arms of the Venus of Milo have been lost, and any attempt to restore them must partake more of the solution of a puzzle than anything else. The analogy I should prefer to make would be with an attempt to finish the *Hyperion* of Keats. What should we think of a firm of publishers who had suggested celebrating the centenary of Keats by the offer of two thousand pounds for finishing *Hyperion*? We should most of us agree at once that the notion was ridiculous. We should say that Keats deliberately laid aside *Hyperion* because he came to the conclusion that, good as it was, it was no better than

Milton. He felt that in that particular style of blank verse narrative it was impossible to go beyond Milton, and here, I am afraid, my own analogy breaks down because there is nothing to lead us to suppose that Schubert laid aside the Unfinished Symphony because he felt that in those first two movements his art was turning back. On the contrary we should be more inclined to suppose that he laid it aside because in these two movements he had succeeded in speaking with a new voice. They are something different in music; they have a directness of personal appeal, an intimacy of simple emotion, which no composer had achieved before, and which, I may add, no composer has achieved since.

"Schubert did as a matter of fact rough out the scherzo pretty fully, and one of the first duties of the Columbia Company will be to give us a record of this half-wrought scherzo as quickly as possible. We have no evidence that Schubert had any ideas for his finale, but we may feel fairly confident in assuming that he did not wish to spoil the first two movements with one of those diffuse symphonic finales to which he was so prone. It may be, of course, that he was quite unaware of having said anything new in the first two movements. They may have been, what one is tempted to suppose so many of his brightest inspirations must have been, a happy accident of genius; and yet the care he bestowed on what was then a somewhat novel orchestration forbids us to suppose that he regarded these two movements as anything akin to an improvisation. On the whole, I think we may fairly decide that the Unfinished Symphony was unfinished because Schubert did not know how to finish it; and if we make this assumption I feel that it relieves our consciences over the artistic value of the competition. Had the Unfinished Symphony been left unfinished through death, as *The Mystery of Edwin Drood* was left, or as R. L. Stevenson's *St. Ives* was left, had we indeed been assured that the composer knew what he wanted to say, it would, I think, have been ridiculous to invite composers a hundred years afterwards to re-create a stifled inspiration. If we knew that the subject of the finale was in his mind as he lay dying, then any attempt to invent that unheard strain would have been, I cannot help feeling, something like sacrilege. I believe that the composer who embarks on this task is justified in rejecting the sketch of the third movement which Schubert wrote down, just as I think we may assume that Schubert himself had rejected it. At the same time, if a composer could take that scherzo and by some alchemy of his art transmute it with the help of modern orchestration, he would, I think, be justified in doing so. However, this is speculating about something I know nothing about, for I have no idea if the unfinished scherzo offers any prospect of successful transmutation.

"It is impossible for me to guess by what standards the judges will make the final award, but I sincerely hope that they will close their ears to anything in the nature of a pastiche. Nothing would be gained for music by a piece of musical tushery. We know that behind this competition is the desire to probe the melodic invention of the present, and I am not suggesting that any deliberate rejection of melody should gain the prize; but we have to face the fact that a symphony left unfinished in the year 1822 is to be finished in the year 1928. We may remember that the symphony was not played in England until 1867, and that every year since it has grown nearer to the heart of simple humanity. We know that it is the main gate by which people have entered the splendid realm of musical appreciation, and therefore any attempt deliberately to narrow this gate would be in the highest degree deplorable. The world is growing older. It has grown much more rapidly older in the last century than ever before. If only this competition could inspire some musician to express 1928 not in the terms of 1828 but with the heart of 1828 and the mind of 1928! Contemporary music, whatever else may be said in its favour, does lack heart; it suffers like every other form of contemporary expression from a plethora of cerebration. You often hear people complain that the novel no longer tells a story. That is not really what people miss; they would not really be grateful to any novelist for sacrificing what he has added to the novel in order to maintain the plot. What they mean is that the contemporary novel fails to hold their attention, and they fancy that if there were more of an obvious story their attention would be recaptured. But again it is the heart that is missing. The modern novel has become too much like a dream, interesting to the person who wrote it but to nobody else; and is not this one of the characteristics of contemporary music? I always feel when I am listening to an ultra-modern composition that it meant a great deal to the man who wrote it, but that by excess of cerebration he has failed to give it a heart.

"They fail, these modern musicians, to touch authentic life; and we listeners, realizing that we can only approach their emotion through our brains, retreat from it because we distrust cerebral emotion for its insecurity and suggestion of impermanence. The fashions of the mind change more quickly than the fashions of the heart. We distrust a work of art that requires us to be incarnate in the artist's conception before we can appreciate it. There is a conspicuous lack of objectivity at present in all the arts, one of the causes of which may be the excessive attention that humanity is devoting to objective utility. The impulse that drives a man to design a motor-car is an entirely different aspect of the creative instinct from that which drives him to write a poem, and the objectivity of the material world preoccupies contemporary minds so intensely that man himself seems to have become instinctively more subjective. He is much more concerned with the expression of his own idea of beauty than with the creation of beauty that will communicate its idea to others. He is not prepared to part with his ego, because his ego is the only fact of which he can pretend to know anything and also the only fact in which he can rationally believe.

"I myself suppose that the modern musician is incapable of melodic invention because he is in such a state of confusion about values—spiritual, aesthetic, political, biological, and all the rest of it—that he lacks the necessary self-confidence to produce a melody. I think that Beethoven at the end of his life anticipated some of the hesitation of the modern artist, and it may be that Schubert, of whom, it will be remembered, Beethoven said, 'Franz has my soul,' was beginning to lose *his* self-confidence. I seem to detect that doubt in his sublime last work—the Quintet in C.

"I often wonder whether we are right in saying that Beethoven struck a profounder note in his last quartets. We may be mistaking complicacy for profundity. Some of that profundity may be the gasps of a man who is out of his depth. Beethoven may not have quite known what he was wanting to say, and for that reason he may not have managed to say it clearly. That state of mind is common with writers, and even commoner with philosophers, who make cat's cradles of their minds and hide their confusion by building round them a wall of jargon. I hope that the young composer, or it may be the old composer, who wins this prize, will win it because he will have managed, in spite of the clash and din of his world, in spite of the confusion and doubt within himself, to speak as intimately and directly to the human heart as Schubert spoke. He will have to preserve at the back of his mind a resolve to add something to the sum of the beauty created by man, and in these days that will be a valuable resolve for an artist. The beauty of ugliness has been over-emphasized at the present moment, for there never has been, there never is, and there never will be any beauty in ugliness. That ugliness may offer the artist an opportunity to display his cleverness, that ugliness may be extremely interesting, that ugliness may have an

M

artistic value I am not prepared to deny, but I do deny that it will ever achieve beauty.

"Let us put on one side the aesthetic aspect of the matter and regard it from a practical standpoint. The struggles of the great composers are familiar reading. We are tempted sometimes to suppose that great music can only be produced through suffering, but I do not think that I am wrong in claiming that it was easier to be poor a hundred years ago than now. The material claims of existence are much more insistent now than they were then. A democratic society is a much harsher critic of genius than an aristocratic society. A Prince Lichnowsky is a much more practical patron of art than a municipal council, and we may feel fairly confident that no great musical genius on the threshold of his career was ever stifled by circumstances a hundred years ago. Can we feel as certain of that now? Can we feel positive that no young composer has been diverted from his resolve through the necessity of earning a livelihood? What, I say to myself, must inevitably be the feelings of a contemporary musician at the beginning of his career to-day? His training may be accomplished with the help of scholarships and so his academic future assured; but any young man of to-day who announced that he proposed to earn his living by writing symphonies and string quartets would be considered as foolish as if he had announced that he intended to earn his living by writing epics and odes. We simply must recognize the fact that the modern conditions of society do not offer any musician or any poet even the means of keeping himself from actual starvation, unless he is prepared to make his music or his poetry subsidiary either to some other profession or deliberately to turn his art to commercial advantage.

> The harlot's cry from street to street
> Shall weave old England's winding sheet,

wrote Blake. God knows, the prostitution of the female body is a horrible thing; but the prostitution of the male mind is not less horrible, and we have, not merely in England but everywhere else in the world, to face the fact that we are deliberately tolerating the possibility of such a prostitution. A year or two ago I was turning over the pages of a book in which were entered the unprinted, unperformed works of contemporary musicians, and that long, weary heartbroken list has haunted me ever since. That was merely a list of works written by the members of one small London club. How many tomes would be required to chronicle the unpublished, unperformed music of Europe?

"My great pleasure in the gramophone is always that it may ultimately make a musical career less heartrending than it must be now. I consider that the display of practical patronage by the Columbia Company deserves our admiration and our gratitude. Nothing may come of this competition, but at least an attempt will have been made to encourage composers all over the world to write half a symphony under the spur of fame; and if Franz Schubert may be aware of this prize for the completion of his unfinished symphony I do not think he will resent it. He will remember his youth and his Vienna and his table in the inn yard where he wrote so many songs that afternoon. Of all the musicians I can remember there was none who would have been less likely to resent his works being made an incentive to youth or a consolation for age. This will seem a sentimental plea to more austere minds than my own; but the music of Schubert does not favour austerity of judgment. When I read every day of prizes of a thousand pounds being offered for the solution of cross-word puzzles, or for finding the first horses in a race, or for any of the other innumerable enticements to waste contemporary time, I cannot feel that art is being desecrated by the Columbia Company. On the contrary, I feel that they have done a more practical thing for music than has been done for a long time, and I hope that their name will be associated hereafter with a work of art which will be for ever a pride to their house."

By the beginning of 1928 it was clear that the old sound-box was doomed and that its place would soon be taken everywhere by the electric pick-up. No doubt, for a time the old battles would be waged by the supporters of this or that pick-up but the introduction of electricity would put many of us out of the contest at the start. I looked at my big Balmain horn—the old Balmain pagoda as I used to call it—which glided along in a bath of mercury and had given me the best reproduction available as yet with the various sound-boxes whose merits and demerits were for ever discussed. I looked at the Lifebelt sadly, recognizing that soon its day would be past.

P. Wilson who had come down to Jethou as the representative of our Expert Committee and had endorsed my enthusiasm about that little gadget had gone over completely to electric reproduction. I felt I must try to follow him, but though I wrote with apparent light-heartedness about the future I knew that some of the fun of the gramophone for me was gone, because I should never be able to understand how a pick-up worked.

"This year," I announced with a brave attempt at bluff, "I shall devote myself as soon as possible to electric pick-ups.

"Wilson is such an electrical person that I sometimes wonder if he isn't himself a walking accumulator. At any rate he has done something to Balmain, from whom I had a letter the other day recanting all his prophecies about electrical reproduction. He wrote of the latest electrical reproduction with the enthusiasm of one willing to be a martyr for the new faith, and, if I am to believe him, Big Bertha will stand in my library soon like that immense prehistoric skeleton in the entrance hall of the Natural History Museum. Rumour says that Gilman,[1] fighting desperately in the last ditch of the old order with a doped fibre, has also surrendered, but up to the time of writing I have not had any positive information from him on this point. My own feeling at the moment, after seeing the picture on page 307 of the Christmas number, is one of pious hope that when I see something like that gazing at me in my library I shall be able to work without a gas mask. I can't help feeling a little nervous about that Igranic High Resistance Potentiometer, which looks uncommonly like the fifteen-inch guns of a battleship. The Bulgin Panel Light seems a nasty customer, and the Varley Anode has as sinister an expression as I have ever seen. Then there are some things called Dubiliers, which sound rather like Dublin Fusiliers of the Robot type, and when I read further that the resistance required for two ohms is $\dfrac{6-5.5}{0.25}$ I am not surprised that the Varley Anode, which is prepared to resist 100,000 of them, looks so pugnacious. There is also a picture of the fuse bulb and holder, but I see no sign of the holder except a note of interrogation in the middle of the bulb. I expect that is what I shall turn into before this year is out."

The Schubert Centenary Committee wisely decided to give up the idea of finishing the Unfinished Symphony and the Grand International Prize of £2000 was to be awarded for an unrestricted composition dedicated to the memory and immortal genius of Schubert. Furthermore ten first prizes of £150 and ten second prizes of £50 were to be awarded in ten zones.

"If the expenditure of £4000 cannot produce a remarkable symphonic composition," I commented, "we shall have to form our own conclusions, and the Columbia Company may reasonably

[1] The late Lionel Gilman had been a great supporter of ours from the beginning.

conclude at the end of it that their obligation to encourage contemporary music will have been for the moment sufficiently honoured. I expect some duffers will go about saying that great works of art are not produced for money. Nobody supposes that they are, but there may be some great music hidden away that deserves material reward, and it is precisely to discover if such great music exists that the Columbia prizes are offered."

Chapter 16

IN 1924 I had acquired the Shiant Islands—the Enchanted Islands is the Gaelic equivalent—in the Minch, and I was trying every year to spend more and more time in Scotland. This was impossible at first because Herm had involved me in debt to the tune of £14,000 and I had to work pretty hard to pay off my obligations. Fortunately there was no income tax in the Channel Islands and therefore I was all clear by 1930. There was a bad moment in 1925 when Mr. Churchill was Chancellor of the Exchequer because kow-towing to a silly agitation in the popular Press about authors who were supposed to be living in luxury on the Riviera and thereby depriving the Treasury of millions he inserted a clause in his Budget compelling publishers to deduct tax at full rate from authors' royalties. This preposterous piece of discrimination was not contested by the Society of Authors, and the few wretched authors hit by it were incapable of doing anything about it. Probably the sum total of revenue the Treasury lost from the sum total of authors living abroad did not exceed £10,000. I held my lease of Jethou from the King as Duke of Normandy but it was administered by the Treasury. I wrote to Their Lordships to ask whether if I sold my books outright they would be taxable at source and was informed by them that they would not be. So for a time I had to sell outright. Twenty years later I bought back these books written during those strenuous nights and days.

I could not afford to live in Scotland yet, and I look back with gratitude to the perpetual music of the gramophone which sustained me morally, mentally, and almost physically throughout those seven years.

An echo of these difficulties may be heard from July 1928 when I had been in the Highlands and the Hebrides:

"Several correspondents have been writing to protest against my writing too little for *The Gramophone* and refusing to accept my weekly articles in the *Sunday Pictorial* as a substitute. I would beg such readers to remember that I produce two novels a year, and this year I shall be adding to my two novels the first volume of my War reminiscences, not to mention a big original film and a great deal of journalistic work unconnected with the gramophone. It is almost true to say that I never stop working, and it must be remembered that the output of gramophone records now must be five times as large as it was when I first started the paper. Another valued corres-pondent writes this month deploring the loss of amateur status which the paper has gradually achieved. We all look back with regret on the happy-go-lucky days of youth, but alas, that first fine careless rapture cannot by the laws of nature endure. Moreover, it must be remembered that the gramophone itself is a much less amateur instrument than it was, and that if we started the paper to-day we should not be able to start it in quite the same spirit as we started it in April 1923. Pioneers have a difficult task, it is true, but from another standpoint they have a very easy task. In old days there was always the chance of some happy fluke in recording which gave one an opportunity to wax lyrical. Nowadays recording is on such a high level of excellence that we miss these happy flukes. However, there will be plenty of excitement for me when I get my electric apparatus installed and when I get back to my Balmain, separation from which has been the only fly in the amber of these recent weeks."

I was becoming all the time more and more deeply involved in what was called the Scottish renaissance. That October I presided in Inverness at one of the two "grand concerts" which bring the National Mod to a close. The Mod is more or less the equivalent of the Welsh Eisteddfod. It was the greatest pleasure to get some of the winning singers recorded by Columbia.

As I remember, it was in that autumn that the B.B.C. asked me if I would take on a weekly gramophone hour. I told them it was impossible for me to come to London weekly and suggested that my brother-in-law Christopher Stone should be invited to tackle the job. Christopher did not relish the notion at first, but he agreed, and thus began his remarkable career as a broadcaster. I do not think I exaggerate if I say that for many years he was the listening public's favourite.

In November 1928 I was deep in Nationalist politics, but I turned aside from them to write a few words about Schubert.

"On November 19th one hundred years ago Franz Schubert died of typhus just over two months before his thirty-second birthday. 'Schubert has my soul,' the mighty Beethoven had said of him when he lay fighting death in March of the previous year. Hüttenbrenner, a friend of Beethoven and Schubert, had brought the dying colossus

some of the younger man's songs, of which, turning over the pages,
he had declared, 'Truly in Schubert lives the divine fire.' It was to
a date shortly after this that legend ascribes the visit paid by Schubert
when Hüttenbrenner and Schubert stood beside the bed of the dying
man and he spoke those famous words, 'You, Hüttenbrenner, have
my heart, but Schubert has my soul.' A few days later Schubert was
one of the torch-bearers who escorted the dead Beethoven to the
cemetery to the music of the funeral march from the Sonata Op. 28.
On the way back Schubert stopped with some friends to drink wine,
and after lifting his glass to him whom they had just buried, filled it
again and drank to him who was to be the next. Twenty months
later he died himself.

"These and many other stories of the beloved genius whose
centenary we are celebrating this month will be found in a book by
Mr. Newman Flower[1] which I commend to every reader who
wishes to learn something of the life and surroundings of one who
more kindly than any other composer has led humble aspirants into
the magical world of great music. Readers will learn from this
biography a great deal about the life of an artist, and I should like
to think that some of the thousands whom the Unfinished Symphony
has admitted to a refuge from the toil and care of this twentieth-
century world will give themselves the trouble to ponder for a few
hours the existence, in a nineteenth-century world equally full as
ours of toil and care, of that dear and lovable little man.

"When we were thinking last year about the death of Beethoven,
we were also aware of the fierce struggle of a Titan to live longer and
do more. Schubert seems to have passed from them a hundred years
ago, as might a butterfly in November, and like one of his own
prodigal melodies which are finished as simply as the fragrance of
flowers in a dusky garden whose perfume is caught for a few footsteps and lost again too soon. It is idle to speculate to what lengths
or depths Schubert would have taken his music had he lived his full
span. I have myself always felt profoundly sure that the genius
fated to early death instinctively crowds into his brief life an output
that is more indicative of what he is than of what he might become.
If Keats and Shelley had been destined to live longer we should
never have had their glory of premature blooming. The plant that
knows it is doomed to die soon, either because it is growing in unkind
soil or because it is aware of some radical weakness in itself, will
often flower and seed more profusely than its companions better
placed.

[1] Sir Newman Flower.

"The soul of Beethoven was too tremendous a responsibility for that little man to whom he entrusted it. Yet it would not be fanciful to hear Beethoven's soul in that last great Quintet for two violins, viola and two violoncellos. And is it too fanciful to perceive in that funeral march of the Trio in E flat major, which was performed at a concert on the anniversary of Beethoven's death, an echo of his funeral, and in the way he turns the sombre little tune to favour and to prettiness, a feeling of great embarrassment in the possessor of that too mighty soul?

"Let that pass. We devotees of the gramophone may be sure of one thing and that is how much Schubert would have enjoyed making the world-wide appeal he is able to make to-day. How near all the great composers are to us—so much nearer with their centenaries than most of the great poets and painters. It seems impossible to doubt that music has still greater wonders of art to unfold, or that we shall not soon get another Schubert to give out his melodies. He would not go so ill-rewarded now. But to Schubert will always remain the honour of having been the first to express in song this new self-conscious world of ours. He is truly the first modern song-writer."

By the beginning of 1929 we were beginning to get worried about the N.G.S. and I preached a little sermon in January:

"I want to say a few words about the National Gramophonic Society this month. To be frank, we are not getting the support from our readers on this side of the Atlantic that we get from the other. I fully recognize the growing embarrassment for the purse of the riches which the recording companies offer us every month, but there have been several occasions lately when I have had to ask myself whether there is still any real need for such a society as ours. It is beginning to look as if the greater and lesser recording companies were providing all the chamber music that the public at home can absorb, and it was with this feeling of uneasiness about the value of the N.G.S. that I recently put out a 'feeler' in the matter of song recording. I should like to be able to announce that the response I received was more encouraging than it has been, but though several enthusiasts have acclaimed the idea and given us the benefit of their suggestions, the general response has not been lively enough to encourage us to proceed any further with this scheme at present. We are still receiving enough support for our publications of chamber music to warrant our continuing with them, but if we are merely going to record charming Quartets of Haydn and Mozart, which will inevitably sooner or later be given to us by the recording companies, I shall have to consider seriously the value of our activities, which are, as may be imagined, a great additional strain upon an already overworked staff. At this point let me print a delightful letter we have received from Mr. William Braid White, whose monthly articles are a most refreshing feature of the *Talking Machine World* in America, which is by far the largest magazine of its kind in the world:

" 'May I thank you most heartily for the perfectly charming records which came a few days ago, giving me the latest fruits of the activities of your wonderful society. The recording in the case of both the Mozart flute quartet and the Haydn "Sunrise" quartet is beautifully done, and it is difficult to say which of the two is better. Music-lovers the world over owe you a tremendous debt of gratitude. The example of the N.G.S. has been very possibly the greatest single force in compelling the commercial manufacturers of records to take their courage in both hands and go forward along artistic lines. It is difficult to know where the record situation would be to-day if it had not been for the high-mindedness and intrepidity of you and your associates.

" 'Thanks to you, we have to-day permanent records of some of the loveliest and least known, both of classical and of modern work. Lovers of chamber music will never cease to bless your name, and among those who sing your praises daily I beg that you will number the name of William Braid White.'

"Encouragement like this does make us feel that it is worth while to persevere, and to Mr. Braid White's spontaneous and generous praise I must add my thanks to that group of enthusiasts who manage the excellent American monthly review called *The Phonograph*. They have never failed to recognize the value of our enterprise, and never hesitated to give it the prominence which we at any rate think it deserves. We are also indebted to some of the most enterprising firms in the U.S.A. for their efforts to make our Society's existence felt over that side. But once again I ask myself, what about the future? It has always been my dream to give opportunities of being heard on the gramophone, not merely to combinations of players, but also to composers, and it has naturally been a great pride and pleasure when such a combination as the International String Quartet is recognized with the scarlet and gold of the H.M.V. Celebrity discs. I do not mean to claim that the International String Quartet could not have reached that eminence without our help.

I am enough of an optimist to believe that all really good things finally gain recognition, but I do claim that a society like the N.G.S. if it were accorded the support it deserves, might hasten that recognition, not merely as I said before, of combinations of players, but also of composers, and it is precisely in the reception that our readers seem inclined to accord to all modern music that I find my chief reason for doubting the value of our work in the immediate future. Whenever we have sent out a voting list we always find that the majority records its vote in favour of old music against new, and if we examine our sales we shall find that most of the contemporary work we have recorded has been comparatively poorly supported, and I ask myself what earthly chance we should have of obtaining the least recognition for the work of our modern composers.

"So long as the big recording companies were shy of publishing chamber music I saw no reason to deprive our supporters of such works as the Brahms Clarinet Quintet, but now that the established works of chamber music are gradually finding their way into the catalogues of the big recording companies, I am anxious to start publishing work that would have no chance at all of being published without our help. I do not ask our public that they should immediately invest their hard-earned money in the often doubtful achievements of modernity, but I do ask them to spare a little more of their money for the lovely and perfectly safe achievements of the past which now adorn our list. By doing so they will give us financial confidence and enable us to make a few experiments with the present.

"The circulation of this magazine increases every month and reflects the increasing popularity of recorded music, but the support accorded to the National Gramophonic Society not merely does not increase, but it shows an inclination to decrease, and so long as that tendency exists it will be impossible for us to extend the utility of the Society. To put it briefly, we cannot afford to take the least risk of publishing any work for which we do not know in advance if there is a genuine demand. This musical conservatism of the public is noticeable all round. Indignant enthusiasts who write and complain of the duplication and re-duplication of stock pieces of music forget that such a duplication and re-duplication is entirely due to the public itself. There does not exist in any recording studio a sinister passion for compelling every barytone to sing the Prologue to Pagliacci, but what does exist is a weary consciousness that, if the new barytone should make his début with an entirely new song, there would be no market for it. There are probably few great discoveries still to be made in the world of cooking, but those mighty geniuses who discovered and bequeathed to posterity such combinations as cucumber with salmon or red-currant jelly with roast saddle of mutton, and a hundred others equally inspired by the genius of gluttony, had not merely courage themselves, but demanded courage from their clients. I do wish that a little of this empirical daring could be cultivated in musical audiences of to-day.

"With a circulation four times as large as it was when we started the National Gramophonic Society we cannot sell any more records than when we first began, and we are now compelled to ask ourselves whether our continued existence serves any really useful purpose to the art to which we are all supposed to be so much devoted."

That month of January was made memorable for me by the broadcast of a dramatized version of my novel *Carnival*.

Eric Maschwitz, who was editing the *Radio Times*, made the version, and it was one of the first productions undertaken by Val Gielgud who had not long been appointed Director of Drama at Savoy Hill. In those days it was believed that half an hour was as long as people could listen to a play. *Carnival* began at 9.50 p.m. and went on until midnight. It was a tremendous success. I received over 400 letters from enthusiastic listeners, and what above all made it a success was a scene in which the girls of the ballet sang old music-hall songs of fifteen years earlier, the leading performer being Miss Hermione Gingold. The B.B.C. learnt the appeal of old songs on that January night and for the last twenty-five years old songs have been staple entertainment. The panel for effects was used for the first time. I myself read pieces of narrative linking the scenes, which was an uncanny experience because I was alone in a remote studio and dependent for my cues on the flicker of a green light. No arrangement had been made then for the narrator to listen through earphones to what was going on and he sat in absolute silence, wondering each time whether they had forgotten to flick him his cue.

I chose the incidental music myself, and I certainly could not have done that four or five years earlier. As it was, the whole of the music was chosen over a lunch-table in under an hour, and to judge by the enthusiastic letters from listeners well chosen. For this the gramophone deserved all the credit.

An indication of my reaction to electric reproduction was the fact that on some excuse or another I put off saying anything about the installation on Jethou for four months. Even then I was writing:

"I have not reached in my own mind a clear view of electric reproduction. I do not mean by that that I have any doubt of its gradually superseding our present method of reproduction, but I fancy that a general use of electric devices is a great deal further off than at first I thought it was. At present the chief objection to electric reproduction is not the complication or expense of it, but the inclination of every electrical enthusiast to love his machine a little bit more than he loves his music and the difficulty of resisting the temptation to show off to listeners the sheer volume of sound he can extract from it. The result is that always at some time or another the record will be trying to give more than it is capable of giving. You find exactly the same tendency among Wireless enthusiasts. One day I shall see a miracle; that will be when a Wireless enthusiast enters a room in the middle of a performance and sits down in the nearest armchair without turning one of his knobs. I already detect in myself a desire to 'give it a little bit more'. Alas, in the middle of last month the unforeseeable happened and a 'resistance' burned out in my wonderful new electric instrument, so the intensive course of listening to electrical reproduction was interrupted and I was driven back to Balmain's Big Bertha which, spurred on by its electrical rival, performed with what even for her was exceptional brilliancy."

Presently I roused the musical world to a fury by suggesting that we should give names to pieces of music.

"Most of us have at some time or other regretted that discouraging system of nomenclature in music which depends on opus numbers and keys, and I do feel that the time has come when, without offending the susceptibilities of purists, we might make some attempt to give easily remembered names to various pieces of music which at present possess nothing except a number to distinguish them from their peers. Even the most modern painters, who pretend to scorn the representational, still cling to readable titles, however remotely such titles may seem to bear upon the subject depicted. Why is Schubert's *Unfinished Symphony* the most popular in the world? Surely because at the back of many people's minds is the idea that death cut short his accomplishment. A romantic story has been woven into the very texture of the music, and many listeners find in its gentle melancholy an illustration of their own fanciful reflections. This is just the kind of melody, they feel of that second movement, which a young man at death's door might snatch from the threshold of eternity. Later on, when they find out more about Schubert, they learn that death had nothing to do with the unfinished state of this symphony, and that it was unfinished only because Schubert never made up his mind how to finish it. However, by the time this has been discovered the music has become familiar and the destruction of a pretty story does not matter.

"Which of the two quintets is the more popular, and which so long as it has a name will go on being the more popular? The *Trout* Quintet. Yet the beauty of that last great quintet known as Opus 163, which actually *was* written almost at the point of death, is immeasurably greater, more poignant and more vital than the dainty charm of The *Trout* Quintet. Suppose now that the late Auguste Van Biene had never toured the world with that play called *The Broken Melody*, what a splendid title 'The Broken Melody' would have been for that last great quintet. Do you remember the way the sublime melody of the adagio is suddenly interrupted by a kind of feverish gaiety, as if the composer had been frightened by the unearthliness of the strain he had evoked and had tried to flee from it back to ordinary life? If there is anything in music more moving than this I have never heard it. Yes, in spite of Van Biene, I feel inclined to call this quintet *The Broken Melody* quintet. Will any reader provide a more suitable name? The *Trout* Quintet only got its name because Schubert used the theme of his song *The Trout* for one of the movements, and for the same reason one of his quartets is called *Death and the Maiden*. It is significant that this Quartet in D minor is the most popular. Yet the Quartet in A minor or the Quartet in C minor would be equally popular if they had names instead of numbers and keys. The glorious Trio in B flat gained its popularity on the gramophone from that remarkable recording of it with Casals, Thibaud, and Cortot. 'I want that trio played by Casals, Thibaud and Cortot,' was the way most people ordered it from their dealers. Will some reader suggest a name for that? The other trio of Schubert's in E flat, which was one of the first records published by the National Gramophonic Soicety, might appropriately be called the '*Funeral of Beethoven*' trio, because it was composed about the time that Beethoven was buried, and the second movement is a funeral march.

"I am prepared to be reminded that the most popular of all Beethoven's symphonies has never had a name. I allude to the Fifth, of course, but even if it has never had a name it has always had a fanciful story attached to it, about 'fate knocking at the door'. And I am sure that many people still think of the Fifth Symphony in C minor as the one which begins with fate knocking at the door. The two next most popular symphonies of Beethoven are the Third and Sixth, both of which have names. The *Eroica* Symphony, in addition to having a name, has a story about Napoleon attached to it, and the *Pastoral* Symphony answers to its description so obviously that it needs no story. Schumann described the Fourth Symphony as a slim Greek maiden between those two Norse giants the Third and Fifth. Why not call the Fourth the *Greek Maiden* Symphony? I find myself now, after playing all the nine symphonies over and over again, considering the Fourth Symphony to be the one I love best of all. For the Eighth Symphony why do we not use Beethoven's own name for it, the *Little One*? And for the Seventh why not take the hint from Wagner, who called it 'The Apotheosis of the dance' and refer to it as the *Dance* Symphony? The Ninth we haven't to bother about, for that is generally known as the *Choral* Symphony.

"The most popular of Haydn's symphonies is the *Surprise,* to which name is attached the story of the composer's practical joke on the old ladies in the front row. Several of Haydn's symphonies have names, and it is worthy of remark that these are the ones which seem to get themselves into the public's head first. Several of Haydn's quartets, too, have names. The *Sunrise* and the *Emperor* come to the mind. I don't think that any of Beethoven's quartets have been given names except the Tenth, which is called the *Harp* quartet, but this is a bad name because to the lay ear it gives an impression that the harp is being used as an instrument. Even such a clumsy title as the *Rasoumovsky* quartets has helped to fix in the public mind the identity of the Seventh, Eighth and Ninth of Beethoven quartets.

The most conspicuous examples of popularity being won by titles occur among the Beethoven sonatas. I don't believe for a moment that the *Moonlight* sonata would have occupied the place it does as a best seller if it had not had that title which Beethoven himself never gave it, any more than he named the piano and violin sonata in F the *Spring* sonata, though just because it is called the *Spring* sonata it has become the most popular of Beethoven's violin and piano sonatas, except the *Kreutzer*. Another name, you see, and one, moreover, used by Tolstoy for a novel. After the *Moonlight* sonata surely the next best known is the *Appassionata,* and after the *Appassionata* the *Pathetic*. There is a great opportunity for some ingenious amateur to fill in the gaps in nomenclature among Beethoven's thirty-two piano sonatas.

"Which is the most popular symphony of Mozart? Undoubtedly the *Jupiter*. What a boon it really would be if we could get the quartets of Mozart allotted names that we could remember! It takes half an arithmetic book (after every quartet of Mozart) before we know for certain which one is being played, and I am sure lots of readers have bought duplicates of Mozart quartets which would never have been bought if they had not been confused by contradictory numbers. Gramophone companies are not the only concerns that would welcome a new system of nomenclature particularly for chamber music. I fancy that the B.B.C. would be grateful for a few names instead of numbers. Half the idiots who write in and grumble about being given chamber music would write and say how much they had enjoyed the performance if, for instance, the first movement of Brahms's quartet in A minor, Op. 51, No. 2, were called 'Your lips are hot, honey, but my big toe is cold', or if Beethoven's Op. 131 in C sharp minor were called 'Your goo-goo eyes, sweetie, are swimming in my heart'."

Percy Scholes rallied to my support and we had to stand back to back to repel the onslaught of the purists.

"My old friend Robin Legge declares in the *Daily Telegraph* that I am wrong in supposing that a composition with a name to it instead of a number would impress itself more on the public fancy; but he rather plays into my hands when he says, 'So far as I am aware publishers were responsible for practically all the more familiar titles now attached to most important compositions that bear them.' Precisely! And presumably they found that it paid them, or they would never have gone on attaching unauthorized titles to great works. The point I wished to make was that the vast extension of the musical audience during the last five years calls for some attempt from everybody interested in music to make the most of it. I maintain that it has definitely helped the popularity of Beethoven's Violin Sonata in F to be called the *Spring* Sonata, just as I would equally maintain that it has helped the popularity of Beethoven's Fifth Piano Concerto to be called the *Emperor*. Neither of these titles was given by the composer, though I fancy the great man himself was always feeling out toward programme music, which he would never admit himself and which none of his commentators has ever admitted since.

"I do not ask for any alliance between music and literature in giving names. There is much to be said for the onomatopoeic methods of the savages in the hinterland of the three Guianas where, for instance, a motor-car is called a wackawacka, because that is what it sounds like. It may be possible to find titles on the same principles for various unnamed musical compositions, which would obviate the necessity that all good musical critics dread of tainting them with literature. I have always thought that it was a great mistake when modern painters, in their flight from the representational, did not abandon their literary baggage to the pursuing Philistines. When the first exhibition of the Post-impressionists was held in London somewhere round about 1910, I went to look at them accompanied by a friend who was always extremely sensitive to any advance in art. Standing in front of one picture, I said to him, 'Surely, my dear X, you cannot maintain that it is possible by looking at this picture to obtain an impression of a dog fight?' After studying it for a minute or two he said, 'Yes, I think I see what the painter is after.' 'Do you?' I retorted; 'then you are cleverer than he is, for this particular picture is labelled in the catalogue *Woman Swimming*.' But if the painter had called that particular picture *Mingle Mungle* or even *Hi-tiddley-hi-ti*, all argument about its programme would have been at an end, and I fee 'sure that both X and myself would have reached a truer idea of what the painter was really after. For Robin Legge to argue with me that it is no handicap for a quartet of Mozart to be called Quartet No. 72 in C sharp minor (K 1122) is, I think, rash. If the Fourth Quartet of Beethoven had been called the *Summer* Quartet, and if the Sixth had been called the *Autumn* Quartet, I am convinced that the great public would remember each of them much more readily, and for the life of me I cannot see what objection there is to affixing such harmless labels."

Then Basil Maine launched an attack in the *Morning Post*:

"Let me insist to Mr. Maine that I am not asking for names to be given in the spirit of modern programme music. The *Archduke Trio*, for instance, is surely a harmless name to give Beethoven's Trio No. 7 in B flat major, Op. 97. But there is one sentence which I must take out from the rest of the article and pin up for a moment. 'It is well,' said Mr. Maine, 'to look upon this feverish interest in music with suspicion. It is akin to an alcoholic reaction; inevitably, a period of depression must follow.' I do not think that any depression will follow if musicians are able to supply the world with great works of art in the same proportion that writers continued to give the world great works of art after the invention of printing. I may personally think that the invention of printing was a disaster; I may personally think that the invention of the gramophone and wireless

N

was a disaster; I may personally think that the invention of the internal combustion engine was a disaster; but whatever my personal opinion may be, the only possible attitude for me to adopt is a determination to make the most of and get the best out of all these inventions.

"There was a significant article by Mr. Ernest Newman in the *Sunday Times*, in which he practically put forward the theory that the only musical form certain of enduring vitality was opera. Now where is Mr. Laurence Binyon's definition of music as material which is no material? or Walter Pater's highest art in which form and matter are one? Musicians have a right to suspect this feverish interest of the public in music; but the public is equally entitled to suspect the creative ability of modern musicians to produce the goods. At present the public looks like being starved between the stale and the indigestible."

Percy Scholes asked:

"Why do my fellow critics oppose the Editor of *The Gramophone* who is giving publicity to a practical general proposition? There is no finer spirited or more thoughtfully conscientious set of men in Britain than the London music critics, and they are (most of them) genuinely wishful for the greater popularity of the art they serve. But their treadmill life is necessarily narrowing. Except for one or two younger men who are sent by their senior colleagues to occasional competitions, festivals and the like, they don't see life. They daily perambulate just that short well-beaten track that leads from the Aeolian Hall to the Wigmore, from the Wigmore to the Queen's, and the Queen's back to the Aeolian. At this time of the year they occasionally get half-a-mile further afield to Covent Garden and on Saturday and Sunday a few of them actually go right out to Kensington Gardens district and accept the musical hospitality of that sincere music lover, the Prince Consort. Occasionally there comes as a blessed relief a provincial festival, Leeds, Gloucester or Norwich, perhaps. But all their life through (and some of them have been at this sad game for twenty, thirty or more years) they are attending the conventicles of the elect. They are good Christians, but they know little of any preachings to the heathen or any answering of sceptical objections in Hyde Park.

"Here is the editor of the British Music Society's *Bulletin* telling us:

"'The proposal set forth by the Editor of *The Gramophone* does

not take into account the fact that if all the big works in the gramophone lists were christened, the buying public would be in exactly
the same difficulty as before, for how shall a man tell whether the
Fire alarm sonata has a greater claim to his attention than the
Steeplechase quartet?

" 'You see, the dear fellow simply can't grasp the point. Of
course *Steeplechase* Quartet doesn't tell the man in the street any
more about the quality of the quartet than did *Quartet in A flat*, Op.
93. What *Steeplechase* does, that *A flat*, Op. 93 doesn't, is to give the
composition a "handle" by which the man in the street can take
hold of it. If he hears the "Steeplechase" broadcast, and likes it, he
can tell his pals in the train next morning and discuss it with them,
and they will know what he's talking about and give their views
too.' "

My own last words were:

"Mr. Percy Scholes's entry into the discussion about names has
provoked a re-opening of the discussion by Feste in the *Musical Times*
of August 1st. He argues wittily and well, as one would expect,
against the proposed sacrilege by Mr. Scholes and myself; but at the
end of his article the reader is left with the impression that Feste
resents any extension of the popularity of music. This is what he has
to say about the man in the street:

" 'But the man in the street usually has his *Radio Times* at hand,
and in any case the work is described by the announcer before being
played. Is the man in the street so lazy, or such a fool, that he cannot
write down a key or a number as easily as a fancy title? I, for one,
am getting very tired of the man in the street to whom art and
artists are supposed to salaam so abjectly. If His High Mightiness
doesn't think good music is worth a little trouble, let him go without
it.'

"Very well, then, let the man in the street go without music,
and if musicians prefer to exist in an archaic mumbo jumbo world
let them do so; it will not worry the man in the street, that is a sure
thing. The point Mr. Scholes and I have tried to make is that for
the benefit of musicians, but by no means necessarily for the
benefit of music, we wish to give the classics the benefit of what the
classical composers would certainly have given themselves if they
had been writing to-day. It is not even as if opus numbers provided
an accurate time table of the composer's work, or we should not get
a quartet of Schubert written at the age of seventeen labelled Opus

168. The comparative lack of fertility of contemporary composers compared with that of their predecessors may insure that an opus number will label a quartet or a quintet with sufficient distinction, a single string quartet or quintet may be all that he has written in either form.

"An American commentator on this argument argued with singular ineptness that the César Franck Symphony was one of the most popular symphonies, and that the absence of any kind of label was a proof that I did not know what I was talking about. But who wants to give a label to César Franck's only symphony? It is perfectly easy to remember César Franck's sonata, or César Franck's quintet, or César Franck's quartet. It is when one asks people to remember the dozens of string quartets by Haydn or Mozart that one wishes for a more memorable description than Op. 76, No. 5. I have never suggested treating them as programme music, but if one quartet of Mozart can be called the *Huntsman* quartet, why cannot another with only an opus number be called the *Blue* or the *Green* quartet, or anything else that may seem vaguely appropriate? To argue as Feste does that such titles as the *Pathétique* and the *Appassionata* are tolerated because the consensus of musical opinion has decided that they fit, is to throw up the sponge in favour of Mr. Scholes and myself, who are only anxious to find titles which the consensus of musical opinion will accept as suitable. If *any* titles not given by the composer himself are justifiable, then all titles are justifiable and if Feste enjoys the notion that the Prussian Academy of Arts and Sciences is now collecting evidence to obtain the passing of a law in Germany for the safeguarding of the musical classics, it is only one more piece of evidence of the conspiracy among intellectuals to Teutonize this country. If Mr. Scholes and I label the whole 1248 works which comprise the opus numbers now in existence, we should certainly not achieve such a disservice to music by placing the classics under the tutelage of the Prussian Academy of Arts and Sciences.

"The ill-concealed chagrin with which so many musical critics regard the violation of their pet sanctuaries would be laughable if obscurantism were ever laughable. Some of them have written more like gamekeepers than critics about my suggestion, more as if they were trying to preserve salmon than sonatas, quails than quartets. The disrepute into which many a composer and painter and writer falls when the vulgar herd begins to enjoy his work is a notorious phenomenon. Small-minded exclusiveness has been as much the enemy of art as it has been of religion. What maggot in the human brain makes a work of art more desirable because it can only be enjoyed by the few?"

A quarter of a century later I remain obstinately convinced that Scholes and I were right and that our shocked antagonists were wrong. I find that I am still in agreement with what I wrote at this date about the future of music and art in general:

"I have lately had occasion to read the life of Robert Schumann and I have learnt two facts which particularly interest me. One is that it was Schumann's desire to call his First Symphony in B flat *A Spring Symphony*. He intended to give the movements separate titles: *The Coming of Spring, Evening, Happy Playmates*, and *Full Spring*. However, in deference apparently to academic prejudice, he gave up the idea and merely wrote a letter to the poet Böttger to tell him that it was a poem of his about spring which had inspired him to write the symphony. In a letter to Spohr he disclaimed any intention of descriptive colouring, though he wrote to another musician, who was going to conduct the symphony, urging him to breathe into the orchestra some of that longing for spring which had obsessed him when he was composing it. The trumpet call at the beginning was to be a summons bidding Nature awake. After that the music was to suggest the tender green of spring and the quiver of butterflies' wings. No sooner has Schumann committed himself to this than he hastens to assure the conductor that these are only fancies which came to him after the symphony was finished. Then he obviously feels that he is being insincere and adds that he cannot help thinking of the last movement as spring's farewell, for which reason he does not want it to be taken too lightly.

"All this reveals a most interesting struggle in a composer's mind. Schumann, of course, was the perfect highbrow, and though in his day the mark of highbrowism was an exaggerated sensibility which would horrify modern Bloomsbury, the state of mind which revered Jean Paul Richter was essentially the same as that which nowadays reveres Freud. There is always in the highbrow attitude the spirit of a close corporation. It is always a distinction to be able to enjoy what the mob is incapable of enjoying. Schumann would have enjoyed such a display of sensibility as that *Spring Symphony*, if he could have been sure that he was not being obvious; but he was not prepared to ignore academic prejudice, and being himself a critic he dreaded the mockery of critics. So in the end the *Spring Symphony* became the First Symphony in B flat, Opus 38.

"It will be remembered that Beethoven was always anxious that his *Pastoral Symphony* should not be accused of being what we now-adays call programme music. Musicians have always perceived the danger to music in allowing it to be what I may call materialized. Yet, if we examine the development of music, we cannot help recognizing that it has evinced an unbroken tendency to materialize itself more and more; and it seems to me that the gramophone and the radio between them are going to quicken the pace of this materialization. I have no doubt whatever that the only future for art in our present megalopolitan civilization—forgive these long words, but the monstrous swarming of modern city life demands verbal monstrosities to express it suitably—the only future for art, I repeat, lies with music.

"The tendency of literature, unless we are to accept a phenomenon like James Joyce as a mere freak of morbidity, will be to develop into a personal use of words. That means the writer will gradually usurp what was the function of music, for if every writer is to have his own vocabulary it is clear that most of his emotion and thought will be incommunicable. It is perfectly easy for any impudent charlatan of words to trade on the eccentricity of a man of genius like Joyce. Paris is haunted at the moment by numbers of half-baked young Americans who are under the impression that they stand for some new and vital creative impulse in the mind of man, but who are actually mere hobbledehoys of a primitive culture. But we need not go to Paris to find *les précieuses ridicules*, or *les précieux* either. We may find them in Hampstead and Chelsea without difficulty. The other day a young highbrow hostess asked me if I admired James Joyce's last book. I told her I could not understand more than a word here and there, and that I doubted if she could. She assured me she could understand it perfectly, so I issued a challenge. I said I would read now half a page from Joyce's book, now improvise myself in the same style; and I offered if she could tell me once where Joyce left off and I began, or if she could explain what I meant by one sentence of my improvisation, I would buy her this book, which cost three guineas. She was not once able to tell when it was Joyce and when it was myself, and so I kept my three guineas and took leave to doubt whether she understood much of Joyce. All that is not a criticism of Joyce's writing, but it *is* a criticism of his audience. Some people maintain that Joyce is a forerunner, and that one day everybody will understand this language of his. That kind of statement about a hundred years hence is easy to make, because we shall none of us be here to prove it right or wrong; but if Joyce's latest vocabulary is not understood by his contemporaries it is far less likely to be understood by posterity. Who will claim that the mighty work of Rabelais is better understood to-day than when he wrote it?

"And as the experimenters in new literary forms are reaching out toward what they suppose to be a richer language to express the more intricate complicacy of modern life, so too are the painters determined to become less and less representational; and music, which hitherto has been able to do much of what literature and painting and sculpture seem ambitious to do in the future, tends to become more and more representational. I wish somebody better equipped than myself would trace in the history of music the gradual development of the personal appeal. Anyway, by the time of Schumann it had become as direct in music as it had long ago become in poetry, so that he need not really have felt any qualms about calling that first symphony *A Spring Symphony*. Nevertheless, if that symphony were played to an audience of a thousand people and not one of that audience were aware of the emotion which had inspired the music, I would wager that perhaps not half a dozen, perhaps not even one, would be able to recognize the emotion of spring, however carefully the conductor tried to make the music take on hues of tender green and flutter like a butterfly. That being the case, it is plain that any attempt to give titles to untitled music based on a pretended emotion or reaction to them would be ridiculous, and particularly ridiculous if such a system of nomenclature were to be applied to the works of masters like Haydn and Mozart whose music, however personal it might seem to their contemporaries, affects us nowadays by its remoteness and beautiful externality.

"So let me make it clear once and for all that I do not and never did want to give names which would impute a representational or emotional meaning to works which at present are only known by opus numbers and keys. At the same time, if the life of the composer can provide an appropriate name, by all means let us take advantage of it. If we had not known from Schumann's own correspondence that this particular symphony had been inspired by spring we could have found for it another name; we could have called it *The Rusty Pen* Symphony, because it was written with a rusty pen which he picked up on Beethoven's grave. What possible harm could such a title have done? It would certainly have fixed in the mind of the public that particular symphony of Schumann's, and it would at the same time have been a link with the past.

"Has any critic seriously considered what the effect of that is going to be? Has any critic asked himself what would be the state of a man who could claim that he had read everything in the world worth reading? Yet even within my lifetime I may hope to have heard in my own room all the music in the world worth hearing. If musicians would get together and use the gramophone in the way it should be used they would be able to knock out bad taste in music. It is far too late to do anything with the unimaginably vast accumulation of literature. Moreover, literature in future is likely to become more and more purely utilitarian, and to keep up with it will be such a tax on people that the literature of the past will be read only by a few Eng. Litters engaged upon potting it down and making it digestive for the megalopolitan swarms of the dreary future. Two hundred years hence all these desperate efforts of to-day to put new life into poetry, into prose, into painting, into sculpture, and into drama may have ceased, and the whole of artistic expression may be concentrated on music. Why I am anxious to persuade people into listening to good music is because I dread to see the continuity of culture completely broken. Nobody who reads the literary critics of to-day can be anything but impressed by their lamentable absence of equipment. They are clever, but so few of them have read enough. The abandonment of Latin and Greek has already been shattering in its effect on the younger generation. Do let us try to preserve the continuity of musical culture. The gramophone has given us the opportunity.

"We must not be deterred by the kind of prejudice that kept Schumann from calling his B flat Symphony *A Spring Symphony*. If we cannot overcome the obstinate refusal of the average man to like the best in music, let us cheat him into liking it, because after all, he will never appreciate it until he likes it. Do not let us weigh down music with great names in the way we have weighed down literature. We all agree that Milton was a great poet but how many of us have read *Paradise Lost* from beginning to end? That need not happen in music, because we have the time and we shall gradually have the opportunity to know all the great music of the world. We shall have no *Paradise Losts* and *Divine Comedies* and *Iliads* and *Odysseys* and *Don Quixotes* and *Aeneids* unread by the many. The trouble with cultivating good taste in literature is the impossibility of finding the necessary time to do it automatically. Should a man retire to a cottage with the nine Beethoven symphonies on gramophone records and play them over and over again because he had nothing else to play if he had any ear for music at all, he would at the end of a year surely have better taste in music than he had at the beginning of it. Shut that same man up in a cottage with *Paradise Lost* and *Paradise Regained*, and it will by no means follow that at the end of of it he will have any better taste in literature. You may find people in remote villages who will have read of great literature nothing except the Authorized Version of the Bible, who read it day and night and yet who in spite of drinking from that glorious source are as incapable of appreciating other great literature as if they had never read a line of the Bible. The field of literature is too wide for this process of good taste to work as automatically as it does in the case of music.

"To return to a discussion of titles for music, not with any notion of interpreting the composer's mood, but merely to mark a date in his life. Take, for instance, the Fourth Symphony of Tchaikovsky, which is by far the most cheerful piece of music with the exception of the *Caprice Italien* that Tchaikovsky ever wrote. We might expect, remembering the dreadful gloom of some of his compositions, that when he wrote the Fourth Symphony he was enjoying a period of relative happiness. On the contrary, in 1877, he had made a most undesirable marriage with a woman he did not love and had separated from her nine weeks later. He had left Moscow utterly worn out, in bad health, without much money, and in a state of despair. As soon as he reached Petrograd, or Leningrad, or whatever we are to call it, he had collapsed and spent some time on the verge of brain fever, and finally with his brother Anatole had left Russia and gone to live in Switzerland and Italy. At that time he was writing about himself as 'a finished-off man', but the music he wrote during this period was the Fourth Symphony. It is dedicated 'To my Best Friend'. Who was that? It was Madame von Meck, a widow with eleven children and a large fortune, ten years older than himself. She managed with beautiful tact to make him accept a yearly allowance of money, and thus be able to write what he wanted without worry, so that perhaps the high spirits of the Fourth Symphony is due to financial relief. Yet, if I may be egotistical for a moment, the more worried and depressed I am the more easily I write comedy. On the other hand, I have never yet, thank Heaven, been reduced to the state of melancholy in which poor Tchaikovsky spent so much of his life. He was hypochondriacal and homosexual, and among other notions he had an idea that his head was coming off, so that sometimes when he was conducting he used to hold it on with one hand. Surely there would be no harm in calling the Fourth Symphony of Tchaikovsky the *Best Friend* Symphony, and if by doing so I could induce two or three of these spoilt men in the street to give themselves the pleasure of getting acquainted with this symphony I should not feel I had committed a great crime against art.

"And now I must say a few words about the second fact in Schumann's life which particularly interested me. His wife, the great pianist, could not bear chamber music. In looking up the life of Tchaikovsky to check the dates for my remarks about the Fourth Symphony I reminded myself of something I had forgotten, which was that Tchaikovsky himself could not for a long time stand chamber music. He, too, found the timbre of the string quartet unpleasant, and it was not until he was thirty-one years of age that he wrote the string Quartet in D major. But even when he surrendered to the string quartet, he held out against the trio, and when Madame von Meck begged him to compose a pianoforte trio he told her that it was torture to him to have to listen to a piano with violin and violoncello. Finally, however, he surrendered and composed that exquisite trio in memory of a great artist—his friend and benefactor, Nicolas Rubinstein.

"Looking back to a time when it was something worse than boredom for me to listen to chamber music, and finding in it now a pleasure which I cannot hope to express in words, I shall ride my hobby-horse once more round the ring and beg all readers who still think that they cannot endure chamber music to try again. Let them remember that Tchaikovsky and Clara Wieck both disliked it once upon a time."

At the same time as this outcry by musicians against my sacrilegious proposal I find myself going to war on behalf of literature.

It began thus:

"I was thoroughly exasperated by a record of Walter Glynne singing Sanderson's *Until*, and what is called *Annabelle Lee* (Leslie). It does not matter what happens to the words in a song like *Until*, and if Miss Marjorie Hayward chooses to play a violin obbligato like the leader of a night club orchestra that does not matter in a song like this, but when a composer called Leslie debauches with his dull music one of the loveliest lyrics ever written, and when that delightful tenor, Mr. Walter Glynne, makes half-a-dozen mistakes in the words of that lovely lyric, it matters very much. It matters very much, too, that the Editorial Staff of His Master's Voice should confuse Edgar Allan Poe's poem spelt *Annabel Lee* with a Tom Fool dance tune called *Annabelle Lee*."

More in sorrow than in anger His Master's Voice protested with grave dignity in a letter to me:

"With reference to your criticism in the issue of *The Gramophone* this month of Mr. Walter Glynne's record of *Annabelle Lee*, I am enclosing a copy of this song as published by Messrs. Cramer and would suggest that you compare this with Mr. Glynne's record, when I think you will find that Mr. Glynne gives a word-perfect performance according to the published copy. If you agree that this is so you may perhaps consider it due to Mr. Walter Glynne to correct the charge of 'half-a-dozen mistakes' made in your article.

"With regard to the spelling of the title, you will see from the attached copy of this song that we have been guilty of no other error than an adherence to the printed copy, which is necessary for identification purposes, although we are quite aware that Edgar Allan Poe did not spell the title in this manner."

I replied:

"I hasten to acquit Mr. Glynne of carelessness with regard to his singing of the words as published in the song, but at the same time I must impute a more culpable carelessness to him and to the Gramophone Company and to Messrs. Cramer, and to the late Sim Reeves and to the late Henry Leslie, the composer, whose name is printed in large letters on the cover of the song whereas Edgar Allan Poe's name appears only on the inside. Here is the poem as written by Poe:

ANNABEL LEE

It was many and many a year ago,
    In a kingdom by the sea,
That a maiden there lived whom you may know
    By the name of Annabel Lee;
And this maiden she lived with no other thought
    Than to love and be loved by me.

I was a child and she was a child,
    In this kingdom by the sea;
But we loved with a love *which* was more than love—
    I and my Annabel Lee;
With a love that the wingèd seraphs of heaven
    Coveted her and me.

And this was the reason that, long ago,
   In this kingdom by the sea,
A wind blew out of a cloud, chilling
   My beautiful Annabel Lee;
So that her highborn *kinsman* came
   And bore her away from me,
To shut her up in a sepulchre
   In this kingdom by the sea.

The angels, not half so happy in heaven,
   Went envying her and me—
Yes!—that was the reason (as all men knew,
   In this kingdom by the sea)
That the wind came out of the cloud by night
   Chilling and killing my Annabel Lee.

But our love it was stronger by far than the love
   Of those who were older than we—
   Of many far wiser than we—
And neither the angels in heaven above,
   Nor the demons down under the sea,
Can ever dissever my soul from the soul
   Of the beautiful Annabel Lee.

For the moon never beams without bringing me dreams
   Of the beautiful Annabel Lee;
And the stars never rise but I feel the bright eyes
   Of the beautiful Annabel Lee;
And so, all the night-tide, I lie down by the side
Of my darling—my darling—my life and my bride,
   In *the* sepulchre there by the sea,
   In her tomb by the sounding sea.

"I have printed in italics the four words changed in the song version and the lines omitted altogether. It may seem a trifle to print 'that' instead of 'which', but it has been well said that the proper use of 'that' and 'which' is a great test of whether a man can or cannot write good English. Poe wrote 'which' with a full sense of its value. He wrote 'which' to follow up the 'with' which precedes it. He wanted to avoid the double 'th' of 'with' and 'that', and finally he wanted to emphasize the greatness of the love by using 'which'. 'Which' is a stronger relative pronoun here than 'that' would have been. A love *that* is more than love sounds conventional and cold as a phrase when put beside a love *which* is more than love.

So much for the first mistake, which looks like a mere trifle until it is analysed.

The next mistake is outrageous, and it proves that this feeble composer missed the whole point of the poem. It is the highborn 'kinsman' not 'kinsmen' who came, and that highborn 'kinsman' was Death. Highborn kinsmen sound like nothing but the sentimental Gothic vapourings of the mid-Victorian misses for whom the composer was writing. Even if the highborn kinsman is not taken to mean Death, the singular evokes a more menacing picture than the weak plural.

"The next mistake is the printing of 'but' instead of 'for'. Of course, the justification for this would be that the two preceding verses were omitted, and that 'but' is a more suitable conjunction than 'for' to introduce the poet's next statement. At the same time, the 'but' by anticipating the 'b' in 'beams' kills the music of the words. Poe wrote 'for', and he followed up the 'for' with the 'v' in never. He followed up that with the 'f' in 'beautiful', and he picks it up again with the 'f' in 'feel'. The short vowel sound in 'but' ruins the broad vowel sounds in 'beams' and 'beautiful', and though there is no broad vowel sound in 'bringing' the double consonant softens the explosive effect of the 'b'.

"The last mistake is the substitution of 'her' for 'the' in the last line but one, thereby wrecking the poetic intention of the last line completely, quite apart from spoiling the alliteration of 'the' and 'their'. Surely everybody with any notion of language will perceive the value of the contrast between the cold despair of the definite article and the warmth of passion which the use of the possessive pronoun rekindles as it were, so that what was dead becomes alive again.

"It is the failure of musicians to appreciate the difference between a 'that' and a 'which', a 'but' and a 'for', which ruins ninety per cent of the English lyrics set to music. The music of a song is provided, or should be provided, to suit the words; the words of a poem should not merely be an excuse for a musician to show off a tune that has come into his head. When I suggested recently that various pieces of chamber music might have names allotted to them for the benefit of the public, musicians all over the world waxed most indignant at the notion of such sacrilege. Yet musicians have committed far more crimes against poets than poets have ever dreamed of committing against musicians. It is certainly a great crime for some poetaster to write words to a melody like Schubert's Serenade or Chopin's Nocturne in E flat, but it is just as great a crime for a composer to take a poem like *Annabel Lee* and drape it with his own scanty talent. The habit of leaving out the name of the author of the words encourages the musician to suppose that his musical doggerel is of more importance than the words. It was nothing short of impudence to call this song '*Annabelle Lee*, by Henry Leslie', without any mention of the poet's name on the cover, and call him Edgar Poe on the inside page."

Chapter 17

THE success of the *Carnival* broadcast and close association with various people at Savoy Hill suggested that the time was ripe for a weekly review of broadcasting. We moved the offices of *The Gramophone* from Frith Street to Soho Square in November 1929. Christopher Grieve (that is Hugh MacDiarmid the poet) came down from Montrose to edit the paper, and in the expectation that the wireless trade would be as intelligent as the recording companies and makers of gramophones we felt confident that *Vox*, the new paper, would be a success. Unfortunately the last thing that the wireless trade wanted was to encourage the B.B.C. to improve their programmes. On the contrary they would have liked the B.B.C. to cater exclusively for the little man who was buying a wireless set then as to-day he is buying a television set. The popular Press was continuing to moan about the 'highbrow' tendencies of the B.B.C. and the wireless trade firmly believed that these 'highbrow' tendencies were spoiling business. The B.B.C. itself at top level would not help an enterprise which they feared might lead the younger members of the staff astray. The enterprise in fact was premature, and a year later all that was left of *Vox*, *The Radio Critic* and *The Broadcast Review* was the incorporation of their names in *The Gramophone*. If at that date anybody had prophesied that serious radio criticism would be a feature of the Press within a few years he would have been laughed at.

While I was in the Outer Hebrides in that summer of 1930 I received a long letter from one of the original subscribers to *The Gramophone*, the burden of which could be summed up in one sentence.

"Is there already a tendency to the hardening of the arteries which comes with advancing years? In spite of signs of increasing prosperity I sadly miss the youthful fire and zeal which gave us the tests and competitions for gramophones and sound-boxes and the gramophone congress. The voyages of the Elizabethan mariners have given place to the ordered monotony of modern life."

In one of those islands of the West I wrote an editorial for our August issue in which I tried to answer some of the questions of my correspondent. I said that his letter had provided me with a suitable text for a sermon (a sermon as much to myself as to my readers) for the month of August because that letter made me wonder whether *The Gramophone* itself had not reached the August of its life.

"There is a verse in one of the old ballads which I cannot quote correctly, being far from any books, but it runs something like this:

> I saw a dead man's ghost beyond the Isle of Skye,
> And when I looked again, behold! that man was I.

"I have spoilt the quotation, I am afraid, but it is so appropriate to myself who am at this very moment beyond the Isle of Skye that I cannot resist using it. I wonder if I can make clear without either appearing hopelessly weak or hopelessly insincere how profoundly I agree with my correspondent's views, while at the same time postulating that the change he deplores was inevitable from the start. In doing so I shall have to be even more egotistical than my readers must think I usually am. My life up to date has been conducted in a series of violent enthusiasms which I prefer to call passions, and which many other people would prefer to call crazes. Difficulty and opposition have been the fuel which have fed these fires. When once the object has been attained I have usually turned to another. Among such enthusiasms was my intelligence work in Athens during the war. From one room, one typewriter, one assistant, and an allowance of £50 a month to deal with the problem of checking German espionage and propaganda in Greece I ended two years later with forty officers, a dozen clerks and secretaries, a dozen typewriters, and an allowance of £9000 for a month's work. Need I add that the personal touch was not quite so obvious in August 1917 as it had been in August 1915? Worn out in body and mind I was finally given indefinite sick leave, though kept in uniform until the end of 1918 lest I should suppose myself free to express what I thought of the mess that was being made of the Balkan situation. Within another five years I had the bitterness and humiliation of seeing the betrayal of Greece by that despicable Coalition Government which would have betrayed anybody or anything in order to get clear of Mr. Lloyd George's leadership. I had also the bitterness and humiliation of being too ill to feel that I could be of the least use in helping the struggle of Ireland against that same execrable

Coalition Government, for which the people of England like a flock of sheep had bleated their votes. In my spiritual discomfort, so deep a discomfort that I did not dare try to express it with my pen, I found a measure of solace in acquiring the islands of Herm and Jethou. There followed the disappointment of discovering that even an island so small as Herm might involve the destruction of one's individuality, and that the odious incidents of modern life were conspiring to make mechanical and commercial what should have been a genuine freedom.

"It was during the financial stress of trying to support more than my over-driven pen was capable of supporting that *The Gramophone* appeared in my life to provide a new passion. The moment I chose to launch the new magazine was sufficiently unpropitious to give a crusading zest to the enterprise. Nothing seemed more improbable than the attainment within a few years of what at that date looked unlikely ever to be attained. There was so much to do. Radio had just appeared, and people were prophesying the complete disappearance of the gramophone as a medium for music. The wretched support which the gramophone was receiving from professional musicians gave no encouragement to the recording companies to attempt on any scale the publication of anything except a snippet of good music. I need not recount the tale of the gramophone's progress during the last seven years, but it is surely obvious that the magazine which takes its name from the instrument should, with the mechanical perfection of that instrument, perfect itself mechanically at the same time. I do not feel that it would have been possible for us to maintain the attitude of irresponsibility which characterized our first period, for though the big recording companies were extraordinarily patient with our amateur irresponsibility, they could not have continued to accept us as the leading organ of gramophonic opinion unless we showed ourselves ready to settle down to a certain staidness.

"The attitude of H.M.V. and Columbia toward the Gramophone Congress, the discontinuance of which our correspondent deplores, was a warning that we must put a term to our activities. I think myself that both H.M.V. and Columbia could have afforded to take part in the Gramophone Congress and encourage it; but I thoroughly appreciate the reasons which prevented their seeing their way to doing so. Without the support of the two leading recording companies, the Congress was too incomplete to serve its full purpose, while the financial worry and the physical strain upon the staff was too much of an anxiety with which to saddle ourselves unless we were convinced that such a Congress was a representative gathering.

"I regret as much as our correspondent those competing instruments and those gold medals which were awarded so solemnly. But I do not believe that such competitions would any longer be effective. I do not believe that any audience could sit still and listen nowadays to hours of electrical reproduction and remain sane. After the performance of the first two or three instruments the voting for respective merit would become a farce.

"In estimating the reasons for the decline of *The Gramophone* into a humdrum respectability our correspondent must remember that the general levelling up and standardization in musical reproduction are themselves discouraging to the Celtic predilection for being against the Government, because even the most unreasonable Celt is discouraged by lack of opportunity to criticize.

"I am genuinely diffident about my own qualifications for judging a record. As a musical critic I regard myself as nothing more than the average man of fairly good taste who knows how to express in a readable way his personal impressions. I readily confess that I am no longer capable of writing about records in the *Sunday Pictorial* every week, and then all over again about the same records in *The Gramophone* every month. I may be asking too much in asking my friends to read what I have to say every week in the *Sunday Pictorial* at the cost of twopence, but I am not asking so much as if I were to suggest that they should guarantee me the necessary income to make my views on records exclusive to *The Gramophone*. Moreover, even if they did offer to do this, I should hesitate to take advantage of such an offer, because I do believe that the immense audience of over two million readers which the *Sunday Pictorial* provides every week is worth a great deal of cherishing.

"And then there is the question of the attention paid to theme songs and dance records. I agree with our correspondent that there is an apparent inconsistency in my attitude which looks unpleasantly like selling my soul for cash. I have never, however, pretended to have been converted myself to theme songs or the films in which they can be heard. Many people, and among them Christopher Stone, think that my attitude is rather childishly obscurantist, and they point out that I have no right to edit a paper called *The Gramophone* unless I am willing to give every aspect of the gramophone an equal chance; I cannot discover any good argument against such a contention. I am afraid that as it is I have given a great deal of liberty to my own eccentric opinions, for it is no good pretending that my opinions are regarded as anything else by most people. I have seldom considered expediency when only myself is involved, but *The Gramophone* for good or for ill has grown too big to be the medium of one man's voice, and it would be unfair to the many commercial interests involved if I were to refuse to recognize that some surrender of one's personal prejudices is inevitable. I fear my correspondent will detect sophistry in my plea unless I admit quite frankly that the financial aspect of *The Gramophone* is as important to myself as to any one of those who are associated with me in it. Considering how much I have done of both, I am prepared to maintain that my enthusiasm for novel writing and gramophone criticism has managed to retain as much of the first fine careless rapture as any man can hope to retain who derives his livelihood from self-expression. Still, I recognize that what I have to say about the gramophone must now, after writing so much about it, be liable to show signs of professionalism. The same is no doubt true of some of the novels I write, and I think it was a desire to feel the constructive urge behind my criticism which led me to be enthusiastic enough to believe in the value of Radio criticism.

"The rapid development of the B.B.C. into an immense fossil of Mr. Everyman, which pathetically enough Mr. Everyman in the flesh fails to recognize as himself, was too daunting even for my self-confidence. The B.B.C. is, in fact, the perfect expression of English genius, and as such beyond criticism. The faults of the B.B.C. are inherent in its constitution and in the character of its audience. No change of personnel could do anything to improve it. I regard it with the same unqualified admiration I should give to any of the great inanimate works of mankind, and in writing that last sentence I am only too well aware how nearly in miniature *The Gramophone* is in danger of going the same way as the B.B.C. And yet what can we do nowadays? The trend of evolution seems everywhere to achieve progress at the expense of the individual just as the individual himself develops at the expense of his separate senses. We feel less, see less, hear less, smell less, taste less, than our ancestors; and yet, in the total of what we accomplish with our senses we imagine we understand more. There is nothing which survives the ruin caused by mechanical perfection.

"At the present moment I am engaged with a few other people in trying to secure the independence of Scotland. The task before us is so tremendous that our enthusiasm is unbounded, and yet already I am beginning to dread that glorious moment when we shall achieve our aims and there will seem nothing left remarkable beneath the visiting moon, I believed at first that we should have at least twenty years of uphill struggle, but within a couple of years we have effected such a change in opinion already that within another five years we may be already regretting the days when to be a Scottish Nationalist was to proclaim oneself an unpractical political idealist.

"The longer I live, the better I realize the deadly nature of success. Compare the achievements of French art after the Franco-Prussian War with the achievements of French art to-day. Why have Empires declined and fallen? By being too successful. And I suppose that *The Gramophone* is suffering from prosperity.

"My experience of the National Gramophonic Society has not increased my belief in the willingness of the public to support art for art's sake. It is no use shutting our eyes to the fact that the sales for big musical works are depressingly small, and that, if it were not for these wretched theme songs and the mass production of musical rubbish generally, the recording companies would not be able to give us any big works at all. Our present civilization is based on successful commerce, and it is no use expecting a recording company to be more altruistic than an artificial silk company. I regard a civilization based on commerce as disastrous, and I am old-fashioned enough not to be able to improve on the old platitude that money is the root of all evil.

"When beyond the Isle of Skye I turn on the wireless and listen to the reports of speeches made by notable personages it nauseates me to hear nothing but their sordid remarks about commerce and industry; but if millions of sheep are determined to bleat round a golden calf I am not going to invite the directors of H.M.V. and Columbia to retire into the Egyptian desert like St. Anthony and there practise the major austerities. I should be the first to applaud Mr. Alfred Clark or Mr. Louis Sterling if either of them took it into his head to fast upon the top of a column like St. Simeon Stylites and despise the material world of to-day; but I am not going to suggest to either of them that he should do it because I know perfectly well that if they did the shareholders of H.M.V. and Columbia would at once look for new managing directors, and that the new managing directors would take care that plenty of new theme songs were published every month. I cannot see why we should expect big commercial concerns to show an idealism which the average individual is incapable of showing himself or even of appreciating in others. I am afraid that I am writing as if I were disillusioned, but a bitter wisdom is not necessarily disillusionment. I recognize fully what the correspondent from whose letter I have quoted means; I am ready to admit that much of what he says is deserved. He is good enough to pay a passing compliment to my editorials, but he must remember that I have reserved to myself the right of a proprietor editor to say what he likes. If I had been pinned down to reviews of records each month I fancy he would find my editorials showing sad signs of wear and tear. Nobody is better aware than Christopher Stone and myself how much we owe to the devotion and loyalty of our original readers, but we could not stay where we were and depend on them and their support without gradually going back, and neither of us could afford to run *The Gramophone* as a merely philanthropic, or should I say philharmonic, affair. Perhaps the necessity to earn our own bread and butter makes us more lenient to the desire of the recording companies to earn their bread and butter; perhaps, too, we are gratefully conscious of the debt we owe to their support and loyalty without which the support and loyalty of our die-hard readers would have been of little avail.

"Another correspondent wrote to point out that it was mere priggishness to scoff at the popular songs of the moment and accept with reverence due to antiquity a popular song of an earlier moment like *Sally in Our Alley*. He maintained that the words and the tune of 'Sally' were as cheap and as commonplace as those of any contemporary effusion. Our correspondent is right in calling *Sally in Our Alley* a popular song of the moment, but he is wrong in supposing that its vitality depends in the least on its age. There were hundreds of popular songs contemporary with *Sally in Our Alley*, not one of which is known to anybody nowadays unless he be one of those people who delight in turning over the pages of dusty 18th-century and 17th-century song books. A collection like D'Urfey's *Pills to Purge Melancholy* contains many verses both bawdy and polite and many pleasant little tunes, but they have no vitality—not so much vitality even as say an early volume of one of Francis Day and Hunter's albums of the year's popular songs. No, the magic of *Sally in our Alley* does not depend on its antiquarian interest. The magic is the same magic as the cuckoo's call holds for us when we first hear it in April, as the sweep of the first swallow, as the primroses budding, as the flowers we see blossoming on the window-sill of some squalid tenement. The words of the song are artless and simple enough, and yet since first 'Sally' was sung what other Sally has taken her place? The melody, too, is artless and simple enough, and yet it is always unmistakably the melody of 'Sally'. If any song writer of to-day could wed such simple and artless words with a tune equally simple and artless, but always unmistakably itself and no other tune, why, then his sweetheart might live as long in the hearts of English people as Sally has lived. The conditions of our time do not favour the immortalization of Sallys. Our Sallys nowadays are mostly American and the songs about them last about as long as a piece of chewing-gum. The fact is that nobody writing popular songs at the moment is writing sincerely, that indeed for many years nobody has been writing popular songs sincerely. It may be that the author of 'Sally' only called her 'Sally' because he wanted her to live in an alley, or it may be that he put her to live in an alley because he wanted her to be called Sally. It does not matter; he has managed to convince generation after generation that she was called Sally, and that she and he did live in their alley. It may be that a song like *Daisy Bell* will endure; but I doubt it, because I think that the accidental decorations of Daisy's career like the bicycle made for two and the carriage will not have the power to stir the fancy of the future. Moreover, in the case of *Daisy Bell* the tune really is banal and never unmistakably itself. *Daisy Bell* is a fairly representative song of the last fifty years, which has stood revival with some success, to put up against *Sally in our Alley*; will anybody back her to hold her own with posterity? However, there is much to be said for our correspondent's contention. *Sally in our Alley* is nothing but a popular song of many years ago, and there is no reason why a popular song as good should not be written now, no reason whatever, except that the impulse to write songs is very nearly worn out. They will go on being written, of course, and sung and printed and recorded, but they will be as impermanent as most of the other products of their mediocre period."

In December 1930 we left Jethou and went to live for a while on Eilean Aigas, a romantic island in the River Beauly. It was impossible to move either my records or my books until I had decided where I intended to make my home in Scotland for the next few years, and this was a benefit because it compelled me to pay more attention to the records issued monthly on account of the sudden shrinkage of my repertory. Moreover, taking on the reviewing of books for the *Daily Mail* meant that I was no longer writing about gramophone records for the *Sunday Pictorial*. I was now absolved from the need to listen to records electrically reproduced because I had to return to the acoustical gramophone. I was equipped with an E.M.G. and an E.M. Ginn Expert, and what a relief it was!

Later on with outsize horns these two instruments would accompany me to Barra and remain my only gramophones until I left the island in 1945. During these years electrical reproduction was perfected and when I settled in Berkshire I was given the services of the H.M.V. Electrogram de Luxe and Decola both of which magnificent instruments have accompanied me to Edinburgh and provide me with the music to which this book is being written.

That release from the tyranny of knobs the working of which I never grasped acted like magic upon my gramophone arteries about which my correspondent had asked that uncomfortable question. Significantly, in March 1931 I was writing:

"I have played over the January and February records a great deal more often that I can usually find the time to play new records; and once more I have had impressed upon my mind the importance of repetition so far as one's appreciation of music is concerned. Actually there has been very little music published during these two months with which I was not already familiar, but among it was this magnificent First Symphony of Sibelius, which impresses me more and more every time I hear it. I have found nothing else in music that so completely expresses my own state of mind at the present moment as that first movement, and until a Scottish composer of equal genius arises I shall continue to feel that the spirit of Scotland has been more richly expressed by Sibelius than by anybody. It would be absurd to draw a parallel between the relation of Finland to Russia and the relation of Scotland to England, but it is not too far-fetched to claim that the struggle against natural disadvantages of climate and soil has moulded the Finnish character along the same lines as the Scottish. Therefore, when the differences of racial origin have been taken into account, a marked spiritual affinity seems to emerge. I have often thought how much in common there always seems between Ireland and Poland and between the individual Irishman and the individual Pole, but it had never occurred to me to search for similarities between the Scotsman and the Finn. I am ignorant about Finland, and it may be that when I learn something more about it, as I shall certainly try to do now, this attempt to draw a parallel will break down hopelessly. No matter. This great First Symphony has provided the inspiration, or perhaps I should say more correctly the aspiration, to discover something about a country of which I know next to nothing and, as the mental indolence of middle age grows beguiling, one is grateful to a refreshing source of enthusiasm like that provided by this magnificent Symphony."

The Finnish Government had subsidized the production in Great Britain of the first two Sibelius symphonies, and Columbia had issued the Second before we left Jethou. I wrote of it:

"I have not had time to master the work thoroughly enough to be able to offer any useful comments upon it as a work of art; but that is the advantage of the gramophone—one is not called upon to pass final judgments in a hurry. The chief reflection left to me after hearing this symphony was the advantage to an artist of belonging to a small country. If it were suggested that the British Government should contribute a halfpenny toward the recording of any British composer's works we can imagine the response! An American millionaire has just presented £2,000,000 as a token of his esteem and regard for Great Britain. Will the committee appointed to administer this magnanimous gift have the courage to endow a national theatre or opera house? Not they. Precious little of that £2,000,000 will go to help art, I'll wager. Our notion of encouraging music officially is to knight an organist."

I sent at once for the records of the Second Symphony from Jethou and, enjoying now the chance to play it over and over again, I found myself captivated even more completely if possible than by the First. I have already told about hearing the first performance of *The Swan of Tuonela* in Great Britain at Queen's Hall. In that autumn of 1931 a record of it appeared in the H.M.V. Connoisseur Catalogue. That single performance I had heard over a quarter of a century earlier had touched my imagination so profoundly that I was anxious to find out what effect this music would have on one whose experience of life and of music had been so greatly widened since he last heard this symphonic poem. To my intense pleasure, I discovered that *The Swan of Tuonela* could stir my imagination deeply. Much of it consists of a beautiful meditative theme played by the cor anglais, and I confess I find it hard to explain why this theme moves me so much. Perhaps it is the faith and sincerity of the composer himself which are revealed in his music. The swan which glides majestically and sings upon the wide, black, rapid river that flows round the home of the dead seems to be an historical fact to Sibelius. That is where our modern British composers have failed us. They have done no more than carry on the sophistication in which so much of our poetry has languished since the death of Shelley. I should not care to claim that Wagner believed in the historical fact of Siegfried's life and death, but he was able to be completely enough possessed by the importance of Siegfried's life and death to lose all self-consciousness in the telling of it. Compare the four great music dramas of *The Ring* with such a work as Tennyson's *Idylls of a King*, or, if you will, compare *The Idylls of a King* with Tennyson's own *Maud*, and what a wretched piece of prolonged gentlemanliness that drawing-room epic appears.

"Perhaps it was the popularity of the Old Testament which dried up the fount of our racial inspiration. Britons have always had a feeling that they were the Lost Tribes. The identification of themselves with the folk-lore of the Jews has prevented the writing of a great British epic. Music always follows literature, and our poets have provided nothing except lyrics to inspire a few songs. It might be argued that German music knew how to derive inspiration from biblical sources, but the Germans never became enslaved by the less important side of the Old Testament in the way that the English, and still more the Scots, allowed themselves to be during the seventeenth century. What does Milton's *Paradise Lost* mean to us to-day except a few perfect hundred lines of blank verse? Busiris and his Memphian chivalry are as lifeless as an exhibit in the British Museum. Anyway, whatever the cause, we seem unable to produce music of the romantic sincerity which animates such a work as *The Swan of Tuonela*.

"I am dictating these random reflections in an open boat crossing from the mainland to the island of Rum. As I look to starboard and see the Coolins of Skye, jagged grey shapes piercing from a glittering blue sea the October haze, and ahead the fantastic peaks of Rum, and astern the shadowy mountains of the mainland, I ask myself why no composer has been able to dig more deeply for the treasure of our Northern past. Why cannot we produce a Sibelius? I suppose sophistication overtook us before we were ready as a nation to make music, since in every culture music is the last of the arts to develop. These reflections inspired by the thought of the black Swan of Tuonela I have attempted to put into words as I, less majestically and less melodiously than the swan, go rolling across that stream of life which seems to flow from the ultimate North."

The realization of the greatness of Sibelius was followed almost at once by my first opportunity to study Beethoven's Missa Solemnis in D. This had been issued by the Decca Company, which at a time when the prosperity of the gramophone was beginning to suffer severely from the economic depression that was deepening all the time, had courageously set out to compete in the grand style. Some indication of the slump in record buying may be found in the fact that when His Master's Voice tried to obtain the 500 subscribers required for the issue of all Hugo Wolf's songs in three or four albums no less than 117 were provided by Japanese enthusiasts of the gramophone who responded to an appeal I made to our members not to let it be said that we could not muster enough keenness to support the praiseworthy initiative of His Master's Voice. I fear that those eleven Decca-Polydor discs of the Mass in D found very few purchasers, but they provided me with the most tremendous experience in music since my first hearing of the Fifth Symphony at Queen's Hall.

"The summer and autumn of both 1818 and 1819 were spent at Mödling. Beethoven's health at this time was excellent, and his devotion to the Mass extraordinary. Never had he been known to be so entirely abstracted from external things, so immersed in the struggle of composition. Schindler has well described a strange scene which occurred during the elaboration of the *Credo*—the house deserted by the servants, and denuded of every comfort; the master shut up in his room, singing, shouting, stamping, as if in actual conflict of life and death over the fugue *Et vitam venturi*; his sudden appearance, wild, dishevelled, faint with toil and twenty-four hours' fast! These were indeed 'drangvollen Umstönden'—wretched conditions—but they are the conditions which accompany the production of great works."

In these words Grove describes the conditions in which Beethoven's Missa Solemnis in D was written, a composition which was begun in 1818 and finished on February 27th, 1823, during which time he also wrote the great Hammerklavier Sonata in B flat, Opus 106, and the beautiful Sonata in E major, Opus 109, following these with the Hammerklavier Sonata in A flat, Opus 110, and the divine last Sonata in C minor, Opus 111. When the Mass was finished Beethoven almost immediately began to write the Choral Symphony, and these two sublime works were followed during the last years of his life by the last five string quartets, the whole body of music offering to the human soul the most secure assurance of immortality that music has offered yet.

It always seems to me that critics in commenting on the music of Masses are apt to forget the words and actions the music is intended to illustrate and express. However beautiful, however elevating, however profoundly religious Bach's great Mass in B minor may be, it does not express the Mass itself, and whatever may be the greatness of it as music it inevitably fails dramatically and practically. A musician might argue that drama is not required for a Mass; my reply is that dramatic music is now as much required for a Mass as for an opera. The purest expression of ecclesiastical music is Palestrina, but such music can never be written again by the hand of man until an age of faith returns. It is true that Palestrina lived and wrote during the sixteenth century but his music is untouched by the mental disturbance of either the Reformation or the Renaissance. The security of its faith expresses the thirteenth and fourteenth centuries. The great Mass of Pope Marcellus would have been completely intelligible to St. Louis. In judging Beethoven's Mass in D we have to remember that it is an affirmation of faith delivered at a moment in the development of mankind when the last vestiges of a secure geocentric universe had been swept away.

The portions of the Mass available for musical setting make the task of the composer who wishes to give his music form apart from its illustrative aspects a difficult one. Palestrina had to consider merely the professional side of the business, if I may so put it. His job was to write Masses to be sung by an ordinary choir that would not occupy an undue amount of time. Bach was not hampered by any considerations of time, for his Mass was never meant to be performed as a Mass in church. It is, in effect, an oratorio. The later eighteenth century composers like Mozart and Haydn found themselves much handicapped by the conflicting claims of the musical and the ecclesiastical. The ninefold *Kyrie* followed by the long *Gloria in Excelsis*, and the even longer and more varied *Credo*, left little with which to achieve a climax with the threefold *Sanctus*, the *Benedictus* and the *Agnus Dei*, particularly as the *Agnus Dei* had already been partly incorporated in the *Gloria*. Yet, from an ecclesiastical point of view, this disproportion must not be felt in the music, because the most emotionally direct appeal in the Mass, sung after the words of consecration, is the *Agnus Dei*. It is of absorbing interest to see how Beethoven confronts this artistic problem, especially as he had already, in 1807, written one rather dull and somewhat conventional Mass.

The occasion for the second Mass was the installation of his friend, the Archduke Rudolf, as Archbishop of Olmütz. Beethoven was so utterly carried away by his composition that the Mass was not finished until three years after the installation had been held. What may have been conceived originally as a compliment to a royal friend soon took upon itself the whole of the vast burden of Beethoven's humanity. The Mass in D must be regarded as a formal act of faith, and it is in the highest degree significant that this formal act of faith in the doctrine of the Catholic Church was followed by the ultimate expression of Beethoven's individuality unfettered by any doctrinal formality in the Ninth Symphony. If we take those last piano sonatas to express the workings of his mind during the adaptation of it to the expression of Christian truth in the Mass which he was composing at the same time, may we not equally surmise that the late quartets were showing the workings of a mind which, had longer life been granted to it, would have soared even beyond the Ninth Symphony into the Tenth Symphony on which he was already meditating?

Kyrie Eleison and *Christe Eleison* are the only Greek words in the liturgy of the Western Church. Lord have mercy upon us, Christ have mercy upon us, Lord have mercy upon us, each in turn repeated three times. Nothing might be so easily conventionalized as those simple ejaculations uttered in a language twice removed from ordinary speech. But Beethoven from the very start seems determined that there shall be nothing conventional about his Mass. In the first notes of the *Kyrie Eleison* you hear, as it were, the wailing of that Europe distressed and impoverished by the Napoleonic wars, a Europe, indeed, whose emotions were not unlike those we are feeling in our Europe of to-day. After the first *Kyrie Eleison*, the *Christe Eleison* seems to strike a more confident note; when the *Kyrie Eleison* is repeated on the third side it seems in some mysterious way to combine the first *Kyrie Eleison* with the *Christe Eleison*, and to prepare the worshipper for the superb note of triumph with which the *Gloria in Excelsis* opens.

In the Second Prayer Book of Edward VI the *Gloria in Excelsis* by a printer's mistake got moved to the end of the office of Holy Communion, where it is entirely out of place. In the Scottish and American Prayer Books the *Gloria* is not displaced. The first side contains what a critic calls that "almost miraculous stroke of the climax of *Glorificamus Te*" which must be heard, for the wonder of it cannot be expressed in words. The second side of the *Gloria* contains two of the appeals which are afterwards repeated in the *Agnus Dei*, "Who takest away the sins of the world, have mercy upon us." There are some marvellous phrases for the *peccata mundi*, and it will be profoundly impressive to hear the different way in which Beethoven treats them in the *Agnus Dei*. The third and fourth sides of the *Gloria* carry on the note of triumphant expectation with which it opens, and then we come to the *Credo*.

In all earlier creeds the first phrase, *Credo in unum Deum*, "I believe in one God", is expressed in a single phrase, but Beethoven opens with a repetition by soloists and choir of the single word "credo", and the effect of this detached from the dogmatic details of what is believed has an almost defiant character, as if we were to translate *Credo*, I do believe, I will believe, I must believe. At the end of this side, at "Who for us men and for our salvation came down from Heaven", the voices express marvellously this preface to the statement of the great mystery of the Incarnation. It must be remembered that while the *Et incarnatus est* is sung the congregation will be kneeling till the conclusion of that supreme statement of the Christian Faith, *Et Homo Factus Est*, "And was made Man". I know nothing in music which expresses a so completely positive and overwhelming statement of fact. On the third side of the Creed there is a moment of intense drama when the trumpets ring out and the last trump as the choir sings, "He shall come again with glory to judge both the quick and the dead." The trumpet call in the Third Leonora Overture produces a similar dramatic effect, and yet that trumpet call, romantic and exciting as it is, is of an entirely different quality from this awe-inspiring trumpet call of the Last Judgment. The fourth and fifth sides of the Creed are taken up with the repetition of the last four words, *et vitam venturi saeculi*, "and the life of the world to come".

> To see a World in a Grain of Sand
> And a Heaven in a Wild Flower,
> Hold infinity in the palm of your hand,
> And Eternity in an hour.

Thus wrote Blake, and we who listen to the two sides of the gramophone disc which records that last phrase of the Nicene Creed may hear Eternity in that sublime fugue.

The threefold *Sanctus* calls worshippers at Mass to prepare for the solemn moment of consecrating the elements. In so many masses the *Sanctus* opens with a full volume of sound, but Beethoven's music is full of awe as the accomplishment of the great mystery draws near. The *Sanctus* is followed by the *Benedictus*, "Blessed is He that cometh in the name of the Lord, Hosanna in the Highest." It is rash for any critic to attribute a subtlety of intention to the composer for the attribution of which he lacks authority from the composer himself, but I cannot help thinking that by the solo violin which plays such an important part in the *Benedictus*, Beethoven meant to express pathetic humanity, and that the voices which are so much more austere than the violin solo are intended to be voices of celestial life.

One of the problems which has beset all composers who have written Masses, perhaps the chief problem, is how to prevent an anticlimax when they come to write the *Agnus Dei*. I refer, of course, to composers who succeeded the liturgical composers like Palestrina, and who developed what was known as the Neapolitan school, which, in other words, means the writing of dramatic music for the Mass. The *Agnus Dei* is being sung while the consecrated elements are on the altar, and yet, with slight variation, the same ejaculations have already been uttered in the course of the *Gloria* before the Consecration. "O Lamb of God, Who takest away the sins of the World, grant us peace." This concludes the musical part of the Mass.

Beethoven, by a stroke of superlative genius, succeeds in making his *Agnus Dei* a more tremendous utterance than anything he has previously written in the course of the Mass. I said that in the opening of *Kyrie* one felt the wailing of a disheartened and war-ravaged Europe. During the *Agnus Dei* we hear on the drums the booming of the guns that bombarded Vienna; we hear the martial sounds of trumpets and the clash of war; and at the end we hear that tremendous appeal for peace, *Agnus Dei, Qui tollis peccata mundi, dona nobis pacem*. This is succeeded by that beautiful prayer for peace which begins, *Domine Jesu Christe, qui dixisti Apostolis tuis, Pacem relinquo vobis, Pacem meam do vobis*.

Writing for the eleventh edition of the *Encyclopaedia Britannica* in 1910, Professor Donald Tovey said:

"In the *Agnus Dei* the circumstances of the time gave him something special to say which has never so imperatively demanded utterance since. Europe has been shattered by the Napoleonic wars. Beethoven read the final prayer of the Mass as a 'prayer for inward and outward peace', and, giving it that title, organized it on the basis of a contrast between terrible martial sounds and the triumph of peaceful themes, in a scheme none the less spiritual and sublime because those who first heard it had derived their notions of the horror of war from living in Vienna during its bombardment. Critics who have lived in London during the relief of Mafeking have blamed Beethoven for his realism."

We can say now that the circumstances of the time make this grand utterance more imperative even than when Beethoven first delivered it, we who in 1955 have lived through so much more than the relief of Mafeking. When I listen to that Mass in D on two long-playing discs with the N.B.C. Symphony Orchestra, conducted by Toscanini, the hydrogen bomb seems more evil and yet at the same time less fearful. Music like this revives and sustains the human soul. *Agnus Dei, Qui tollis peccata mundi, dona nobis pacem.*

The Ninth Symphony opens in a mood of mystic perception; the only conductor I have heard who seemed to grasp the full significance of this mood was Koussevitsky. Some of the humility of the Mass in D persists in this first movement. Man is in the presence of God, and he does not feel perfectly sure of himself. Throughout that first movement Beethoven seems to be preparing us for some tremendous revelation, and to my mind there is nothing more tragic in art than the failure of the Ninth Symphony after the triumph of the Mass in D to provide that revelation. By making the second movement a scherzo Beethoven seems to cut himself free abruptly from any will to surrender further to the mood of humility. It is as if he had lost faith in a Divine revelation, and had set out to arrange his own revelation. Hence the jangle and discordant clamour which he, Beethoven, not God, is going to lull. Beethoven appears throughout the Ninth Symphony as a kind of Prospero, and indeed it would not be difficult to find a parallel between Shakespeare's last play, *The Tempest*, and Beethoven's last symphony. After the Scherzo comes the Adagio, as lovely as any of Beethoven's lovely adagios, and yet somehow unsatisfying. The usual criticism of Beethoven's slow movements is that he overdoes them. The linked sweetness is too long drawn out. My own feeling is that this adagio at any rate should be impugned less for its length or direct appeal to emotion than for its insincerity. It was really too easy for Beethoven to write these lovely adagios, and the sound of this last one in our ears touches the heart of mortality but leaves it mortal.

Beethoven was evidently much puzzled to know how to lead up to his innovation of a choral finale, for it must be remembered that his original scheme for the Ninth Symphony had not included such an ending. So he conceived the idea of a kind of competition for the right tune, and in turn the three preceding movements present themselves as candidates. He dismisses the first abruptly, almost casually, and yet ironically enough he was never so near to the threshold of transporting his hearers into eternity as in that first movement of the Ninth Symphony. After rejecting the melody of the first movement, he rejects the scherzo, but in rejecting the scherzo he goes further and reproves it. We detect megalomania here, that curse of genius. "Stop this wrangling and jangling," say the strings. "I, Beethoven, have a panacea for all the ills of humanity." He rejects the third movement tenderly and almost reverently, as if awed by the beauty of his own creation. "Beautiful though you are," he seems to say, "I must reject you, because I possess something even more beautiful, but more capable of being appreciated by everybody, high and low."

With this begins the march leading up to the singing of Schiller's Ode to Joy. Musicians often have execrable taste in literature, and the banality of Schiller's words inevitably suggests that the music Beethoven gave to them is equally banal. The fatal facility of humanitarian ejaculation reflects itself in this music. "All men are brothers!" "Liberté, Égalité, Fraternité!" "A land fit for heroes to live in!" "Make the world safe for democracy!" Slogans like these require a good easy tune to march to. If Beethoven had lived to see some of the results of that facile humanitarianism he might have cancelled the end of the Choral Symphony as he cancelled the dedication of the Third Symphony to Napoleon. Yet, this anticlimax is paradoxically one of the peaks of Beethoven's supreme genius. The finale of the Ninth Symphony may offer too facile a solution of life's problems, but the simplicity of the man himself in accepting such a solution destroys the memory of the egoism and the fits of megalomania to which he was subject. The inspiration of it seems almost as naïve as the inspiration of some of those rondos in his earliest work.

It has always puzzled me that the Communists have never taken advantage of this melodious expression of the mechanized emotion of human brotherhood. Even the Soviet leaders could join in such a chorus. For us to-day the real finale of the Ninth Symphony is the first movement and the answer to that fluttering of the human soul in search of God is the Mass in D.

Still listening

Chapter 18

IN October 1931 I was elected Rector of Glasgow University but managed to attend to my duties and work hard enough at books and journalism to find myself financially all square by September 1932. My third volume of war memories was published that October, and a prosecution under the Official Secrets Act was launched, culminating at the Old Bailey in January 1933. This cost me about £5000, all in all, though the actual fine was trifling, and any hope of having to work less hard vanished. I retired to the island of Barra and there between the Atlantic and the Minch I spent most of the next twelve years in congenial company with books, music and laughter. Apropos of music and laughter I may mention that for the last twenty-five years Lord Samuel and myself have been collecting examples of the misuse of the adverb "literally". Unlike most collectors we present each other with our best specimens and in August 1933 I noted:

"Last week Lord Samuel sent me this beauty from the *Radio Times*:
" 'When, at the age of twenty-four Strauss hurled *Don Juan* into the concert-room, a bomb literally burst in the ears of the musical world.' "

That must have caused more discomfort than the performance at which a famous violinist's double-stopping "literally swept the audience off its feet".

It was in that August, I think, that Dame Ethel Smyth suddenly arrived in Barra at the start of a tour up through the Outer Hebrides. She was seventy-five years old, and still in the full vigour of her rich vitality. Indeed, the only sign of age was her deafness. I remember standing with her in half a gale beside the great cockle strand and discussing the work of D. H. Lawrence. I had to shout every observation at the top of my voice, feeling like the boatswain's mate trying to communicate with the boatswain in a storm. I remember too telling her at the top of my voice a story which gave her much pleasure. A week or two before I had been driving with a couple of old Barra women round the island in a hired car and presently ahead of us we saw a gloomy-looking fellow in blue dungarees coming along the road. At sight of him the two old ladies collapsed into irrepressible laughter and continued laughing after we had left the blue dungarees behind. I asked what they were laughing at, but it was a minute or two before their mirth could be got sufficiently under control to answer.

"That man!" they gurgled, with renewed spasms of merriment, adding his name in Gaelic.

"What's so funny about him?"

"He doesn't believe in a future life," they gasped, and then began to laugh again in a very rapture of mirth.

Dame Ethel was captivated by this view of the atheist, and announced her intention as soon as she returned to London of telling . . . well, one of our most distinguished atheists, who, still alive, views the prospect of extinction after death with philosophic equanimity. She told me much about the agitation for women's suffrage, when she was imprisoned for awhile at Holloway, but she would not talk about music. Like Elgar she professed to take no more interest in music. The conviction she had that the work of women in music never received its due had become an obsession; I did not venture to ask whether she had noticed that not a single one of the great composers had inherited his music from his mother. Dame Ethel talked freely about her early days as a student in Germany and of meeting Brahms whose table manners she deplored.

"I once saw him eat all the sardines in a tin and then pick it up and drink the oil that was left, some of it dribbling down his beard, of course. It was a severe shock to my romantic awe of him."

We arranged a *luádh* for her in the parish hall, when a dozen women sang the refrains of the waulking songs as they swung the length of blanket or tweed from side to side to shrink it with many a thud on the corrugated board, one very old lady leading the singing with verse after verse of the song chosen. Dame Ethel was enchanted. Dr. Johnson was also enchanted by such an occasion when he was at Raasay during his tour with Boswell and anxious to know what the words meant. Dame Ethel was equally anxious and I called upon the rich voice of the late Father John Macmillan to translate.

When the waulking was done, Dame Ethel asked if it would be in order for her to offer a dram to the now exhausted singers. I was kicking myself for not having brought with me a bottle when Dame Ethel pulled up her skirt and produced from a concealed pocket a full bottle which she took round with a dram glass to every woman in turn.

We shall be celebrating Dame Ethel Smyth's centenary three years hence on next St. George's Day. It would be extravagant to claim that she was a great composer, but she was assuredly a very great woman, with a good deal of the man in her, be it added. Sir Henry Wood used to tell a story of coming into his study one day to see somebody leaning out of the window and presenting to the room only the back of a pair of breeches. Thinking it was a young man who had come to see him about mending a bicycle, Sir Henry said. "Ah, there you are at last," and as he spoke thumped heartily the posterior of the breeches. The figure leaning out of the window looked round in surprise; it was Ethel Smyth.

The summer of 1934 came before I was able to dispose of my life lease of Jethou and therefore to contemplate building a house on Barra which would hold all my books and records.

My wife recalled in *The Gramophone* what the little island had meant to us:

"Stacks and stacks of them!" sang the beggar in Hassan. . . .

"A long, low room, gold and black, with cool green light from a garden which has been allowed to show what a garden can do if left to itself for a year or two; a deserted room, but a room that has lived and still seems to breathe. Created by an artist, built by only two pairs of hands, this room was once a centre of inspired activity, literary and gramophonic, and now houses a collection of landmarks in the evolution of the gramophone. Most of the furniture of daily life has been removed. Gramophones remain, and heaps of records.

"Some twenty-five cases, each weighing apparently a ton, await transportation in various parts of the house, but in the long room there are shelves full of unclassified discs.

"Single-sided Galli-Curcis are discovered. These were the first loves of the Editor and must be kept. *Una voce poco fà*, wrinkled and faded, shall go on the old Balmain with the Wilson horn which has floated serenely for two years in its mercury bath, quite indifferent to time and neglect. The result is astonishing. Have we progressed so much? Only the scratch and the ludicrous orchestral accompaniment give it away. The angelic quality of the voice could hardly be more truly given than it is on this obsolete machine.

"This 'obsolete' machine went up with the room. Before the walls were finished in 1926, Mr. Balmain and the rest of the Expert

Committee arrived at Jethou bearing with them the largest gramophone horn then known to man. It was put up and tested during a few days of delirious excitement, shared by a dozen or so Siamese cats who had the added thrill of a brand-new room to explore.

"In 1928 it was decided that a radio-gramophone must be introduced in Jethou. Down came the experts again, and the thing was done. There was no electric installation on the island, so the prison, a small round impregnable fortress, was turned into an engine-room, and the H.M.V. cabinet, which had been the mainstay of our gramophonic life since the early days before the paper started, was fitted with a pick-up; a square was cut out of the bookshelves to make room for a loudspeaker. To tell the truth, I thought this new noise quite unbearable, though it was the latest thing and first-rate of its kind. . . . Amplification spells vexation . . . but I soon got used to it, and even enjoyed it, which may or may not be a good thing. The Editor was enthusiastic and used to sit writing in an ocean of sound. But I sometimes came in and caught him playing that old Balmain.

"And now it is farewell to Jethou. Time to move on after ten years of it. Leave others to enjoy the fruits of so much work and thought; the garden, ten years ago a sad waste of bracken and weeds, now glorious with enchanting rare flowers and shrubs; the long room designed so curiously to hold the books and records that accumulated month by month. The records! We unearthed some good things before we left, but there was a mass of pre-electric stuff really not fit to give away. What more dignified end could be devised for them than to be warmed gently on the stove and fluted to fantastic shapes and launched on to a milky sea carrying paper sails on a perfect evening in June? To join the floating puffins at their play, to race along the rushing tide and end perhaps at Alderney, perhaps even on the coast of Normandy? This was the fate of a small fleet that put out to sea on June the Eleventh, 1934, but their departure seemed to make no difference to the shelves in the long gold room."

We went to South America soon after this for me to give some lectures in Buenos Aires, Rio de Janeiro and Monte Video. Many gramophone enthusiasts in Buenos Aires made haste to call when we arrived and I was urged to give a talk about their beloved instrument. As arrangements had been made for me to give one more lecture than those on the programme arranged by the Foreign

Office I was able to include the gramophone. The large hall was packed out. I gave one broadcast, speaking extempore into the microphone for twenty minutes to the almost continuous accompaniment of flashlight photographs. The microphone was in an outsize studio surrounded on three sides by glass like the tank of an aquarium, through which the public were allowed to gaze at the speaker, though they could not hear him. I arrived ten minutes before the time my broadcast was due to start but when the moment came the director (I need hardly say that he was a Scotsman) told me he was going to put on a record of *Roses in Picardy* to give listeners an opportunity to compose themselves for my discourse and allow the Scottish sheep farmers in Patagonia a few minutes' grace. It was all delightfully informal and a contrast to the hushed robotry of the B.B.C.

In Rio de Janeiro the Association of Brazilian Artists invited me to an audition of Brazilian records arranged for my benefit, and I had the privilege of meeting the Brazilian composer Villalobos, besides several others. The records played were all presented to me afterwards, and the British Customs charged duty upon them as if they were discs I had imported from the United States because the examining officer could not turn Brazilian money into British. The Customs officers have always been strict about gramophone records, but I have never seen one of them try to stop the importation of a Continental edition of a current English novel which for years it was their duty to do.

That decade of the 1930's was a difficult time for the recording companies owing to the financial muddle into which the world had got itself. Naturally some of their difficulties were felt by *The Gramophone*. One of the casualties of the mid-'thirties was the National Gramophonic Society. However, it had served its purpose, and the measure of its ability may be gauged by the fact that over ten years later all the works of chamber music originally recorded by the N.G.S. had now been recorded by the big companies. I am proud to think that the contribution which the little society we launched so casually, soon after we had launched *The Gramophone* just as casually, made to chamber music is commemorated in a work unlikely ever to be superseded—Cobbet's *Cyclopedic Survey of Chamber Music*. In November 1935 I was welcoming the Schubert Quintet in C major which the N.G.S. had issued about six years before and which was now being issued by H.M.V. recorded by the Pro Arte Quartet with Anthony Pini as second 'cellist.

"This quintet, written in the last year of Schubert's short life, remained unheard and unknown until the composer had lain twenty-two years in the grave. It is one of the greatest pieces of chamber music ever written—indeed, perhaps *the* greatest piece of chamber music ever written—and the astounding thing about it is that, although the sublime beauty of it is apparent at a first hearing to the man with any kind of cultivated musical taste, with each successive hearing the sublime beauty of it becomes always more apparent. To my ears the *adagio* of the second movement is the loveliest melody discovered by mortality. We hear a faint indication of it in the variations of the *Death and the Maiden* Quartet, but when Schubert wrote this *adagio* he was already so near to death himself that it almost seems, as we listen, that he is looking beyond this world and actually perceiving the life of the world to come. I hope when I lie upon my own death-bed I may pass from this small green world of ours to the sound of that melody. And the whole Quintet is a succession of moments of seraphic music. The first movement is only a breath less lovely than the second, indeed to many it is even lovelier. What composer after such a first half would not have let down his listeners with the *scherzo* and *presto*? And what composer after such a *scherzo* and *presto* could have produced such an exquisite fourth movement?"

However, during that difficult decade our circulation did not drop heavily and I was never in the least doubt that the policy of encouraging the growing taste both in Great Britain and the United States for records of the best in music was the right one. A valued correspondent was writing to us from New York:

"Not much more than a year ago classical recorded music here in America was in a bad way. The Brunswick Company had long since ceased releasing important German Polydor records under its own label; the American Odeon Company had for years been out of business; the Columbia Company was on the verge of suspending classical releases altogether; and the bulk of Victor discs were foreign H.M.V. recordings issued with the Victor label. The Philadelphia Orchestra was the single, solitary American orchestra making records. It seemed safe to say that the American classical record business faced a decline from which there was no return. It is with distinct pleasure and optimism, therefore, that one reviews the events of the past few months, remarkable for the heartening achievements and renewed interest which seems to have revived the classical disc field in America."

Our correspondent went on to tell us about the records issued in America, and he then wrote some words which I set down here for the benefit of those who believe that commercial radio and television are an unmixed evil.

"The outstanding series of concerts is that sponsored by the General Motors Corporation and presented by N.B.C. each Sunday evening. This unparalleled group of concerts has given us the large N.B.C. Symphony Orchestra, one of the finest in the country, under the direction of great conductors such as Stokowski, Damrosch, Bruno Walter, Gabrilowitch, Eugene Goossens, Toscanini, and others no less famous. At each of these concerts a famous soloist is heard, including Menuhin, Farrar (who was called out of retirement especially for a single appearance; her voice seems but little dimmed by the years), Melchoir, Iturbi, Myra Hess, Lily Pons, Bori, Gershwin, Heifetz, Tibbett, and others. Torrents of violent abuse have been poured upon the American system of commercially sponsored radio entertainment, but surely this unsurpassed series overbalances a huge amount of the trash with which we have been regaled. Not to be outdone, the Columbia Broadcasting system has offered a series of concerts by the Philadelphia Orchestra, later quite adequately replaced by the Minneapolis Symphony under Eugene Ormandy.

"But records and radio were brought even closer together in a recent remarkable programme sponsored by RCA Victor, which served to advertise the most important event in recorded music that has taken place in many months; the reappearance on discs of the matchless Boston Symphony Orchestra. Over an extensive N.B.C. network of stations Victor broadcast on January 22nd part of an actual recording session of this orchestra.

"Thus it will be seen that renewed interest, and certainly renewed activity, has marked the progress of classical music on records in America during the past few months; results should be far reaching and encouraging to those who are assured of the phonograph's place in modern musical life."

Richard Tauber had made his début as a singer on records with an album of Schubert's *Winterreise* issued by Parlophone. It failed to make much mark but it was not surprising that Tauber should have turned to Lehar and all too often to inferior composers in singing whose songs he became a best seller. In 1934 His Master's Voice issued another album of Schubert's song cycle with Gerhard Hüsch as the singer and the comparative success this enjoyed compared with the Tauber album was an indication of the way taste was developing.

It gave me an opportunity to make some remarks about setting words to music:

"A study of Schubert's song cycle *Winterreise* will bring home to anybody the profound change that has apparently swept across human nature; at any rate the human nature with which as northern Europeans we are most likely to be brought into contact emotionally or intellectually.

"*Winterreise* was written by a young German poet, Wilhelm Müller, who at the age of thirty-three died a year or two before Schubert himself. The theme of the twenty-four short poems is one of the oldest in literature, being the 'pangs of despised love'. A young man has been jilted by his sweetheart for a wealthy husband. It is winter time, and from the harshness of the season he illustrates his own sorrow. Life for him is now an eternal winter's journey, for although the streams may melt, the naked trees break into leaf, and the snow-white earth put on once more the green vesture of spring, he will not be able to share in this rebirth of nature. The imagery of the poet throughout except in one lyric is as simple as an old-fashioned Christmas-card or Valentine. There is a weathercock above the false fair one's house, and it suggests the obvious comparison. The tears upon the forsaken lover's cheeks freeze, but they spring from a heart warm enough to melt winter's ice. He searches the snow for her footprints where once they had wandered together over the green meadows. He remembers the lime-tree that overhung the well by the gate of his beloved's house, and now far away from it he seems to hear its branches murmuring in the gentle wind of summer a message of peace. Upon the frozen river he cuts with a stone her name, the day and the hour when they first met, the day and the hour when they parted. And these dates are encircled by a broken ring.

"He dreams of the Maytime, of green leaves, of joyful bird-song, and wakes to see leaves of frost upon his window-pane and to hear ravens croaking on the roof. A post-horn rings out, and he begins to imagine that once again it is the herald of a love-letter for himself. He plays the old game of 'She loves me, she loves me not' with the last dying leaf left upon a tree. When it falls hope will fall with it. He comes to a churchyard. The wreaths upon the tombs appear to him like inn signs inviting him to enter a cool tavern; but the rooms in the inn are all occupied, and he has to turn his back upon 'easeful death'. Finally, he sees a poor old organ-grinder with frozen fingers grinding out music to which nobody listens, and at which the very dogs growl. The forsaken lover asks the old organ-grinder if he shall come with him, and if he will grind his organ to his songs. To this question the answer is given by the accompaniment in a final repetition of the cracked phrase which has tinkled wearily on and on throughout the last song.

"Judged as poetry there is not one of Wilhelm Müller's lyrics which unmistakably escapes from the flood of sentimental outpour-ings by which a century ago northern Europe was inundated, and from the prevailing moisture of which not even the Latin nations succeeded in keeping themselves dry. There is none which in magical poignancy of personal grief comes near to 'Fare thee well, thou first and fairest' or to 'My Love is like a red, red rose', none which in the same language can compare with the best of Heine's lyrics. *Winterreisse* has the tender charm of a faded lover's knot or tattered old keepsake album, and though it might beguile a mood of sentimental reminiscence like a tune on an old musical box, it could scarcely hope to strike a passionate chord from the music of contemporary humanity. The sorrows of Werther himself lack significance for to-day. Yet Schubert's genius has given to this sequence of little poems a pulsating life which will defy for ever the envious cynicism of time. The perfection of the musical setting raises Wilhelm Müller's simple expression of heartbreak to the highest peaks of passionate utterance. The combination challenges the supreme expressions of mortal love, so that when Wilhelm Müller mingles with Franz Schubert the listener finds himself exalted above the gentle undulations of sentiment and riding the clouds with Propertius and Sappho, with Petrarch and Burns, even with Shakespeare himself.

"Nevertheless, it would be wrong to give all the credit to Schubert and allow none to Müller. Schubert could not have turned Müller's sequence of lyrics into that exquisite song cycle without having received from it a positive inspiration. We may fancy that when Shakespeare took hold of some hackneyed old wives' tale and transmuted it by the alchemy of his art into something immeasurably beyond the significance of the original, he was not so much inspired by the tale as saved from the fatigue of invention. Schubert, on the other hand, must have been directly moved by Wilhelm Müller's poetry before he was able to immortalize it by music that never over-weighted the simple and homely theme. That is the real achievement of *Winterreise*.

"It will always be a matter of regret to myself that Tennyson's *Maud* was not written in time to be given music by Schubert. If only that mood of melodious inspiration which produced *Der Lindenbaum*, *Frühlingstraum* and *Die Post* could have been given to *Come into the garden, Maud*, what a song of songs we might have had! During the nineteenth century there were three sonnet-sequences upon the theme of happy and unhappy love—Meredith's *Modern Love*, Mrs. Browning's *Sonnets from the Portuguese*, and Christina Rossetti's *Monna Innominata*. The sonnet form, however, is inimical to music, and except for the setting by Maud Valérie White of the beautiful sonnet from *Monna Innominata* which begins :

> 'I wish I could remember that first day,
> First hour, first moment of my meeting you'

I cannot recall that those intense and often poignant expressions of individual hopes and fears and joys and griefs inspired a single musician.

"We have to acknowledge that the poetical expression of romantic emotion in English was incapable of producing a Schubert, a Schumann or a Brahms to perfect it and so immortalize it with music. Yet if we examine the lyrics chosen by Schubert, Schumann and Brahms for their songs we can claim that except for one or two of Heine's poems the English poetry available for songs has always been immeasurably superior to the German poetry, which rarely seems aware that metrical ingenuity need be taxed beyond alternate feminine and masculine rhymes in six, seven and eight feet. Yet the very monotony of such versification seems able to evoke powers of musical expression that are baffled by the variety and subtlety of English metrical poems. The fact is that English lyrical poetry from the time of Elizabeth has displayed an ever-increasing independence of music, whereas German poetry has always seemed to demand the addition of music if it was not to expire when the mood that called it forth had vanished.

"The failure of the nineteenth century to produce any British composers capable of finding in the volume of great English poetry written during that century an inspiration to hoist himself above the commonplace led to that intolerable alloy of words and music known as the English ballad, the revolt from which has been most unfortunately extended by the younger generation into a rebellion on a grand scale against every expression of art that seemed to them tainted by romance or sentiment, romance and sentiment appearing to them a falsification of emotional, ethical and intellectual values. The result has been a bewildering clearance of old reputations, the dust of which would appear to have temporarily choked the lungs of the demolishers and rendered them incapable of revealing coherently what they propose to set up on the vacant space. One finds a widely held opinion that the twentieth century is playing a part in the development of humanity akin to that played by the eighteenth century. One finds among younger writers a belief, not without its pathetic aspect, that an ability to echo faintly the manner of eighteenth-century prose must indicate that reason has successfully dethroned emotion from the kingdom of their minds. The eighteenth century, however, set about its task of restoring order to a period exhausted by two centuries of religious strife, geographical expansion, and emotional fever with all the confidence of a new experiment—an experiment, let me add, which I am sufficiently old-fashioned to believe was a failure, and directly responsible for the evil course pursued by the industrialism of the nineteenth century. Those of the present generation who discover in the mixture of romance, materialism and complacency that distinguishes the nineteenth century from others a just cause for disowning romance might ponder the advantages of preserving the romance, disowning the materialism, and avoiding the complacency; and in pondering that alternative they might consider the artistically ignominious end of the eighteenth century at any rate in England.

"What I find so tiresome about the self-insistent anti-romantics of the moment is their inability to recognize that in an anxiety to deromanticize the individual they are smearing the world with a greasy and insincere humanitarianism which presents itself to the romantic individual as a much baser expression of romance than is imputed to himself. I call this humanitarianism greasy because it expects to slide over the rugosity of man's disposition by the exudation of a kind of emotional lard. I call it insincere because it is inspired in the vast majority of individual cases not by a desire for human happiness or a love of human nature, but by a selfish devotion to personal comfort and a laziness impudently masquerading as tolerance. The conspiracy of aggressive pacifists to throttle the expression of any sentiment or opinion that might favour what they choose to declare is an indirect encouragement to the martial spirit is one of many instances of this greasy and insincere humanitarianism. They would not merely destroy admiration for the ideals of glory, valour, honour, endurance, and self-abnegation, but they would like to abolish chivalry, romantic love, supernatural religion, and even such relics of an inhumanitarian past as the outward forms of courtesy.

"It is becoming a popular superstition that men of science will soon establish such a control over the glandular secretions of humanity that we may look forward to as successful an achievement of synthetic emotions and morals as of synthetic vanilla. A little more knowledge of the adrenal glands, and the lion will lie down with the lamb. A nicer appreciation of the functions of the thymus gland, and we may protract youth in such a way that old men who now postpone wisdom by playing golf will postpone wisdom by playing football. Alas, this rich prospect does not include another Franz Schubert or another *Winterreise*. Yet who knows? Some mystery still lurks in the pituitary gland, and when that is dispelled we may be able to produce Schuberts as prolifically as we now produce crooning tenors."

However, taste was not in any danger of becoming too good. The B.B.C. was talking about reviving the ballad-concert which drove me to write:

"These lollipop fiends who claim to be in a vast majority should form a Sugar-sprinklers' Association on the lines of the Froth-blowers and secure a wave-length for themselves, where they can dream that they dwell with Henry Halls, and gurgle away their time like a baby with a rubber teat. But let this mental diabetes be isolated.

"The intelligent listener is not deficient in pancreatic juice. Live and let live has worked very well for the gramophone. There is music for every taste. It will be intolerable if broadcasting is handed to sugar daddies and sweeties. The air is already as sticky as the fingers of a candy-sucking child. I have recently been indulging myself in some intensive listening, and I have proved that it is possible for any listener with a minimum of trouble to provide himself with syrup at any hour of the afternoon or evening. So why grumble at the minority which has to work very hard with the knobs to achieve solid nourishment, and then succeeds only seldom?"

Two years of the strictest economy in Barra cottages enabled me to start building a house there and in May 1935 the foundation stone was laid. We moved in on St. Andrew's Day, and in January 1936 I was able to announce in *The Gramophone*:

"Hundreds of records which had been packed away in boxes for five years were again upon my shelves. I have had so much pleasure from having by me again Brahms Piano Concerto in D minor that I must talk about it.

"Apparently this concerto was originally conceived as a symphony in the summer of 1854. Brahms was writing to Schumann about it in the following year, and at the end of 1855 he wrote to Clara Schumann that he had been dreaming he had turned his symphony into a piano concerto, and was playing it with a terribly difficult and grand scherzo for the finale. 'I was quite carried away,' he added. Dietrich in 1862 recalled that he had seen parts of the D minor Concerto projected for use in a sonata for two pianos. If that were so it would account very neatly for the dream, for one might fairly call a piano concerto a cross between a symphony and a sonata. When Brahms was sketching out the C minor Piano Quartet he was trying to keep himself from making love to Clara Schumann, whose husband was in an asylum. Schumann had tried to kill himself in March 1854 by jumping into the Rhine, and from the correspondence of Joachim and Kalbeck we find that the first movement of the D minor Concerto reflects the emotion of Brahms over his friend's attempted suicide. If that be so, it is difficult not to find in the exquisite adagio of the second movement the expression of a mind chastened by tragedy and strengthened by victory over the flesh. In this movement the music of the piano seems to rock gently like a boat upon the calm sea of the strings, and if one sees this movement played one almost has the impression that the instrument itself is being wafted upwards by the violins.

"The Concerto was first performed in public at Hanover, in January 1859, the conductor being Joachim, and the soloist Brahms himself. The reception was cool. Five days later it was played again at Leipzig, where Mendelssohn was king, and it was a complete failure. Writing to Joachim the following day he said: 'The first and second movements were listened to without the slightest display of feeling. At the conclusion three pairs of hands were brought together very slowly, whereupon a perfectly distinct hissing from all sides forbade any such demonstration. . . . This failure has made no impression whatever upon me. After all, I am only experimenting in feeling my way. But the hissing was too much.'

"Not many young men who had written words like this before they were twenty-six would have accepted failure so philosophically."

A note on diabolic music about this time says what I should say again to-day on this topic:

"I was interested to read in our review of that remarkable Columbia recording of Moussorgsky's *A Night on a Bare Mountain* that the music 'sounds really and frighteningly evil'. This was, of course, the composer's intention inasmuch as the night included a witches' Sabbath with the appearance of the god Chernobog and spirits of darkness. On me it made no impression at all of evil, but I hasten to add that neither does the Witches' Sabbath in the Fantastic Symphony which our reviewer says sounds in comparison with the Moussorgsky like the Salvation Army. The only successful transference of evil to music that I can think of is Stravinsky's *Sacre du Printemps*, and even that does not seem to me to reach beyond the evil of unfriendly aborigines. A brigadier-general once told me that he found the music of *Tannhäuser* unhealthy, but I fancy that was only because he was unable to hum it at a first hearing. At the same time Wagner must have hoped that the Venusberg music was expressing evil, and no doubt if we surrender our fancy to the composer's intention we might extract from it the picture of plump nymphs prancing about the stage in pink tights, which used to be the visible expression of it on the stage.

"Orgies in terms of music are usually as unimpressive as orgies on the films, or indeed as orgies in real life. But leave orgies out of it, and think of the failure of musicians to make our hair stand on end or our flesh creep. Who could muster a square millimetre of gooseflesh from a performance of Saint-Saëns' *Danse Macabre*? Who in fact would know that it was a danse macabre unless the composer had given it a title? The music of the magician in Holst's *Uranus* parodies pleasantly all this mock-magical stuff. I am inclined to argue that this failure of music to suggest what we call the supernatural is a valid argument against the objective existence of ghosts. How many genuinely eerie moments can you remember in all music? I can recall but two. The first occurs in the opening bars of *The Midnight Review* by Glinka, where one or two chords definitely make me feel mentally uncomfortable, with a suggestion of gooseflesh. The other is at the beginning of Strauss's *Death and Transfiguration*, which I heard first without knowing what it was supposed to be about, and so was not subject to auto-suggestion. On the other hand, an immense amount of avowedly sacred music fails to suggest supernatural good. Mendelssohn's *Elijah*, for instance, seems to me as unreal in its own way as the expression of what it is trying to express as Wagner's Venusberg music. And even Bach's Mass in B minor, however glorious as music, is to my hearing entirely devoid of spiritual meaning except, of course, in that pantheistic sense which naturally gives a spiritual meaning to all great music. On the other hand, the music of Palestrina affects me as positive proof of the objective existence of God."

Soon after this I was writing about the medicine-men of Moscow:

"The music of Rachmaninoff has been solemnly banned in Russia because it is considered unhealthy and subversive of Soviet ideals. It is difficult to imagine how music can exercise a political influence, and we must presume that the music of Rachmaninoff is credited with this mysterious power solely because the composer himself has refused to acknowledge the sanity of the Communist Party. Or is it that the Soviet leaders discern in Rachmaninoff's music the traditional melancholy of the too-easily surrendering Slav? Certainly the study of his Second Symphony played by the Minneapolis Orchestra under Ormandy does suggest a lack of vitality, or perhaps an unduly prolonged course of sentimental meandering which, although it be extremely agreeable to the ear, does leave the listener just where he was when he started. Yet solemnly to ban such music from performance is surely a little fatuous even for contemporary Russia. We ask ourselves what music the Soviets will consider good propaganda for their political schemes, and fortunately for our curiosity we have the answer in another symphony. The First of Szostakowicz is played by the Philadelphia Orchestra. He is not yet thirty, but he already has a large volume of work to his name, and he has been appointed official composer to the U.S.S.R. Probably one of the objects of a Proletarian composer of the younger generation is the expression of a completely unsentimental and coldly ruthless view of life. Yet, the greater part of this First Symphony consists of music which, save for the difference of idiom, might have been written by Tchaikovsky in one of his most abject moods of sentimental self-pity.

"I have been reading this week a novel by one of the younger Russians, Mikail Sholokhov, which has been accorded official recognition by being made compulsory reading for all managers of collectivist farms, a novel which poor old Maxim Gorky proclaims to be a new *War and Peace*. This is called *Virgin Soil Upturned*. Alas, when the virgin soil is upturned nothing except the rubbish of centuries is revealed, and the sentimentality tricked out with new effects is exactly the same kind of sentimentality we find in the Szostakowicz symphony. Both the novel and the symphony have their passages of what are intended to be that 'brutal realism' which so easily impresses the fireside critic, but which, when all is said and done, is nothing much more brutal than the unpleasant fidgetiness of a child picking its nose. These heralds of a new era will have to get beyond childish fidgets if their jigging about with muted trumpets is to rouse the passion even of their own credulous and complaisant believers. Yet when we have eliminated from this symphony all that seems to have been put into it to conform with the fashion of the moment, when we have laughed at the sudden intrusion of a tawdry piano, at the bursts of shrill screaming by the upper wood-wind, and at the little strutting tunes imitated from Stravinsky, there remains a suspicion in the mind that Szostakowicz may have something to say in the music of the near future. There are many attractive moments in this symphony which repeated playings have not yet spoiled for me, conscious though I am that they are the result of ingenuity rather than inspiration, and I will go so far as to express an opinion that I should tire of the Rachmaninoff symphony before I tire of the Szostakowicz.

"Readers who are anxious to start a course of modern music in the hope of ascertaining the present way of the world will find the First Symphony of Szostakowicz a fairly intelligible primer. I have no doubt whatever that in another hundred years work like this will be buried beneath a dust deeper than now lies over the work of a composer like Spohr, not because more enduring work will necessarily have taken its place, but because I foresee a rapidly increasing impermanence for the works of all the arts."

That September *The British Musician* published some strictures on myself as a lover of music to which I did not reply because I was infuriated by an impudent attack on Sir Henry Wood in the same number.

Under the heading "A Serious Consideration" *The British Musician* says:

"Sir Henry Wood began his forty-first season at Queen's Hall Promenades on August 1st. And he will go on with the concerts till October.

"Is he an artist? Then he must be heartily sick of the business. But if he were sick of the business, then he wouldn't go on with it. He goes on. Therefore . . ."

Therefore we are to suppose by those dots that Sir Henry is not an artist.

"*The British Musician* has been listening to the Promenade Concerts over the wireless. One 'was of the Elgar Enigma, and it was one that for certain made many commencing-amateurs say, "Well, I shan't like *that* sort of music." ' In other words, forty-one years of doing more for musical appreciation in this country than any other individual have changed Sir Henry Wood from a public benefactor into a public menace. Does *The British Musician* really believe that a 'commencing-amateur' will cease in despair to make any further efforts to enjoy Elgar's music because Sir Henry Wood's interpretation of it has snubbed his aspiring soul? Such a 'commencing amateur' would have to be either an incipient prig or a congenital idiot.

"It may be true that Sir Henry Wood at the age of sixty-six may take the more familiar music he conducts as a routine business, but it must be remembered that this familiarity will be just as noticeable in his orchestra as in himself. If papers like *The British Musician* would abstain from giving these commencing-amateurs a most exaggerated notion of their musical taste, by letting them suppose that their failure to enjoy a composition like the Enigma Variations is due to Sir Henry Wood's inartistic interpretation of it, the better it will be for everybody. In my opinion, the remarks of *The British Musician* are a piece of gratuitous insolence offered to a man who has done more for British music in forty years than *The British Musician* will do in four hundred. The record of professional musical criticism is perhaps the least enviable of all professional criticism, and the offensive sneer at Sir Henry Wood in the September number of *The British Musician* adds another ebony-black mark against musical criticism. The last person to deceive himself about his position in the world of music is Sir Henry Wood himself, and if he considers that he can stand the terrific strain of the Promenade Concerts, it is for us to admire him with gratitude, and not insult him with the style of criticism suitable for the local poet's last volume of verse published at his own expense."

Sir Henry Wood was good enough to write and thank me for what I had said and added:
"It is curious that they should single out my performance of Elgar's *Enigma Variations*, as the composer went through the score with me, gave me a souvenir MS. of one of the Variations, and I was

Q

with him at its first performance at St. James's Hall, under Richter—
and heard him direct it many times, making copious notes upon his
interpretation (the same with Falstaff), so if any conductor knows
his Elgar I do."

I can humbly endorse what Sir Henry Wood says from a remark
which Elgar himself once made to me when I told him I had just
been hearing one of his works at Queen's Hall, though which one it
was I do not recall. "Oh, well, I am quite content with that," he said,
or words to that effect.

Chapter 19

I SHALL always be grateful that most of that lamentable decade of the 1930's was spent on a remote Hebridean island, and most of the previous decade in the seclusion of a small isle in the English Channel. Continuously sustained by music and books I built reserves of mental and emotional resistance to the despair with which our ruthless period has tormented so many artists.

Yet that life on the edge of the Atlantic spent among simple and lovable people whose language was Gaelic and whose creed was a Catholicism which had survived the dark storms of the Reformation was not always immune from the intrusion of a cynical materialism.

On a December night I wrote these words:

"What a strange thing music is! This platitudinous ejaculation was inspired by the Beethoven Quintet in C major, which has just been published, played by the Léner Quartet with William Primrose as a second viola. It is a work with which I was not familiar and, whether or not my mind was preoccupied with other matters, it made no impression on me either the first time it was played or the second time. It was played a third time when I was trying to exclude from my mind, in order to concentrate on my own work, all thoughts about late events, and most of all a black rage which had come over me at hearing immediately after the news of the Abdication, the prices on the Stock Exchange read by the six o'clock announcer out of their usual order. Was that the true anodyne for a nation's sorrow, a rise in the shares of some wretched motor-car company? Had Elgar's *Land of Hope and Glory* been played as an overture to this eructation of bad taste? Financial anxiety is intelligible, but decency, even if it was but a piece of humbugging decency, should have kept Stock Exchange prices at such a tragic moment to their proper place in the lees of the news.

"I had cut off the wireless in a fury for some chamber music to be played, and was trying to get away from the present and back to the Greece of the fifth century B.C. about which I was writing, when gradually I became aware of an exquisite melody that was washing

243

away the sense of uncleanliness left by that conjunction of tragedy with commerce. On asking what the music was I found that it was the second movement of this Beethoven Quintet in C major. It seemed incredible that I should have heard it twice without being conscious of this serene beauty. Since then I have played the whole quintet through several times, and each time with an added appreciation of its loveliness. I would not say that any of it had quite the magic of that marvellous opening of the Mozart Quintet in C major, and I certainly should not dream of giving it the emotional profundity of the Schubert Quintet in C major; but nevertheless it has the same quality as the Schubert Quintet in C major, and those who are fortunate enough to have that work on their shelves will do well to put this Beethoven Quintet beside it.

"What is the explanation of my being able to be completely deaf to the beauties of this quintet during the first two playings of it? It is a perfectly simple piece of music; the ear has not to be accustomed to any novel mode. Compared with the later quartets of Beethoven it sounds almost childishly simple. The first explanation which suggests itself is that I was not really listening to it on the first two occasions. Yet I was listening to it much less carefully on the third occasion, the proof of which is that the whole of the first movement had been played through without my being conscious of anything more than that a combination of stringed instruments was performing on the other side of my doorway. The awareness of the beauty of the second movement was as sudden as a view that is suddenly spread before one after climbing a steep hill. I have often preached about the necessity of repetition for those of us who love music but are not musicians. Much of the music we most love has gradually revealed its beauty to us through many repetitions. Still, an early work of Beethoven should not present difficulties in the way of immediate appreciation or depreciation to one who has listened to as much Beethoven as I have during the last twelve years, and that brings me back to my platitudinous ejaculation about the strangeness of music. These surprises are constantly appearing, but one of the troubles is that comparatively so few people are in a position to get the benefit of them."

In October 1938 I was turning over the pages of the latest catalogue of the music recorded by His Master's Voice and reflecting with gratitude on the richness and variety of the contents compared with those of the first catalogue of His Master's Voice the pages of which I had searched for music that was worth while fifteen years earlier. I noted the list of the sixteen royal records which had been made since that first one we had announced as a stupendous novelty in the first number of *The Gramophone*. One royal record was missing, however, and I asked:

"Was it by the wish of his ex-Majesty King Edward VIII that the record of his abdication speech was not circulated? An assurance from the recording companies that this omission is due only to the express desire of H.R.H. Duke of Windsor would allay the resentment which many of the Duke's late subjects throughout the Empire feel over what, until they have some assurance to the contrary, seems a cold and calculated insult on a par with the many other cold and calculated insults which have been offered to a man who has shown his country such an example of courage and sincerity. I possess a record of that abdication speech, the most poignant speech monarch ever made, but my record had to be imported from over the Atlantic and owing to the difficulties of perfect transmission does not do justice to that historic speech. What influence was brought to bear to suppress the record which must have been made in this country? Was it a mistaken sense of fitness, or was it subserviency to the bureaucratic powers that be, or was it merely nervousness which prevented any of the recording companies from putting this record into general circulation? If some bureaucratic mandarin interfered to stop the circulation of this record, the public has a right to hear which particular mandarin it was. The only valid excuse for suppression was that it was in deference to the wishes of H.M. King George VI, which I do not believe, or of H.R.H. Duke of Windsor, which I do not believe either. I have kept silent on this matter until now because I had hoped to see in this new catalogue the record duly listed, but I cannot keep silent any longer now that I am compelled to realize that its suppression is evidently intended to be permanent. Readers of this paper cannot accuse me of giving vent to my personal feelings in this matter during the months since last December, but I feel too strongly about this subject to keep silent any longer, and I consider the suppression of this record a matter against which *The Gramophone* may becomingly protest. I make that protest now. If the recording companies can adduce satisfactory reasons to justify their action in not circulating this record, I shall be happy to apologize for the observations made above.

"When from Windsor Castle H.R.H. Prince Edward made that last speech he was speaking to the world of to-day and the world of to-morrow; such a speech does not deserve oblivion."

In that October I was televised for the first time and what I wrote then I stand by eighteen years afterwards. I believe that it is only a matter of time before we shall be getting all our music by way of television and in this belief I am confident that the future of the gramophone is safe. I know that in Great Britain the fantastic increase in record-playing is due mainly to the introduction of the long-playing disc and to the opportunity that so many more enjoy to-day, of being able to buy records. Yet I believe that television, so hostile to reading, encourages people to listen to music. Perhaps to that may be added a decline in feminine opposition to the gramophone since records began to take up less space and since pater-familias having provided a television set for his wife and family must be allowed to indulge in his own hobby.

At this date reproduction for the average radiogram was far indeed from what it would become within another ten years and I was able with complete sincerity to assure those who still had to depend on acoustical instruments that they would be better able to appreciate the wonderful advance in the technique of recording than the average pick-up of an electrical instrument. I defined the difference between a good acoustical instrument and the average electrical instrument as the difference between home-killed beef and chilled beef. High Fidelity was beginning to be bandied about as a phrase for salesmen, and I asked our technical experts how far the average ear was capable of responding to the difference between notes of 15,000 cycles and 10,000 cycles. When I was told that one of our best reviewers could hear a note of 9000 cycles distinctly but was baffled by a note of 11,000 I began to wonder whether the achievement of high fidelity was as important as what I called the diffusion of the orchestra. I admitted that it had become reasonably "stereoscopic" but I argued that it was still imprisoned.

That imprisonment still endures and I wish that ingenuity could overcome it. The solo voice and the solo instrument remain at the top of the gramophone's accomplishment and close behind them is the string quartet. The full orchestra on a record is the least representative of the real thing. In some ways I am glad about this because if musical reproduction ever became so perfect on the gramophone as to be indistinguishable from actuality it might imperil the future of music.

The future of the drama has already been imperilled by the cinema and I cannot see any possibility of television's not exercising an even more deleterious influence upon it. My hope is, though I fear it is not a lively hope, that excess of mechanical reproduction

will cause a reaction in favour of the performer and the instrumentalist in the flesh. Yet I remember the way in which tinned food is
captivating the human palate and my hope becomes less lively.

Goethe was saying to Eckerman in the twenties of the last
century that the time had passed for the production of a major work
of art because the tranced withdrawal from the immediate present
necessary was no longer possible. The artist's life was at the mercy
of the newspapers. What would Goethe say to-day?

During those twelve years I spent in Barra I made a resolute and
sustained effort to sympathize with contemporary music, and I
can best illustrate this by recalling what I had to say from time to
time about Stravinsky. In 1931 I was definitely hostile:

"The modernity of Stravinsky is of the same quality as the
modernity of D. H. Lawrence, though I think that Lawrence in his
own medium was a greater artist than Stravinsky in his. Yet neither
Lawrence nor Stravinsky has wrought anything like the revolution
their devotees believe and would like us to believe they have. Both
step back in the hope of jumping farther, and both in despising the
conventional track get entangled in undergrowth. There is a
straight and narrow path to the ultimate truth or heaven, there is
a broad and easy road to the ultimate lie or hell; but if one has an
exaggerated belief in one's own unaided sense of direction it is as
easy to stray off the broad road as the narrow and to end in a tangle
leading nowhere. Thus already in his later work we find Stravinsky
wandering in a circle through a thicket of briars, as in the *Capriccio
for Piano and Orchestra*. And in Lawrence's last book, *Son of Man*, we
find him hopelessly bogged in the eerie empty waste of Gnosticism.

"When I play *The Rite of Spring* after playing through the sober
album of Gregorian Chant published in the same month I seem to
see Stravinsky as a tragic buffoon. *The Rite of Spring* may, as Mr.
Osbert Sitwell says, make all other music sound ridiculous. At the
same time, even its most passionate devotees cannot find other music
one-tenth as ridiculous as I find Stravinsky's after listening for ten
minutes to plainsong. Stravinsky wants to take us back and make
primitive men of us again, but as we assist at the sacrifice of the
chosen virgin we are uncomfortably aware that the cloven hooves
we are wearing were made at a bootshop round the corner, and that
the goat's tails we flourish so wantonly are sewn on with Paisley
cotton. It is all playing at 'let's pretend', and the music is really no
more elemental, no more barbaric, no more potent than the ladylike
young men who cluster and pose and skip through contemporary

ballet. Whatever people may think of Gregorian Chant, nobody can think that there is any pretence about it. It endured through the dark ages when there was neither music nor poetry, nor painting. The school of Solesmes has for seventy years been engaged in restoring and reforming this tremendous expression of human faith which as the centuries went on had become corrupted by modern affectations and accretions and mutilations."

In 1932 I was still hostile:

"I have read with interest an article by our contributor Terpander in which he suggested that *The Rite of Spring* and *The Symphony of Psalms* were the equivalent in music of James Joyce's *Ulysses* in literature, and went on to argue that those born and brought up in a system of life in which speed was not the chief ingredient are incapable of grappling either with Stravinsky or Joyce. This is specious; but what young people are apt to forget is that speed is not necessarily an enrichment of the human mind, and that those of us who are sceptical of the advantages which mere speed may be going to confer on humanity demand, and rightly, some evidence of this benefit. It is possible to imagine a future for mankind under the influence of mere speed as much impoverished as the existence of the common house-fly, which, when not feeding on muck, is moving restlessly and vaguely, though swiftly, round a chandelier. Physical speed to have any value must be accompanied by mental speed. The capacity for moving about must never exceed the capacity for moving about to some purpose. Existing more quickly is not quite the same thing as living more fully. The music of Stravinsky, the prose of James Joyce and the sculpture of Epstein may seem to some of us merely stimulants to a jaded and devitalized generation which has persuaded itself to believe that an imaginary fullness of its mental life compensates for the emptiness of its actual experience. I am ready to accept the prophecy of Terpander that all art in the future will develop along the lines laid down by his idols because I am equally convinced that, if the world develops along the path it now seems to have chosen, there will be no art at all within a comparatively short space of time, and I need not feel the least ashamed of declining to be in at the death.

"On the other hand, I suffer from moments of optimism in which I seem to discern a slowly growing reaction, and in some moods I can fancy that the succeeding generation may easily surprise the stalwarts of Stravinsky and Joyce and Epstein by an obliteration more complete than any obliteration with which these stalwarts may have hoped to overwhelm what preceded them. A generation is coming which will inherit speed without having to strive for it, and which, by inheriting it, may therefore do something with it. I have been entertained by the attitude of the intelligentsia toward the publication of D. H. Lawrence's book *Lady Chatterley's Lover* without the obscene words. When it appeared in its original form I said it reminded me of a novelette which the cook had left downstairs in the kitchen and with which the page-boy had amused himself by writing rude words in the margin. Now that it has been published without the rude words the advanced critics are inclined to suggest the commission of a sacrilege, because finding the novel without any artistic value or even human interest thus mutilated, they must either admit that it was a bad book, or else attribute a mystical and exaggerated importance to the rude words. I cannot help suspecting that some of Stravinsky's influence may be his ability to use rude words in music. However, no aesthetic argument can be based on that assumption; obviously it is impossible to prove obscenity against a musician.

"The fact is that art has never been free from some kind of taboo, and if outrageous behaviour in public of one kind was allowed to the performers in a Greek comedy, in tragedy no scenes of physical horror were tolerated upon the stage. Our most modern exponents of art demand absolute freedom from any prohibitions, whether dictated by sensitiveness, good taste or decency. Once this freedom be granted, art will cease to exist. I recognize the difficulty of deciding what in music wounds sensitiveness, outrages good taste, and affronts decency. Once this freedom be granted, art will cease to exist. I recognize the difficulty of deciding what in music wounds sensitiveness, outrages good taste, and affronts decency; but I do believe that 'atonality' may at last expire of negation."

By 1933 I was beginning to succumb to the rhythmical mastery of Stravinsky:

"The continued repetition of *The Soldier's Tale* has endeared it to me, and I can imagine myself playing it over indefinitely. The reason for this lack of fatigue and increasing appreciation is the rhythmical quality, a rhythmical quality, moreover, which expresses itself in a pattern. It is obvious that if one is going to have a wallpaper one is less likely to be fatigued by a conventional pattern than by a series of emotional illustrations. To take an example. If one were offered a choice between a pattern of pomegranate leaves and fruit and flower and a series of pictures of Claudius poisoning his brother in the orchard, or of Maud coming into the garden, we should, most of us, choose the pomegranate pattern. Yet, I do not feel that I can accept the suggestion that an ability to sustain infinite repetition is a mark of aesthetic superiority.

"After listening over and over again to *The Soldier's Tale*, I have discovered it to be a satisfying rhythmic exercise, but I find its intellectual and emotional content no larger than I thought it was, and I am convinced that no amount of repetition will reveal any more. I find that a comparison between *The Soldier's Tale* and Ravel's *Bolero* will certainly establish *The Soldier's Tale* as a superior creation. The *Bolero* makes an immediate appeal, but it will not stand a repetition indefinitely, and the *Bolero* is as much of an attempt at pattern as *The Soldier's Tale*. The *Bolero* is a pattern which fails probably because it is too obvious. Another weakness of *The Soldier's Tale* seems to me its programme. I do not feel that our appreciation of the music is in the least helped by being told the story of the Devil and the Princess.

"Let me quote : 'The Princess, becoming inquisitive, is anxious to know something of her husband's past life. After giving certain details, the Soldier expresses a wish to visit his mother once more. The Princess persuades him to venture the journey. As he crosses the frontier, the Devil confronts him with a violin and plays. The Devil thereupon drags his unfortunate victim to perdition.'

"No doubt on the stage the dancing would be effective enough, but when we do not see the dancing and only read the programme, all this talk about devils and soldiers and princesses merely interferes with the objectivity which is extolled, for clearly, if half a dozen readers and I try to visualize for ourselves the action of which the music is an illustration, we shall each individually visualize something entirely distinct.

"I can thoroughly enjoy *The Soldier's Tale* as a display of rhythm, but my very enjoyment of it is due as much as anything else to the purity of its rhythmic effect, and the programme is a boring intrusion with which I can dispense. I deprecate the widely spread enjoyment of music not as music but as incidental music to some drama of the listener's fancy. If a correspondent wrote to me that when he listened to the second movement of Beethoven's Seventh Symphony he had a vision in his mind's eye of thousands of angels in pink flannelette marching up a mountain of glass, I should express the same polite interest I express when somebody tells me about the dream he had last night; but I should feel a withering boredom within myself at having to listen to such nonsense. If people wish to provide a setting for music, let them do it; but let them keep quiet about it, and not inflict that setting on other people. Why handicap an enjoyment with a burden which has to be thrown away before we can get down to the music?

"The explanation of our discontent after a long repetition of Beethoven and Brahms, or of any of the music of the nineteenth century, may be that mankind is passing into a new stage of evolution, and that our discontent with Beethoven is due to our realization that we have stepped beyond him. This does not mean I think Stravinsky has stepped above Beethoven. Still less does it mean that in a later posterity's evaluation of musical genius Stravinsky will be granted a fame or a merit anywhere near to Beethoven's. Yet, however unpleasant it may be for reactionaries like myself, we have to face the emergence of a new human being as different from ourselves as we are presumably different from paleolithic man. I myself view that new era with the liveliest feelings of horror, but I am not sufficiently unimaginative to suppose that the signs of violent change everywhere apparent are a temporary condition.

"As emotion precedes reason in the development of the individual so in any fresh development of the race the emotional reaction will take a similar precedence. Already the emotions of the younger generation are much more profoundly different from ours than most of us in middle age seem to grasp. And it is this emotional change which is so rapidly and so ruthlessly discarding the emotional stimuli of the past. The new epoch beginning will proceed in due course to the exhaustion of itself in giving birth to the mighty creative geniuses who are probably years away from being born yet. Whether it is worth while for old-fashioned people (and old-fashioned now means something much more tremendous in its difference than perhaps it has ever meant before in the history of the human race) to procure for themselves a dim apprehension of what is coming by attempting to understand the infantile stammerings of this new epoch, already to be heard in the most modern art, is a decision which every old-fashioned individual must decide for himself."

By the end of 1934 I was becoming a champion of Stravinsky:

"I have been wondering whether some of the failure of extremely modern music to establish itself unmistakably as a fruitful branch instead of suggesting that it is to the main stem of music what an old gardener of mine used to call 'a cantankerous growth' may not be due to using unsuitable instruments. For 600 years the development of wind instruments lagged behind the development of strings, with the result that so late as 1685 an orchestra in any sense in which we use the term nowadays was still an impossibility owing to the hopeless predominance of thick-reeded oboes with which neither the flute that had displaced the recorders nor even the bassoon, itself a kind of bass oboe, could compete. The problem was solved when Christopher Denner of Nuremberg in about the year 1690 invented the clarinet, a single-reed instrument with a cylindrical and not a conical tuble.

"It took many more years before the reconciling sound between pipe instruments and double-reeds established itself in the orchestra. Apparently Rameau was the first to use clarinets, in 1751; but it was not till twenty years later that Haydn, and Mozart finally and authoritatively, made them an essential part of the orchestra. I suppose that the only wind instrument as distinctive as the clarinet invented since is the saxophone, which was welcomed enthusiastically by Berlioz, but which has never established itself except as an instrument for musical ventriloquism rather than music. It may safely be added that it never will, the chief reason being, I believe, its essential lifelessness, a quality which it shares with that gurgling, gargling diplodocus, the cinema organ. The vile use made of the trumpet in dance bands is presumably an attempt to counter the saxophone's lifelessness, like cutting the heart out of a sleepy pear with a sharp knife.

"Berlioz, in spite of his welcome to the saxophone, did not make use of it. His principal contribution to orchestral development was to increase the brass and percussion at the expense of the wood-wind, and it was left for Wagner to rearrange the orchestra in the right proportions. The most notable instrument that he added to the orchestra was the tenor tuba, which he used with irresistible effect. Since Wagner's time various instruments have been added. In Holst's *Planets* we get a bass flute, a bass oboe, additional timpani, a bass drum, a xylophone and a celeste; but except for the percussion additions no effective use was made of the rest, a statement which can easily be checked by following a recorded version of the *Planets* with the score. Other modern composers have introduced such eccentric instruments, if instruments they can be called, as wind machines, rattles and sheet metal; but no composer has discovered an instrument which will compensate listeners for a lack of thematic material.

Yet now that thematic material is beginning to acquire an entirely different significance from any used in European music during the last 200 years we are surely justified in demanding from the Bartoks, the Schönbergs and the Stravinskys the employment of instruments expressive in their own sounds of the mental condition which is being communicated. In literature, for instance, a writer like James Joyce smashes syntax in the way a modern composer smashes tonality, but he goes further by smashing language itself, and has a right to claim that in his use of words he is using the equivalent of new instruments, whether to the ultimate profit or loss of literature need not be argued.

"The study I have been able to make of Stravinsky's music has led me to suppose, whether rightly or wrongly, that Stravinsky is entirely dissatisfied with every instrument at his disposal, considering it an old-fashioned and inconveniently sophisticated medium of sound. Take, for instance, *Les Noces*. This is a cantata with dances, presenting a wedding in a Russian village. The orchestra consists of four pianos, four timpani, xylophone and bells, tambourine, triangle, cymbals, bass drum, side drum, drum without snare, and two small cymbals. Turning to *The Musical Companion* I read 'the peculiar tone of the side drum . . . is the result of the snares (lengths of catgut) that are stretched across the lower parchment coming into rapid contact with the parchment itself. This, in its turn, is set in vibration by the action of the drum sticks on the upper parchment . . . the snares can be loosened . . . this produces that unique muffled sound usually associated with . . . military funerals.'

"From the combination of percussion instruments Stravinsky contrives to extract a noise unlike any other noise you can hear except on certain records of Oriental music. In fact, the impression on the listener is that a strange series of instruments is being employed, the composition of which I was unable to recognize, apart from the piano, which oddly though it be used, remains unmistakably the piano. Presumably Stravinsky has arranged this combination of instruments to suggest the primordial urge of sex with a kind of relentless rhythm, for obviously the musical accompaniment at a real Russian wedding would not sound in the least like this.

"The vocal part of the cantata is carried through by a quartet of British artists under the conductorship of Stravinsky himself, but for all the use their English is to the listener they might as well have been singing in Choctaw. At the very end of the second side I distinguished 'Bless me, my father, your child'. On the remaining four sides I distinguished 'To the church', 'We kiss there the silver cross', 'Grant me your blessing, father dear', 'Raise your voices', 'Leaving their homestead', and about a dozen isolated words besides. This is not good enough. Four experienced singers should be able in twenty minutes of almost incessant singing to give their audience more help than this. If they cannot make themselves clear in their own language it would be better to leave the words in the original Russian. Isolated ejaculations run the risk of making the whole performance sound absurd, and the strain of trying to distinguish the English words detracts from the music, which is already handicapped by our not being able to see the accompanying dances.

"At the same time, I thought our reviewer was unduly impatient with *Les Noces*. I like a tune just as much as he does, but when rhythm is used with such mastery as it is used here by Stravinsky, I am more than willing to forgo any tune which might be supposed to express the hymeneal atmosphere. Let us be honest and admit the improbability of any tune written now being capable of conveying anything more than the conventionally sentimental side of wedlock. Let us remember that if Stravinsky had wanted to do that for the thousandth time, by what we know of the sentimental tunes he has deliberately written, he could have written as good a tune as anybody alive. It is another question when we ask ourselves whether he has succeeded in persuading the majority of his listeners that they are sharing in the primordial emotions he has tried to rouse from the long sleep imposed by what is called civilization. A composition like *Les Noces* ought not to be caviare to the general, because by the very nature of the subject it is an appeal to the general. Stravinsky cannot afford to live by hole-in-the-corner highbrow appreciation, and I assume that the recording of this cantata in English is a minor sign of his awareness of that.

"We may presume that the popularity of dance records is primarily due to a hunger in both the uncultivated ear and the cultivated ear for a rhythmic accompaniment to the unrhythmic noise of contemporary life. I have noticed repeatedly an increasing dread of quiet. 'It must be dreadfully quiet here most of the year' people will say to me with a shiver, commenting on the kind of place that suits what nowadays seems my eccentric fancy. And again you will hear, 'This place is so quiet. It gets on my nerves.' There is no use shutting our eyes to the fact that noise is becoming as necessary to human nature as warmth to cats. Yet people do not listen to noise; they are merely aware of it. Hence their use of music. They do not want to listen to it. They want to be easily aware of it in the background. There was a time when dance music was played by the B.B.C. under the impression that people danced to it. That delusion has long been cured. Dance music has become the staple noise emanating from a loudspeaker. I cannot help feeling that ears habituated to the jejune rhythm from nine out of ten, nay ninety-nine out of a hundred, of the current dance tunes might with very little perseverance be captivated by the marvellous rhythm of *Les Noces*. Ravel's *Bolero* was entirely a triumph of rhythm. When it was first performed it enchanted even the critical. Then it was discovered to have enchanted the undiscerning herd, and it was voted cheap. Of one thing I am certain, which is that both Ravel's *Bolero* and Stravinsky's *Les Noces*, accompanied by a percussion orchestra, are immensely exhilarating. Yet what will tell in favour of the *Bolero* and against *Les Noces* is that the former is a pleasant noise, and that the latter, owing to our unfamiliarity with the combination of instruments used, is an unpleasant noise."

Finally, in 1936 I was paying a tribute to Stravinsky as a musical thinker:

"I strongly advise readers to get hold of Igor Stravinsky's *Chronicle of My Life*. The interest of what Stravinsky has to tell us about his actual music is equalled by the faithful way in which his book reflects the European malaise since the war. One asks what would have happened to a Beethoven if the life of his time had kept him as continuously on the move as Stravinsky has been kept. Yet notwithstanding the air of restlessness which pervades the whole volume the impression of the composer's own personality suggests a singular tranquillity of mind due no doubt to the sheer hard work at whose mercy every creative artist always lies. 'I consider that music is, by its very nature, essentially powerless to express anything at all, whether a feeling, an attitude of mind, a psychological mood, a phenomenon of nature, etc. . . . Expression has never been an inherent property of music. That is by no means the purpose of its existence. If, as is nearly always the case, music appears to express something, this is only an illusion and not a reality.

"'Music is the sole domain in which man realizes the present. By the imperfection of his nature, man is doomed to submit to the passage of time—to its categories of past and future—without ever being able to give substance, and therefore stability, to the category of the present.

"'The phenomenon of music is given to us with the sole purpose of establishing an order in things, including, and particularly, the co-ordination between *man* and *time*. To be put into practice, its indispensable and single requirement is construction. . . . It is precisely this construction, this achieved order, which produces in us a unique emotion having nothing in common with our ordinary sensations and our responses to the impressions of daily life.'

"I cannot recall any passage of musical criticism which states with such clarity what music is. It washes away like a stream of crystal water the accumulated dust of the sentimental rubbish with which nineteenth-century musical criticism was cluttered up. Stravinsky shows lucidly in these observations why it is so difficult to write any musical criticism which steps outside technical criticism, and therefore why literature usually manages to go to pieces when it concerns itself with music. If a literary critic were to preoccupy himself entirely with the technical criticism of a novel he would be read only by those few professional novelists who are themselves preoccupied with the technique of their craft. The literary critic, however, is not tied down to technicalities. He can discuss the probability of the story. He can test by his own experience of human nature the characterization of the novel before him. And most valuably of all from the point of view of interesting his readers, he can attempt some estimate of the emotional depths and shallows. He can, in fact, write if he will an absorbing essay which may be read with pleasure by those who have never read the work that is being criticized.

"The musical critic, on the other hand, from the moment he steps aside from the technical achievement of music itself, is completely at the mercy of his impressionism. 'Music is the sole domain in which man realizes the present.' It would be possible to claim that no poem means the same to any two persons, at any rate in the fullest sense of the word 'means', but it can be definitely asserted of any piece of music. Moreover, no piece of music ever means exactly the same to one person even at two immediately consecutive hearings. It may have been this peculiarly present tense in music which led Bernard Shaw to describe it as a drug, because one of the properties of a narcotic drug is to heighten to an extraordinary extent the importance of the present. We may safely assume, too, that our mental condition during sleep is of an immensely extended and enriched present compared with anything we experience when awake. Practically our whole knowledge of dreams is limited to those we recollect from the edge of sleep when consciousness has already obtruded upon unconsciousness. I know of no instance when a person woken from a deep sleep, in which he was talking aloud, has been able to relate the circumstances in which in sleep he was talking. I feel pretty sure that music affords human beings their nearest approach to the freedom of profound sleep. It has become a stock joke to rail at the notion of the paradisial eternity spent in playing a harp before the throne of God, but so far as it is possible to conceive eternal bliss in terms of this world an eternity of music is as near as we can approach to the conception. When I am in the middle of listening to a great work of music I always have a feeling that it is never going to finish. Take, for instance, that marvellous last quintet of Schubert's, and try to imagine when you are in the middle of listening to it that it ever began or ever will end. Apropos of Schubert here is an extract from Stravinsky's *Chronicle*:

" 'One day when Scriabine with his usual emphasis was pouring out ideological verbosities concerning the sublimity of art and its great pontiffs, I, on my side, began to praise the grace and elegance of Schubert's waltzes. . . . With an ironical smile of commiseration he said: "Schubert? But look here, that is only fit to be strummed on the piano by little girls." '

"I was glad to note that Stravinsky attaches great importance to seeing the music played. I have even noticed that people listen better to the gramophone when they are staring at the horn, and I consider that the external horn instrument always controls an audience better than a camouflaged cabinet. 'Those who maintain that they only enjoy music to the full with their eyes shut,' says Stravinsky, 'do not hear better than when they have them open, but the absence of visual distractions enables them to abandon themselves to the reveries induced by the lullaby of the sounds, and that is really what they prefer to the music itself.'

"And, oh, how good Stravinsky is on Beethoven! He relates how in his youth he had been alienated from Beethoven by the 'intellectual and sentimental attitude'; and how 'cured and matured by age', he approached him objectively to recognize in him 'the indisputable monarch of the instrument. It is the instrument that inspires his thought and determines its substance.'

"I find that as I grow older I, too, in my humble way marvel more and more at the 'giant instrumentalist' that predominates in Beethoven. I recall those drums suddenly coming in at the end of the rondo of the *Emperor* Concerto, or his many magical uses of the horn, or the unique starkness of the violin at the beginning of the Violin Concerto, or his unequalled appreciation of the power of the double-bass both in the Fifth Symphony and in the Ninth Symphony. Indeed, I can think of no instrument the potentialities of which were not enriched by his genius. And I can recall no other composer for whom this claim could be made. Stravinsky is severe on those who

R

make the 'error of regarding instrumentation as something extrinsic from the music for which it exists', as he goes on to point out that the 'unhealthy greed for orchestral opulence of to-day has corrupted the judgment of the public'. This is profoundly true, and we only need compare what Sibelius can do with an ordinary orchestra with what Strauss so often fails to do with an unusual orchestra to realize the truth of this. Tone-colour has been the ruin of most modern composers, and its effect on music has been as inimical as elaborate scenery was disastrous to the drama."

The outbreak of the Second World War seemed for a while to threaten *The Gramophone* with extinction. The shortage of paper, the heavy purchase tax upon records, the fall in advertisement revenue, the loss of most of our subscribers overseas and a dozen other difficulties of various kinds seemed for a while insurmountable. Fortunately, Cecil Pollard, the London Editor, and Christopher Stone did not lose either heart or head, and thanks to their pertinacity, cautious optimism and solid hard work the long and wearisome storm was at last weathered.

An echo of that exasperating time may be heard from some comments of mine on the action of the Chancellor of the Exchequer in raising still higher the purchase tax on records:

" 'If I were to begin life again, I would devote it to music. It is the only cheap and unpunished rapture upon earth,' wrote Sydney Smith to Lady Carlisle all but a hundred years ago, in 1844. Sir Kingsley Wood was not then born. Thus he was spared from being laughed at by the wittiest of all Englishmen. Nor do I feel perfectly convinced that if the Reverend Sydney Smith had been driven to comment upon the present Chancellor of the Exchequer's tax on music he might not have used, perhaps for the first time in his life, a barbed shaft.

"In view of the fact that the British Council is spending a certain amount of public money on obtaining recognition abroad for British music by subsidizing the publication of records of the work of various distinguished British composers, it seems faintly idiotic that Sir Kingsley Wood should immediately proceed to increase the already outrageous tax on every kind of gramophone record, and thus on representative British music. It may be unjust to blame the Chancellor himself; he may be happily ignorant that there are any British composers of note. Nevertheless, when he sat down after his Budget speech like an amiable prima donna to receive a shower of bouquets from his fellow-members of the House of Commons, somebody should have told him that between music and lipstick there is something more than a distinction without a difference. Of this difference the Chancellor of the Exchequer—or shall we say more charitably his advisers at the Treasury?—is obviously unaware. It would, and should have been, easy to exempt from this preposterous tax records of good music. If the Treasury officials do not know what good music is they could consult their colleagues in the Civil Service on the Board of Education who have been devoting a good deal of attention to the encouragement of good music. The Treasury might even have consulted the British Council and thus have avoided the absurdity of taxing British lovers of British music to pay for the advertisement of them abroad. Sir Kingsley Wood looks at a gramophone record as Wordsworth's Peter Bell looked at a primrose. To him it is a gramophone record, and it is nothing more. Whether it be a Bach sonata or the last bit of drooling sentiment about blue birds over the white cliffs of Dover, to Sir Kingsley Wood it is a luxury. We all remember how the little man hoped to tax books and was dissuaded only when he found himself treading on the toes of religious prejudice about taxing the Holy Bible. However, what is the use of jibbing? All we can do is to hope that the German defences of Europe are not so impenetrable as the stupidity of bureaucrats: and if the Government wants to intern the Muses for the rest of the war their devotees must be as patient as the devotees of tobacco who are now keeping the country in Spitfires, and of whose patriotic extravagance we can surely say: 'They also serve who only sit and smoke.' "

One of the works commissioned by the British Council was the Piano Concerto of Arthur Bliss which was first performed in June 1939 at the Carnegie Hall, New York, by the New York Philharmonic Orchestra, conducted by Sir Adrian Boult, with Solomon as the pianist. Then in 1943 it was issued on records at a popular price performed by the Liverpool Philharmonic Orchestra with the same conductor and soloist. It was the patronage of the British Council that made this possible for which the wretched British taxpayer who was already paying for the British Council's patronage was rooked by the Chancellor of the Exchequer to the tune of 66 per cent purchase tax in order to enjoy the result.

It gave me immense pleasure to be able to greet this recording of the Piano Concerto with enthusiasm because I had not been able to be so enthusiastic about some of Arthur Bliss's earlier records, and he

himself is always a joy to me, though to get him on to the printed page
is beyond my ability. It is too much like trying to catch a bird by
putting salt on its tail. I wrote at the time:

"I agree with our critic in condemning the 'reactionary attitude
which refuses to accept the sane melodic and harmonic language of
to-day'. I think it was fair to condemn what twenty years ago seemed
wilful eccentricity and seems to-day more than ever like wilful
eccentricity. I do not believe that I admire this last Quartet more than
the *Conversations* of twenty years ago only because during those
twenty years I have perforce been educated into such admiration by
ever increasing familiarity with the idiom of contemporary music.
If Arthur Bliss had composed his *Conversations* last year and they had
been recorded last month I should have been as much irritated by
them as I was when I originally heard them. The advance he has
made since then does not appear to be a greater advance than it
really is because I have gone half way to meet him along the road. I
have remained obstinately still all these years and waited for modern
music to come to me without making any anxious effort to go to it
except in the case of Stravinsky. I enlarge upon this point because
I see myself as the musical man-in-the-street and do not set up as a
herald of musical progress. I know that if this latest Quartet of Bliss
can give me aesthetic pleasure it can give as much pleasure to many
of our conservative readers who, like myself, are won over with
difficulty even to the sanest melodic and harmonic language of
to-day."

When Elgar died Arnold Bax became Master of the King's
Musick, which is the equivalent of Poet Laureate. Arnold Bax was not
a member of the Savile and therefore I did not have an opportunity
of seeing as much of him as I should have liked, for he was a most
attractive figure. It had been a suggestion of John Barbirolli that the
National Gramophonic Society should record his Oboe Quartet and
I believe that was almost if not the very first recording of his music
that was made. We had to wait until 1944 for the recording of one of
Bax's symphonies, and this was conducted by Barbirolli with the
Hallé Orchestra under the sponsorship of the British Council. Bax
once suggested that I should write a libretto for an opera based on
the West Highlands to which he was devoted, but I have always been
deterred from the experiment of writing the libretto for an opera by
the conviction that it would be drowned by over-orchestration or
starved for lack of melody. Of that Third Symphony I wrote:

"If richness of orchestration has a positive value Bax is certainly a master. I have often wished that one of our modern masters of orchestral colour would re-orchestrate a Brahms or Schubert symphony. Beethoven like Sibelius never failed to achieve magical effects of orchestration with the conventional material, but Brahms and Schubert both have some arid wastes of orchestration. Then there are the symphonies of Schumann. Surely they would gain immensely by complete re-orchestration? This suggestion is offered in the faint, the very faint hope that such a task may inspire one of our modern composers to rediscover melody. Harmony alone is the League of Nations without the United States. One is surprised that it is as good as it is, but in the end one is left unsatisfied. I cannot believe that a composer like Bax is incapable of sustained melodic invention, and throughout this Third Symphony there are brief snatches of exquisite melody. He counts himself a romantic and therefore I do not understand why like so many other modern composers he often seems to be rapping himself on the knuckles for daring to indulge in a tune. Throughout this symphony the listener is carried to celestial heights, only to be dropped, sometimes at the end of a parachute but more often without one, to earth. I wish I could divine the reason for this. I must add hastily that those readers who write to me in despair of, as they say, making anything of modern music, need not suppose from what I have written above that this lovely rhapsody so magnificently recorded is going to be fashionably difficult. Certainly I should not expect any listener of my calibre to begin to grasp what this is all about before a third or fourth playing, but that is all to the good and those who neglect the opportunity now given to them of studying Bax will miss a very great deal."

I once asked Sir Arthur Bliss, who succeeded Sir Arnold Bax as Master of the King's Musick, what was the fundamental objection of contemporary composers to melody, and he placed the responsibility on the distraction of the time in which we live. This may be true but I suspect that there is also a fear of the obvious. In a criticism I read of Sir William Walton's opera *Troilus and Cressida* he was being reproached by some anxious modernist for his occasional surrender to outworn operatic idiom which meant in other words that he had been able to make some of the music immediately intelligible.

Sir William Walton was another composer to be sponsored in wartime by the British Council, and the choice was made of *Belshazzar's Feast* as a piece of music worthy to represent the national spirit at such an hour. To quote what I wrote in 1943:

"I have no hesitation in declaring that so far no music has reached us from the pen of a contemporary Russian composer with as much vitality and explosive force as this. In view of the fact that Marshal Stalin himself has encouraged Russian composers to translate into terms of art the emotional mood of Russia at this time, it is clear that he attaches more importance to music than our own genially Philistine Chancellor of the Exchequer. I will hazard that Walton's music will convey to our Russian allies much more of the spirit of Britain than all the wordy propaganda put together.

"However, let us leave propaganda out of it and consider *Belshazzar's Feast* merely as entertainment, which we have every right to do in view of the price we have to pay for it. Every time I have listened to this magnificent recording I have enjoyed it more. Naturally it is a barbaric noise, for so, no doubt, was Belshazzar's feast when it was first held, and it is the most colourful piece of noise I have listened to for a long time. The effect is rather of an explosive sunset, and that again, no doubt, was what the original feast resembled. Dissonance merely for the sake of dissonance I am old enough to find irritating; but when dissonance is used with genuinely dramatic effect I am still young enough to enjoy it with anybody. The alliance between Walton and the Sitwells was always a happy one. *Façade* is an affectionately remembered pleasure. So when we find that Sir Osbert Sitwell has arranged the verbal scheme of what with memories of Mendelssohn's *Elijah*, I hesitate to call an oratorio we can expect a Biblical anthology of the finest discernment.

"The dancing and revelry of the feast are expressed by the composer in jazz, which suggests more authentically than the pseudo-orientalism of Saint-Saëns in *Samson and Delilah* the hideous megalo-politan swarming of twenty-five centuries ago. Inevitably it is tempting to discover a kinship between those dead civilizations and the projected civilization of Nazism, but I doubt if it could be sustained. If imperial Babylon and Nineveh and Egypt depended for their grandeur on human slavery, so, too, alas, it must be admitted did the city-states of individualistic Greece. It was Aristotle who said that slavery was necessary because without it men of leisure could not exist, and that without men of leisure there could be no intellectual progress. Still, *Belshazzar's Feast* does express one mood most welcome to us at the moment, and that is exultation in the sudden collapse of a tyrant.

"Apart from the excitement of the music, which is a genuinely impressive excitement owing nothing to the meretricious use of strange instrumental combinations and blitzkrieg dissonances, the recording is itself a triumph."

I am tempted to bring to an end my record of music on the beloved island of Barra with a long excerpt about Beethoven's piano sonatas from *The North Wind of Love*, for nothing marks so clearly what I had learnt from and about music during the years since I wrote that chapter in *Sinister Street* a quarter of a century earlier. I abstain, for I fear it would seem like showing off.

Chapter 20

I WAS sixty-two when the Second World War finished and I decided that it was time to give up isolation and live within reach of London. So we moved to an old manor house in Berkshire within easy reach of London and of Oxford. I had not been there a year when I was asked by the Indian Government to undertake a history of the achievements of the Indian Army during the war. I left England in October 1946, travelled in India, Nepal, Burma, Malaya, Egypt, Libya and Eritrea, and as far as Hong Kong, flew back from India in July 1947 to the battlefields in Italy and Tunis, spent a week or two at home, flew back to India and returned to England by way of the Seychelles and Kenya to arrive back in May 1948 at the moment when the three hundred and first number of *The Gramophone* was going to press.

I was continually being greeted wherever I went by readers of *The Gramophone*. I knew from correspondence how widespread was our circulation but the evidence of it was always a most agreeable surprise. In Mysore the Maharaja, who received me in the music-room of the Palace the end of which was occupied by a large electric organ, told me that he had been taking in *The Gramophone* since 1932 when he was a schoolboy of thirteen. He had secured all the earlier numbers since and he said that the intimacy of the paper had been one of his great pleasures and was good enough to add that my own writing about music had meant much to him. This astonished me because His Highness is himself a musician of high accomplishment, and I had never expected anything I wrote about music to appeal to people who really knew something about music. The Maharaja went on to say that he wished to start a society for making the work of Nicolas Medtner better known and he generously offered to subsidize such an undertaking. By a coincidence he had written to tell his Trade Commissioner in London to get into contact with myself about this project and the letter had just been posted when he heard of my proposed visit to Mysore.

The Maharaja was as good as his word about the recordings of Medtner, and the pleasure it gave to the old composer who was near to his end at the time was most moving. His Highness also subsidized later a series of splendid concerts in London, but they were not attended as well as they should have been. I wish that the Maharaja of Mysore had been twenty-five instead of five years old when the National Gramophonic Society was started.

A year or two ago I attended a debate at the Oxford Union when the House supported a motion regretting the disappearance of private patronage. Such a motion in the arid 'thirties would have been considered so morbidly reactionary that it would have been lost by a large majority. In the more vital 'fifties it was handsomely won. People like Mrs. Coolidge in the United States, Walter Cobbett in the United Kingdom and the Maharaja of Mysore shame any government of any country which, having put the means of patronage beyond Maecenas, fails to take his place. Our own country stands very low in that disreputable list.

Soon after my return from the East the long-playing disc which was already the rage in the United States became a bit of an editorial problem. When accounts reached Great Britain of its success there was naturally much eagerness to know when the long-playing disc would cross the Atlantic and whether it was worth while bothering any more about the existing 78 records. The trouble was that the combination in Great Britain of His Master's Voice, Columbia and Parlophone known as E.M.I. did not know because in the United States Victor and Columbia were engaged in a battle. It was my job to allay the impatience of the enthusiast in order to get through the transition period until the long-playing disc had established itself. Fortunately Decca was able to go over to the long-playing disc almost at once and this served as a febrifuge. I set on record my admiration for the courage of Mr. E. R. Lewis first of all in backing his belief in Decca during that inauspicious decade of the 'thirties when the gramophone came as near to a slump as doesn't matter and secondly in launching the long-playing disc in Great Britain about a year before the mighty combination of E.M.I. started.

Reproduction was keeping pace with the steady improvement in recording. I was no longer able to claim that the acoustical instrument was superior to the electrical instrument, and with the Electrogram de Luxe of His Master's Voice and the Decola of Decca I could sit back and listen to music reproduced as thirty-two years ago I never dreamed it would be reproduced within so comparatively short a time. I would that every crusader could have as happy an end to his fight as I have enjoyed.

The upward surge in the monthly circulation of *The Gramophone* from about 10,000 at the end of the war to what may be well on the way to 70,000 by the time these words are in print speaks for itself.

S

But I must not seem to claim too much for myself as a crusader. The development of the gramophone would have happened if that Hepplewhite model of a Vocalion had never been put ashore on the isle of Herm. Nor was I endowed with any unusual prescience. I have the luck to be one of those minority men who lives to become a majority man. I am in fact the man-in-the-street who walks rather quickly and so sometimes finds himself a couple of streets ahead of the others.

The Gramophone entered upon its thirty-first year within a day of the Coronation of Her Majesty Queen Elizabeth II whose Royal grandfather's and grandmother's first record we were announcing in our first number. We took advantage of the fact to record our homage:

"It may be doubted if any paper has been able to celebrate its entry into its thirty-first year within a day of the Coronation of a Queen. In June 1923 such a prospect would have seemed a fairy tale of the future, and it is with an emotion of profound gratitude for this astonishing and happy coincidence that in the name of our readers, our contributors, our staff and our advertisers I declare our fealty to a young Sovereign and affirm our conviction that under Almighty God she will lead this old country out of present difficulties into a future truly glorious. Nobody who has listened to that recorded voice can be deaf to the sense of destiny that inspires it. Simple faith is manifest behind every word The Queen has spoken. I am paying no conventional tribute of loyalty and though I lack the eloquence to express all that they feel at this moment I will ask our readers throughout the world to join with me in this tribute to our young and much beloved Queen.

"We wish Your Majesty the achievement of every high hope, the consummation of every noble ambition, and the completion of every fine design. We wish Your Majesty the happiness and the glory of a long reign rich in renown, preserved from war and devoted to the fulfilment of the Divine purpose.

"Music is the only common tongue of humanity, and with the music we love we offer Your Majesty our homage in this most memorable month of June. From Iceland in the North to Invercargill in the South and from Tokyo in the East to San Francisco in the West the readers of *The Gramophone* whether they be Your Majesty's subjects or not, will say with me

'God Save the Queen!' "

It is appropriate that my record of music should be played to a close in Ireland, for it was in the city of Cork just over seventy years ago that I first expressed what I owed to music when that hurdy-gurdy of long ago calmed the panic set up by a Punch and Judy show.

In 1950 Dr. Tom Walsh of Wexford wrote to tell me that he was starting an operatic study circle through the medium of gramophone records and invited me to come over and address the preliminary meeting. An invitation from Ireland has always been the most difficult for me to refuse and I accepted. We were gathered in the old jail of Wexford and as I have never feared to speak of 'Ninety-eight I felt completely at home.

After talking away about opera and the gramophone I was suddenly moved to ask why Wexford should be content with studying operatic records. Why did not Wexford with its traditions of Balfe produce an opera for itself?

Some weeks after this Dr. Tom Walsh let me know that Wexford intended to hold a Festival of Music and the Arts in 1951, of which I had been elected President! Balfe's opera *The Rose of Castile* was to be performed with professional singers in the leading parts and a chorus gathered from the neighbourhood. There would be films of operas, a concert by the Symphony Orchestra of Radio Eireann, a concert of chamber music, an exhibition of handicrafts, and I know not what besides. Certain alterations were being made in the old Wexford theatre which dated back to the thirties of the last century.

In due course the Wexford Festival of 1951 was an accomplished fact and the success warranted its repetition in 1952. Unfortunately on the eve of crossing over to attend I was laid low with one of these tiresome attacks of acute sciatica which have laid me out at intervals for the last forty years and more.

The Festival had been even more successful in its second year and by 1953 the Municipality of Wexford had realized that it was a genuine occasion and decided to open it by the simultaneous illumination of hundreds of fairy lights strung across the narrow streets of that delightful town, which by the way has a population of about 20,000. The opera given in 1953 was Donizetti's *Don Pasquale* which was produced by Peter Ebert, gifted son of a gifted father. Bellini's *La Sonnambula* was the choice for the fourth Festival, and what that chorus of young Irishwomen and Irishmen did under the direction of Bryan Balkwill was astonishing. Marilyn Cotlow, an American soprano, was Amina, Nicola Monti played Elvine and

Franco Calabrese was the Count. The production of Peter Ebert could not have been bettered.

One of the pleasures of the opening night was to see among the audience so many clergy of various denominations. Indeed, I was moved to observe in a speech from the stage that it might be doubted whether such a representative gathering of the clergy had been seen since the Council of Nicea.

For the fifth Festival at the end of October 1955 a German opera subsidized by the West German Government is to be given as well as an Italian opera.

For me the Wexford Festival has been a joy because the success of it allays that doubt which from time to time has troubled me whether the gramophone was a danger to the future of music. I suppose it was in one of those moments of doubt that I asked why Wexford should be content with studying operatic records. I wish that the whole-hearted and triumphantly successful response of Wexford to a suggestion could inspire other towns in Great Britain and Ireland to a comparable effort. To be sure, every town in Great Britain and Ireland does not possess a dynamic personality like Dr. Tom Walsh, and one is all too sadly aware that killjoy officialdom and red tapery would prevent most towns in Scotland, England or Wales from displaying any signs of festivity after eleven o'clock at the latest. The Edinburgh Festival turns into an Edinburgh Fast by then. Malvolio takes charge of Stratford-on-Avon from the moment people come out of the Memorial Theatre.

Yet, in spite of the rules and regulations which infest us, it ought to be possible for towns on the other side of the Irish Channel to emulate Wexford over opera.

Malvern has achieved a festival of drama, Aldeburgh and Haslemere festivals of music, and Cheltenham under the combined drive of John Moore and Robert Henriques has even managed a festival of literature.

In a mood of temporary depression induced by the election of the "National" Government in the autumn of 1931 I expressed doubt whether poetry, or even literature as a whole, had any future unless a mundane catastrophe a thousand times more tremendous than the last great war drove humanity back from the road in evolution along which it was moving like a column of ants. I was even beginning to lose faith in the future of music and I believed that with every other art the impulse to make great music would languish and expire while human nature struggled with the Frankenstein of machinery it had let loose.

We are now faced by the possibility of that mundane catastrophe. Is the West entering another twilight such as preceded that long night of the Dark Ages which endured five hundred years?

As I ask that question I hear in the *Missa Solemnis* "Credo" upon "Credo" sound Beethoven's defiant answer for the soul of man. Humbly, I affirm my own belief that music, escaping from its present uncertainty, will adumbrate again man's search for truth, beauty and good during his brief sojourn in the material world, and I speculate hopefully whether East and West may not meet at last through music, for music transcends language.

I had intended to bring this volume to an end with a list of the chamber music recordings now available instead of that skimpy list I scraped together for the first number of *The Gramophone* in April 1923. However, on July 15th, 1955, I was notified by MM. Arthur Honegger and Maurice Yvain, the Presidents of the Académie du Disque Français, that I had been offered the fauteuil of a Membre Correspondant, and I feel that this generous tribute is more appropriate.

"Le fait de votre appui moral ne manquera pas d'être hautement significatif et efficace, et c'est pourquoi le Chef du Gouvernement Français, M. Edgar Faure, Président du Conseil des Ministres, à tenu a signer de sa main le diplôme de Votre Excellence, en qui nous saluons le défenseurde la Musique et du Disque, qui depuis trente-trois ans édite la plus grande revue du monde spécialisée en la matiere: *The Gramophone*. Ce diplome a ete remis le 12 Juillet, à Paris, par M. le Ministre de l'Industrie et du Commerce au représentant de M. l'Ambassadeur de Grande-Bretagne."

Recognition from France is always more deeply prized than that from anywhere, and with those heartening words in French I bring *My Record of Music* to an end.

ACKNOWLEDGMENT

I desire to acknowledge with grateful thanks the permission of the O.U.P. to reprint my article on the Gramophone and Chamber Music from Cobbett's *Cyclopedic Survey of Chamber Music*.

GENERAL INDEX

INDEX TO MUSICAL WORKS